Case Studies in School Counseling

Larry B. Golden

University of Texas at

Patricia Her

University of Texas at

PEARSON

Merrill
Prentice Hall

Upper Saddle River,
Columbus, Ohio

Library of Congress Cataloging-in-Publication Data

Case studies in school counseling / [edited by] Larry B. Golden, Patricia Henderson.
   p. cm.
  Includes bibliographical references and index.
  ISBN 0-13-049484-4 (pbk.)
  1. Educational counseling—United States—Case studies.   I. Golden, Larry B.
II. Henderson, Patricia, Ed. D.
  LB1027.5.C3965 2007
  371.4—dc22

2005030586

Vice President and Executive Publisher: Jeffery W. Johnston
Publisher: Kevin M. Davis
Editorial Assistant: Sarah N. Kenoyer
Production Editor: Mary Harlan
Production Coordinator: Thistle Hill Publishing Services, LLC
Design Coordinator: Diane C. Lorenzo
Cover Design: Kristina D. Holmes
Cover Image: SuperStock
Production Manager: Laura Messerly
Director of Marketing: David Gesell
Marketing Manager: Autumn Purdy
Marketing Coordinator: Brian Mounts

This book was set in Garamond by Integra Software Services. It was printed and bound by
R. R. Donnelley & Sons Company. The cover was printed by R. R. Donnelley & Sons Company.

Pearson Education Ltd.
Pearson Education Singapore Pte. Ltd.
Pearson Education Canada, Ltd.
Pearson Education–Japan

Pearson Education Australia Pty. Limited
Pearson Education North Asia Ltd.
Pearson Educación de Mexico, S.A. de C.V.
Pearson Education Malaysia Pte. Ltd.

This book is dedicated to professional school counselors—our heroes!

Foreword

It is a pleasure to provide a foreword to *Case Studies in School Counseling* because this book is a valuable resource to school counselors who are seeking to enhance their program expertise with innovative approaches to facilitate student growth and development.

Today's young people face myriad issues that those of us who could be their parents or grandparents never faced. David Elkind, the eminent developmental psychologist, in his classic works *The Hurried Child: Growing Up Too Fast Too Soon* and *All Grown Up and No Place to Go: Teenagers in Crisis* points out the rapid nature of change in society. Practical applications of prevention and intervention that address these and other issues can be useful to school counselors.

Most young people entering middle school have come face-to-face with alcohol and drugs, bullying or other forms of violent acts, and sexuality. They need guidance and boundaries if they are to get through this safely and grow into productive citizens. I believe that education comes down to one simple purpose: We are endeavoring to teach young people to assume responsibility for their own lives. The school counselor is the key professional who is positioned to address these issues through both prevention and intervention methods.

Case Studies in School Counseling provides the reader with a variety of approaches for both individual and group work. The organization of the cases provides the reader with a sense of each contributor's environment, the intent of the activity or intervention, and a sequential process for implementing the activity. Each contributor provides a reflection on the meaningfulness of the activity and its impact. Drs. Larry Golden and Pat Henderson bring a wealth of experience in the field of counseling, as both practitioners and counselor educators. The vision they provided in formulating this book is anchored in this experience.

This resource may be a springboard to the development of other approaches to address the needs of the students served. Readers should feel free to adapt the activity to fit their setting and student population. Most importantly, this work displays the ingenuity and creativity that today's professional school counselors possess.

Fred O. Bradley, PhD
Department of Counseling and Educational Psychology
Kansas State University
Manhattan, Kansas

Fred O. Bradley, PhD, is professor and clinical coordinator in the Counseling and Educational Psychology Department in the College of Education, Kansas State University.

He began his professional career as a high school teacher and coach and continues his interest in schools, school counseling, and work with parents and teachers. He has presented literally hundreds of workshops and published many articles and books on a broad range of topics relating to children and adolescents. He is past president of the Association for Counselor Education and Supervision.

Preface

We are true believers in the advantages of a comprehensive, developmental school guidance and counseling program. Such a program helps professional school counselors sort out the needs of their caseloads and set reasonable priorities (American School Counselor Association, 2005). A comprehensive, developmental school guidance and counseling program holds school counselors accountable as well. School counselors are expected to guide *all* students and counsel subgroups of students whose barriers to learning threaten their success in school. They consult with parents, teachers, and administrators. They coordinate resources. They interpret results of student assessments to help students with their educational and career planning. They manage the guidance and counseling program, and they conform to professional standards.

Within the priorities of their program, professional school counselors work with myriad subgroups. They provide guidance to students progressing through normal developmental stages (e.g., early and middle childhood, early adolescence, adolescence, and young adulthood). Counselors offer preventive, remedial, and crisis counseling as well. They work with students, teachers, and parents who come from different cultural contexts (e.g., gender, sexual orientation and preference, family configuration, race/ethnicity, lifestyle, economic circumstances, parental educational level, first language, religion).

Our hope is that this book will bring the work of the school counselor alive for both seasoned practitioners and graduate students. We selected a wide sampling of case studies for this book. We've included developmental cases that address the needs of whole grade levels of students, such as Brenda Jones's delineation of the educational and career planning program that spans the four years of high school. There are cases describing efforts to prevent students from being overwhelmed by circumstances beyond their control, such as McMahon and Gold's group counseling intervention with middle school students facing divorces, and Loew's counseling group for gay high school students. There are cases describing efforts to help students rebound after making unhealthy choices, such as Herschenfeld's counseling of a child who was stealing from her classmates. There are cases describing efforts to help students facing crises, such as Libby's counseling and consulting to assist a suicide-prone student, and Melton's postvention work at a middle school after a suicide. There are cases describing consultation with parents, such as Bryant's work with an African American high school student and his parents. There are cases describing coordinating resources, such as Karcher's experience with a mentor program. There are cases describing professional school counselors' efforts to grow professionally, such as Cook and Storment's description of clinical supervision, and Redcay's description of extending her services to a child with hearing impairment.

Organization

Cases are divided by level: Elementary, Middle, High School. We've organized each of the cases by subheads, as follows.

The School. The counselor describes relevant aspects, such as demographics and location.

Student Need. The counselor describes the client and discusses the presenting problem. Who referred and why?

Goals and Strategies. The counselor explains why particular interventions (e.g., consultation with teachers or parents, solution-focused therapy, play therapy, small group counseling, referral, classroom instruction, career guidance, consultation) were selected.

Process. The counselor provides a step-by-step account of what happened.

Results. The counselor lets us in on what worked or didn't work and why?

Personal Reflection. This section gives the counselor a chance to share personal experiences that may have influenced the handling of the case. With the benefit of hindsight, the counselor tells us what could have been done differently.

Biographical Statement. This establishes the author's credentials and provides an e-mail address. All of the authors have told us that they are happy to respond to reader e-mail. Get in touch!

We think that this book works well as an accessory to a comprehensive text. What you get here is an honest picture of the occasionally brilliant and sometimes slogging work of school counselors. We want you to hear the counselor's voice. It's important to note that, in every case, the identity of clients has been carefully disguised to protect confidentiality.

Acknowledgments

We wish to acknowledge the help we received with editing and proofreading from Chichura Allen, Celeste Chaparro, Katrina Cook, Cari Davis, Terri Kurpgeweit, and Lizette Salinas, graduate assistants in our counseling program at UTSA, and from Matthew Hooper (Pat's own dear son), as well as expert assistance from Production Editor Mary Harlan and Publisher Kevin Davis of Merrill/Prentice Hall. We would also like to thank the following reviewers for their comments and insight: Ann L. Bauer, Cleveland State University; Andrew V. Beale, Virginia Commonwealth University; James Dykeman, Oregon State University; Douglas J. Mickelson, Mt. Mary College; and Rowland L. Savage, Johns Hopkins University.

Reference

American School Counselor Association. (2005). *The ASCA national model: A framework for school counseling programs* (2nd ed.). Alexandria, VA: Author.

About the Authors

Larry B. Golden, PhD, is associate professor in the Department of Counseling, Educational Psychology, and Adult and Higher Education at the University of Texas at San Antonio. Larry was an elementary school teacher for 5 years. Among his published books are *Psychotherapeutic Techniques in School Psychology* (1984); *Helping Families Help Children: Family Interventions with School Related Problems* (1986); *Preventing Adolescent Suicide; Ethical Standards Casebook* (4th ed., 1990); *Case Studies in Marriage and Family Therapy* (2nd ed., 2004); and *Case Studies in Child Counseling* (3rd ed., 2002). You can reach Larry at larry.golden@utsa.edu.

Patricia Henderson, EdD, was, for 19 years, director of guidance at Northside Independent School District in San Antonio, Texas, a district that employs more than 200 professional school counselors. Prior to that, she was a high school counselor for 6 years. Among her published works are *Developing and Managing Your School Guidance Program* and its companion, *Leading and Managing Your School Guidance Program Staff,* written with Norman Gysbers. Pat is currently a consultant in school guidance programming and a school counselor educator at the University of Texas at San Antonio. You can reach Pat at guidance@satx.rr.com.

Discover the Companion Website Accompanying This Book

The Prentice Hall Companion Website: A Virtual Learning Environment
Technology is a constantly growing and changing aspect of our field that is creating a need for content and resources. To address this emerging need, Prentice Hall has developed an online learning environment for students and professors alike—Companion Websites—to support our textbooks.

In creating a Companion Website, our goal is to build on and enhance what the textbook already offers. For this reason, the content for each user-friendly website is organized by topic and provides the professor and student with a variety of meaningful resources. Features of this Companion Website include:

- **Counseling Topics**—17 core counseling topics represent the diversity and scope of today's counseling field

- **Annotated Bibliography**—includes seminal foundational works and key current works

- **Web Destinations**—lists significant and up-to-date practitioner and client sites

- **Professional Development**—provides helpful information regarding professional organizations and codes of ethics

- **Electronic Blue Book**—send homework or essays directly to your instructor's e-mail with this paperless form

- **Chat**—real-time chat with anyone who is using the text anywhere in the country—ideal for discussion and study groups, class projects, etc.

To take advantage of these and other resources, please visit the *Case Studies in School Counseling* Companion Website at

www.prenhall.com/golden

Research Navigator:
Research Made Simple!

www.ResearchNavigator.com

Merrill Education is pleased to introduce Research Navigator—a one-stop research solution for students that simplifies and streamlines the entire research process. At www.researchnavigator.com, students will find extensive resources to enhance their understanding of the research process so they can effectively complete research assignments. In addition, Research Navigator has three exclusive databases of credible and reliable source content to help students focus their research efforts and begin the research process.

How Will Research Navigator Enhance Your Course?

- Extensive content helps students understand the research process, including writing, Internet research, and citing sources.
- Step-by-step tutorial guides students through the entire research process from selecting a topic to revising a rough draft.
- Research Writing in the Disciplines section details the differences in research across disciplines.
- Three exclusive databases—EBSCO's ContentSelect Academic Journal Database, *The New York Times* Search by Subject Archive, and "Best of the Web" Link Library—allow students to easily find journal articles and sources.

What's the Cost?

A subscription to Research Navigator is $7.50 but is available at no extra cost when ordered in conjunction with this textbook. To obtain free passcodes for your students, simply contact your local Merrill/Prentice Hall sales representative, and your representative will send you the Evaluating Online Resource Guide, which contains the code to access Research Navigator as well as tips on how to use Research Navigator and how to evaluate research. To preview the value of this website to your students, please go to www.educatorlearningcenter.com and use the Login Name "Research" and the password "Demo."

Contents

NOTE: Every effort has been made to provide accurate and current Internet information in this book. However, the Internet and information posted on it are constantly changing, and it is inevitable that some of the Internet addresses listed in this textbook will change.

Summary of Cases

Elementary School

Case/Counselor	Client	Need	Strategy
1. Lynette Heckenberg	7-year-old boy in Special Education	Mentally disabled, severe deficits in communication, poor social skills, angry outbursts	Play therapy; classroom guidance
2. Linda Herschenfeld	Third-grade girl	Child unable to own up to stealing	A single direct contact
3. Linda Herschenfeld	First-grade girl	Aggression, coping with impending death of a parent	Child-centered play therapy
4. Carol Hoheisel	Second-grade boy	Difficulty adjusting to arrival of baby brother	Small counseling group for children with new siblings
5. Angie Hood and John M. Littrell	7-year-old boy	Dinosaur fixation	Brief counseling techniques
6. Michael J. Karcher	Fourth-grade boy	At risk for academic failure	Mentoring
7. Patti Loewen	First Nation sixth-grade girl	Bullying other students	Solution-focused individual counseling and small group counseling
8. Shirley Redcay	Second-grade boy with hearing impairment	Adjusting to death of baby brother	Bereavement group; referral to summer camp for children with hearing impairment
9. Catherine Somody	Third-grade boy	Child of alcoholic; custody fight	Supportive counseling; testifying in court
10. Sheila Witherspoon	12-year-old African American boy	Defiance of authority; oppression by racist teacher	Glasser's choice theory; encourage healthy African American identity

Middle School

Case/Counselor	Client	Need	Strategy
11. Montserrat Casado-Kehoe	Seventh-grade students	Adjusting to divorce or separation	Small group counseling
12. Katrina Cook and Courtney Storment	Middle school counselor	Enhancing small group counseling skills	One-to-one supervision
13. Terrie J. House	Eighth-grade Latina girls	Use of substances and rise in teen pregnancies	Small group counseling
14. Jered B. Kolbert	Gifted sixth-grade boy	Underachieving, socially isolated	Individual client-centered and solution-focused counseling
15. George McMahon and Sheila Gold	Seventh- and eighth-grade girls	Difficulty adjusting to parents' divorce	Small group counseling based on Adler and Yalom; psychoeducation
16. Brenda Melton	All students, school personnel, and parents	An eighth-grade girl commits suicide	Implement Emergency Response Plan

High School

Case/Counselor	Client	Need or Presenting Problem	Strategy
17. Rhonda Bryant	14-year-old African American boy	Poor academic achievement and acting out	Family consultation; career guidance; encourage healthy African American identity
18. Neal Gray	16-year-old boy	Child of alcoholic; declining academic performance	Referral for substance abuse counseling
19. Brenda Jones	All students	Planning for high school and beyond	Group guidance lessons
20. Mary G. Libby	17-year-old boy	Suicidal ideation	Consultation; individual counseling
21. Marcia Loew	Gay students	Conflict and harassment	Support group for gay students; solution-focused therapy
22. LeAnne North	All students in a residential high school for the gifted	Anxiety, academic pressure, poor social skills	Classroom guidance; peer counseling

PART I

Elementary School Cases

We Two Can Be Teachers

Lynette Heckenberg

Seven-year-old mentally disabled Luke teaches some useful lessons to novice elementary school counselor Lynette Heckenberg. Luke's special education teacher and his parents describe him as angry and unsuccessful in building relationships. Luke's previous school counselor had determined that Luke was unable to communicate and could not benefit from counseling. Perhaps this was a situation where Heckenberg's lack of experience actually helped! She believed in the power of child-centered play therapy and that carried her and Luke forward.

was a first-year elementary school counselor when I met Luke, the boy who told me, "We two can be teachers." As our sessions unfolded, it became quite clear that I was not the only one with something to teach. Luke taught me much about counseling children with special needs. He was right: He, too, was a teacher. In fact, Luke was one of my best teachers. When I first met Luke, I, like many school counselors, both new and experienced, felt undertrained to counsel children with cognitive and communicative deficits. Luke began my training.

The School

Luke was a student in a self-contained class for children with moderate to severe mental disabilities. The class was housed in an elementary school with two sections of each grade level, kindergarten through sixth grade. Luke's school was located in a small Midwestern town with a population that was ethnically homogeneous but socioeconomically heterogeneous. The student-to-counselor ratio for the school was about 250 to 1.

Student Need

Luke was a 7-year-old with a mentally disabled label and severe deficits in receptive and expressive communication. Luke's self-contained special education teacher described him as angry, restless, distractible, unwilling to try new tasks, and chronically unsuccessful in interpersonal interactions with both peers and adults. Luke's parents had little positive to say about their son. They angrily complained of Luke's noncompliant behavior and their inability to take him out of the house without outbursts. Luke's behaviors were making life more difficult for him both at home and at school.

To make matters worse, Luke's expressive and receptive communication deficits had hindered previous efforts to modify the situation. Luke's speech was difficult to understand. Language-processing delays also made it difficult for Luke to fully understand others' messages. His previous school counselor had determined that Luke was unable to communicate and could not benefit from counseling.

I came to Luke's school armed with training in child-centered play therapy and a belief in the power of nonverbal communication. This belief was bolstered through a counseling relationship with Jordan, a classmate of Luke's.

Jordan was an 8-year-old with an unrepaired cleft palate and cognitive deficits that led to severe deficits in receptive and expressive communication. Jordan, like Luke, had been judged unable to benefit from counseling. However, given the opportunity to use play as a form of expression, Jordan communicated with me quite effectively and benefited greatly from counseling. Jordan began each session by grabbing the head of a long snake puppet and handing me the tail. Thus connected, Jordan would lead me around the playroom and into his play. To this day, whenever I think of following a client's lead, I picture Jordan, who ingeniously used a snake puppet to help me follow his thoughts and feelings as well as his actions. Jordan's success made me hopeful that Luke would benefit similarly from child-centered play therapy.

■ Goals and Strategies

Many children find it easier to express their thoughts and feelings through behaviors than through words. This is especially true for children with cognitive and communication deficits, for whom verbal communication often brings misunderstanding and frustration. Acting out, then, can be both a form of communication and a response to frustration when communication is unsuccessful.

I felt that Luke's acting out behaviors were, at least in part, a function of his communication difficulties. Therefore, my primary goal for counseling was to offer Luke a nonverbal, less frustrating means of expression. Toward this end, I engaged Luke in six weekly 30-minute sessions of nondirective child-centered play therapy.

Play is a developmentally appropriate means of communication that is available to even the most verbally challenged child. While adults generally prefer to communicate with words, children, whose language skills are still developing, communicate more easily through play. Nondirective child-centered play therapy gives a child the opportunity to express thoughts and feelings through play and to be responded to by a counselor who is trained to speak and understand the child's language of play. Play becomes communication.

As Luke played through his six sessions, I attended to, and tried to understand, the feelings and thoughts he communicated through his actions, verbalizations, facial expressions, body language, and play themes. In response, I used language to reflect my understanding of his message, my acceptance of his thoughts and feelings, and my belief in his ability to deal effectively with his world.

Related to my goal of providing Luke with an environment for expressing thoughts and feelings through play, I also wanted to help Luke learn a shared language for effectively communicating his feelings outside of the playroom. To accomplish this goal, I engaged Luke's self-contained special education class in weekly classroom guidance lessons. Hitting was a favored means of communication in this class and was used to express anger, sadness, and even happiness, as when one student hit another to gain his attention to show off a new toy. My aim was to help Luke and his classmates label and express their feelings without hitting or acting out.

■ Process

Luke and I shared six once-weekly sessions of nondirective child-centered play therapy. Summaries and excerpts of these sessions follow.

Session 1. Luke's first session began shortly after a frustrating recess during which other children refused to let Luke join them in play. Luke began the session by trying to tell me verbally about the recess incident. Luke's speech was difficult to understand, and I had to ask him to repeat himself several times. Soon, he was frustrated and ready to give up and leave my office! Luckily, we shifted from verbal communication to play. Luke found the toys he needed to quite clearly communicate the recess incident and his feelings. Luke used a group of animals and gave me a toy man. Over and over, the animals killed and devoured the man.

Luke:	Do that again.
Counselor:	Got him again!
Luke:	Do it again.
Counselor:	They get him every time.
Luke:	Do it again.
Counselor:	You want Counselor to do it over and over.
Luke:	Every time I get him.
Counselor:	He's always in trouble.
Luke:	Yeah. Them don't want him there.

Session 2. In his second session, Luke directed my every move in a game of his creation, repetitively misdirecting me, confusing me, and pointing out that I was doing everything wrong. He made it clear that I was helpless to prevent my inevitable failure. Luke again clearly communicated to me what it felt like to be him. After I got the message he sent with his actions, he confirmed it verbally.

Luke:	You did it wrong.
Counselor:	I keep getting it wrong.
Luke:	Get it right now!
Counselor:	There?
Luke:	No! Where I said!
Counselor:	I'm wrong again (trying another place).
Luke:	No!
Counselor:	I always do it wrong.
Luke:	You won't be winner! Ha! Ha! Ha!
Counselor:	No matter what I do, I won't win.
Luke:	Counselor will!
Counselor:	You will always be the winner.
Luke:	You are loser.
Counselor:	You're telling me and telling me so I will know. (Luke laughs.) It's funny.
Luke:	(serious) Know what?
Counselor:	Hmmm?
Luke:	They always laugh at me.

Session 3. Luke spent the majority of the third session directing and confusing me, again using me as a toy to communicate his thoughts and feelings. He didn't have the verbal communication skills to tell me that he felt powerless, but he quite clearly showed me all about the powerlessness that he felt.

Luke:	Get that on.
Counselor:	You're telling me just what to do.
Luke:	Come here.

Counselor:	I'm following you.
Luke:	You get that and that.
Counselor:	You make all the choices.
Luke:	Come here.
Counselor:	You want me over here.
Luke:	Go over there.
Counselor:	Now I belong over here. You're the boss.
Luke:	Not the boss when at home.
Counselor:	You're not the boss at home, only here.
Luke:	Get this! Open that! And that! And this! Do it!

Session 4. Luke let me know at the beginning of Session 4 what was in store for me.

Luke:	I know what we play.
Counselor:	You have a plan for us.
Luke:	I have plan for you.

He certainly did have a plan for me! He again communicated his feelings of powerlessness and confusion by directing me in play. In this play telephone conversation, I was called by a restaurant.

Luke:	(in phone) What do you want?
Counselor:	(whispered to Luke, not in the phone) What do I want?
Luke:	(in phone) Tell me what you want.
Counselor:	I don't know what I want.
Luke:	Tell me.
Counselor:	You want me to decide.
Luke:	Tell me something!
Counselor:	Hmmm. A hamburger.
Luke:	YOU CAN'T ORDER!!
Counselor:	What should I do?
Luke:	Bye!

Later in the session I remained powerless, as a student to Luke's teacher.

Luke:	You ask me you can go to the bathroom.
Counselor:	Can I go to the bathroom?
Luke:	Yes.
Counselor:	I have to ask you first.
Luke:	Turn off light. (I turn it off.) No! Turn it on!
Counselor:	I did it wrong.
Luke:	Ask you can get a drink.
Counselor:	Can I get a drink?
Luke:	Sit down!
Counselor:	I have to follow all your rules.
Luke:	Get a drink.

Session 5. In this session, Luke did not need to make me as powerless, perhaps because he had fewer feelings of powerlessness to communicate. Together, Luke and I dealt with an imaginary class full of misbehaving students. In Luke's words, "We two can be teachers."

Counselor:	You're not happy about that.
Luke:	Or you.
Counselor:	We are both mad.
Luke:	Make your mad face. They not going.
Counselor:	I need to do something about that with my mad face.
Luke:	Now they are.
Counselor:	They listened that time.
Luke:	To me and you.
Counselor:	They listened to us. We are in charge.
Luke:	Me and you.
Counselor:	You decided that we're both in charge today.
Luke:	Yep. We two can be teachers.

Session 6. In his last session, Luke directed a review of earlier sessions, starting with the most recent and moving back in time. Luke allowed me to coteach awhile, then I was the student named Luke and he was the teacher. This time, however, I was not a confused and powerless Luke. Luke as the teacher helped me as the student know just what to do.

Luke:	Put your arm in the sleeve.
Counselor:	You're helping me. I have you to help me.
Luke:	Come on. Play with kids.
Counselor:	You want me to have fun.
Luke:	Be good.
Counselor:	You're telling me so I know just what to do.
Luke:	Yep.

Luke's review continued with a period of the animals killing the man, as he had done in the first session. Finally, after I told Luke he had two minutes left, he became a bus driver and was ready to take me home.

Results

Like Jordan did earlier, Luke taught me that students with communication deficits can benefit from counseling. Though verbalization was difficult for him, Luke clearly communicated feelings of confusion, powerlessness, frustration, and anger. As Luke's feelings of powerlessness waned, he let me know that, too. My primary goal was to offer Luke play as a nonverbal means of communication. I believe he used it quite successfully.

Pre- and postcounseling administrations of Conners' Teacher Rating Scale also showed changes. Luke went from "pretty much" to "just a little" on the easily frustrated item; from "very much" to "pretty much" on the excitable, impulsive item; from "very much" to "just a little" on the overly sensitive item; from "very much" to "not at all" on the cries often and easily item; and from "very much" to "just a little" on the defiant item.

Communication is a two-person activity. It's incorrect to say "He can't communicate." The more accurate statement would be "*We* aren't communicating." Luke and other children with verbal communication deficits can and do communicate. They send messages that we counselors can learn to receive.

■ Personal Reflection

Luke didn't just teach me that he could communicate; he taught me to be a better communicator. Luke's use of me as a toy gave me the opportunity to receive, and to reflect, his message of powerlessness and confusion. Luke showed me what his world was like, and I let him know that I understood. We communicated in a way that seemed helpful for him.

Luke reminded me that every child has the potential to teach me. Children teach us about themselves and about ourselves as counselors. When I look at children, I imagine them saying a slightly edited version of something Luke first said: "We, too, can be teachers."

Suggested Readings

Axline, V. (1969). *Play therapy*. Cambridge, MA: Houghton Mifflin.

Drewes, A., Carey, L., & Schaefer, C. (2001). *School-based play therapy*. New York: John Wiley and Sons.

Kaduson, H., & Schaefer, C. (2000). *Short-term play therapy for children*. New York: Guilford Press.

Landreth, G. (2002). *Play therapy: The art of the relationship* (2nd ed.). New York: Brunner-Routledge.

Landreth, G., Homeyer, L., Glover, G., & Sweeney, D. (1996). *Play therapy interventions with children's problems*. Northvale, NJ: Jason Aronson.

Biographical Statement

At the time of the case study, Lynette Heckenberg was a first-year school counselor with an MA in counseling and human development. Lynette has subsequently earned a PhD in counseling and human development, with a minor in child development. Lynette is a registered play therapist and a licensed mental health counselor. She uses play to counsel children in both elementary school and private practice settings. You can reach Lynette at lynetteheck@mchsi.com.

A Classroom Teacher's Struggle with Stealing

Linda Herschenfeld

In this very brief case, really more of a critical incident, third grader Sarah has been caught stealing but can't bring herself to accept responsibility. Her classmates ostracize her. With a gentle, yet direct intervention, Herschenfeld, the school counselor, helps Sarah admit her responsibility and move on.

Stealing can be a tricky problem to handle in the elementary school environment. As a school counselor, I am called upon to deal with numerous incidents of this type each year. The act of stealing can elicit very judgmental feelings and punitive actions on the part of an otherwise kind and understanding teacher, counselor, or principal. In my initial attempts to handle this problem as a beginning school counselor, I struggled with ways that best addressed the problem. Stealing carries a certain stigma that often influences how the "offender" is handled. It is of concern that children are often treated in ways that serve to compound their guilt and further lower their self-esteem. I have found that it is important to step back from the emotionally charged subject of "stealing" and focus on the goal of helping the child.

The School

Farrington School has a population of 460 students in kindergarten through Grade 6. It is located in Augusta, Maine, the capital city. The school has a population that consists primarily of Caucasian children who range from middle class to financially challenged. The free breakfast and lunch program serves over 50% of our population. One unique feature of Farrington School is that it is the receiving school for all English as a second language (ESL) students in the Augusta schools. This diverse group of students makes up about 10% of our population and adds a rich dimension to our school as we have students from throughout the world in attendance.

Student Need

Mr. White is a very understanding and competent third-grade teacher. He came to me to recount the troubling events that had occurred in his classroom during the past week. Many items had disappeared from students' desks, including pencils, erasers, and a plastic beaded bracelet. It quickly became clear to Mr. White and the students *who* was responsible for these disappearances. The missing items kept appearing in Sarah's desk. Mr. White confronted Sarah with the evidence, but despite all his efforts, she continued to deny that she had taken the missing items.

Mr. White was frustrated and perplexed. He was sure that Sarah was the culprit but could not break through her denials. He was feeling angry that Sarah had lied to him and that he was unable to "extract a confession." Mr. White was also concerned that Sarah was now being ostracized by her classmates, who were avoiding her to protect their possessions.

Sarah was an attractive 8-year-old girl. She lived in a family that was composed of her mother; older sister, age 10; younger brother, age 6; and mother's boyfriend. Sarah's mother is an immigrant and did not speak English well. Sarah participates in the ESL program. It has been noted by Sarah's previous teachers that she has issues with self-esteem, and her mother has mentioned that she has behavioral problems at home. Sarah is currently involved in small group counseling to try to address these needs.

Sarah's stealing needed to be viewed as a presenting problem. To merely address the stealing or "get stuck" on the stealing focuses on a symptom and does not address the underlying problem. Further, accusing Sarah of stealing and trying to extract a confession served to lower her self-esteem. Mr. White certainly had no intention of causing Sarah to feel bad. He was merely trying to address the classroom problem and put an end to it. However, by asking Sarah *if* she had stolen objects and using a tone that conveyed disapproval, he put Sarah in a difficult position. She already felt guilty about her actions. To be confronted in an emotionally charged way further increased her guilt feelings and prompted her to deny her responsibility even though she knew that Mr. White knew she did it.

This impasse was difficult for Sarah. She felt very badly about herself and was now cut off from the support and nurturing she counted on from Mr. White. For his part, Mr. White felt angry that Sarah had lied to him and was not able to respond to her in his usual caring way. This was the point at which Mr. White came to me looking for a way to resolve this problem.

Goals and Strategies

This was not the first time this type of issue had developed in my school environment. In fact, events such as this had transpired and unfolded in much the same way numerous times before. For this reason, I have developed a simple intervention that addresses all the dynamics that arise when this type of situation develops. Therefore, this intervention is not specific to Sarah's circumstances. There is one caution to using this method: It can be used only in instances where the teacher and the counselor are absolutely sure which student is responsible for the missing objects.

Process

Mr. White was quite eager for me to talk with Sarah because he felt that he had exhausted all his options.

Session 1. I got Sarah from her classroom, and as we walked back to my office, I made sure to set the tone by engaging in friendly conversation. It was important for Sarah to know that I was not angry with her and that I was not taking her to face disciplinary action. Once we were in private, I explained the reason for our meeting.

Counselor:	Mr. White has explained to me that there is a problem in your classroom. Sometimes children want something that belongs to someone else and they take it. When that happens, it's best to return the things and take responsibility for your actions. (Sarah nods her head in agreement.) You are probably feeling bad about this and wondering what you can do to feel better. Giving the things back and apologizing will help. You can feel proud that you were able to admit a mistake and take responsibility for it . . . not everyone is brave enough to do that.
Sarah:	OK!
Counselor:	Let's go talk to Mr. White.

■ Results

Most children, including Sarah, readily take responsibility at this point, return the objects, and say they are sorry to the child whom they stole from. They are also relieved to clear things up with their teacher and return to the warm and caring relationship characteristic of elementary school teachers and their students.

Sarah was able to apologize to her peers, and they were ready to forgive her. One boy said, "That's OK," and the friendship went on as before. Sarah's talk with Mr. White was a bit more emotional. She shed some tears as she told the truth. Mr. White was relieved; he told Sarah how proud he was that she had owned up to her actions. He stated that they would "start fresh" and Sarah agreed.

This represents a positive way of handling a situation that needs resolution without doing further damage to the child's self-esteem. It models a way to put a positive spin on negative actions, that is, focusing on taking responsibility versus dwelling on the stealing and lying. Once the identifying issue is resolved, the teacher, counselor, and student can more easily focus on the underlying issues and the therapeutic work can take place in an atmosphere of trust and positive regard.

■ Personal Reflection

This exchange and intervention is very different from my usual counseling techniques. I am this direct only when dealing with problems of this nature. It is important to let the children know that I know what has occurred and that I still like and respect them. This is achieved by stating the events in a matter-of-fact, nonjudgmental, and impartial way so that the child knows he or she is accepted and valued no matter what he or she has done.

It is important to avoid the word *stealing*, which may be laden with value judgments due to the emotional content embedded in the messages that have been given when others have tried to resolve the issue. This is essential because I do not want to make the children feel guiltier than they already do. Most importantly, I do not ask children if they are responsible for the missing objects; I state it as a fact in an impartial way. This eliminates the need for denial on the children's part. They see that you know the truth, that they are still accepted, and that you are offering a way to resolve the situation that allows them to retain their dignity.

Suggested Readings

Balvanz, J., Johnson, L., & Nelson, L. (1999). A play therapy intervention and its relationship to self-efficacy and learning behaviors. *Professional School Counseling* 2(3), 194–204.

Dudley, C. D. (1997). *Treating depressed children: A therapeutic manual of cognitive behavioral interventions*. Oakland, CA: New Harbinger Publications.

Greene, R. (2001). *The Explosive Child*. New York: HarperCollins.

Morris, R. J., & Kratochwill, T. R. (1998). *The Practice of Child Therapy* (3rd ed.). Boston: Allyn and Bacon.

Biographical Statement

Linda Herschenfeld, LCSW, RPTS, is an elementary school counselor at Farrington School in Augusta, Maine. She has been an elementary school counselor for 12 years. Linda is a Registered Play Therapist-Supervisor with the Association for Play Therapy. You can reach her at lherschenfeld@augusta.k12.me.us.

Emily in the Eye of the Storm

Linda Herschenfeld

Emily is a first grader who acts out aggressively against other children. Emily is also dealing with a painful reality: her mother, a single parent, is terminally ill. Herschenfeld uses play therapy to help Emily express her feelings and cope with her mother's impending death. Herschenfeld does a fine job of demonstrating Virginia Axline's Child-Centered Play Therapy.

D

eath is a challenging issue to deal with in the school community. The school counselor is often faced with complicated tasks, as the death almost always reaches far beyond the particular family that experiences the immediate loss. The feelings this loss elicits radiate out in ever larger circles that affect the family, friends, classroom, staff, and community. School counselors often find themselves in the eye of this storm. Using Child-Centered Play Therapy (Landreth, 1991) can enable young children to express their myriad feelings while in the midst of devastating loss.

The School

Farrington School has a population of 460 students in kindergarten through Grade 6. It is located in Augusta, Maine, the capital city. The school population consists primarily of Caucasian children who range from middle class to financially challenged. The free breakfast and lunch program serves over 50% of our population. One unique feature of Farrington School is that it is the receiving school for all ESL students in the Augusta schools. This diverse group of students makes up about 10% of our population and adds a rich dimension to our school as we have students from throughout the world in attendance.

Student Need

Emily was a physically small and attractive first grader. She resided with her mother and one older sibling. Reluctantly, she came to school each day. Emily had some behavioral issues that caused difficulty between her and the other children. She felt that certain children disliked her and were picking on her. On investigation, I found that, in fact, Emily was the aggressor and the other children were acting in response to her. I had the opportunity to work with Emily and her peers on several occasions to try to resolve differences and to help Emily understand her responsibility in these matters.

It was against this backdrop that Emily learned that her mother was terminally ill. I was never sure how much Emily ever really understood, as she was a somewhat immature and nonverbal child. As the disruptions in Emily's life increased, she began acting out more often. Emily was not able to verbalize her feelings about her mom's condition; instead, she focused on how she hated school, the relatives who were caring for her, and life in general. These feelings were acted out each day by physical demonstrations of anger and verbal outbursts. Obviously, something had to be done to help Emily, and it needed to happen fast.

Emily's mother's condition had drastically worsened with no warning. Mrs. Mitchell had had a positive outlook and expected to get well. Her sudden decline had taken Emily and her extended family, as well as the school community, by surprise. Often, when a school is aware of an impending crisis, planning goes on in advance. In Emily's case, it was as if a whirlwind hit her life with no warning and turned it upside down.

Goals and Strategies

It was obvious that intervention was necessary, but what could be the best approach to this heartbreaking situation? How could I best help Emily cope with the many feelings that were consuming her? Child-Centered Play Therapy (Landreth, 1991) was the natural choice. Emily was young, nonverbal, and feeling out of control. She needed intervention at a level she could handle and in which she could feel control. Child-Centered Play Therapy, because of its emphasis on starting with children wherever they are and following their lead, promised to offer the best way for Emily to get some relief.

Process

When Emily came to her first session, I stated, "You can decide to do almost anything you would like to do." This statement sets the tone of the session. It lets children know that they are being afforded some control of their environment and that they may choose how to engage in the therapeutic process. This same simple statement also lets the child know that the therapist will be there to set limits; hence, the child can feel safe. It was crucial to give Emily some control as her life was totally out of control, and also to provide her with a safety net in the form of limits.

One of my metaphors about Emily was that she was free-falling through space. She had no way to stop herself or get hold of something that would ground her in safety. Child-Centered Play Therapy provides a structure and framework in which a child can express feelings through the medium of play. The therapist *follows* the child's lead and reflects the feelings and meaning behind the child's play. The relationship between the counselor and the child helps facilitate the child's ability to express him- or herself. Limit setting is also a key component of this approach as it allows the child to express frightening feelings in an atmosphere that is safe. The child learns through the limit setting that he or she will not be allowed to hurt him- or herself or others. Hence, the child will be kept safe. (An example of limit setting will follow.) My hope was that Emily would find a way to ground herself through the play therapy process.

Emily came to my room during a particularly difficult week in which she had had many outbursts that were distressing to her, her teacher, and her classmates. While everyone felt sorry for Emily, they were also tiring of having to cope with her. She had visited my office several times that week. Each time I stated, "You can decide to do almost anything you would like." She chose to play with cars or make tools out of clay. She seemed to be using the time as a hiatus from her problems.

On this particular day, Emily reacted differently. When I uttered the now familiar phrase "You can decide to do almost anything you would like," she went over to the dollhouse and began to mess up and knock down furniture from the dollhouse into the sand.

Counselor:	Everything is messed up.
Emily:	Yeah, it's a twister. A twister is ruining the house.
Counselor:	You feel scared that everything is getting ruined.
Emily:	Yeah . . . it's getting stronger.
Counselor:	You can't control it.

(Emily went around the room dumping all the dollhouse furniture onto the floor. Then she began to dump Legos, people, blocks, animals, and so forth all over the floor.)

Counselor: It's really powerful. You feel that everything is getting ruined.

(Emily knocked more things onto the floor. This was done in a very controlled and deliberate way.)

Counselor: No one is safe from this . . . you don't feel safe.

(Emily threw puppets on the floor.)

Counselor: You can't get away from it.

(Emily went for the dollhouse and began to try to throw it on the floor.)

Counselor: (using limit setting) You'd like to throw that on the floor. (Acknowl-
               edgement of feelings)
               That could hurt you. (Statement of consequence)
               I'll help you place it on the floor. (Provide an alternative)

(Emily allowed me to help her take the dollhouse down and place it on the pile of "rubble." In fact, some wooden dollhouse furniture had really broken as it was crushed under other toys or as Emily had accidentally stepped on it.) When everything was on the floor in a heap—and it was a *huge* mess—Emily looked around and said:

Emily: It's not over . . . the twister's not done.
Counselor: It's so powerful. You are having so many powerful feelings.

Emily roughly moved toys from one pile to another.

Counselor: You feel that everything is ruined.
Emily: It's not just a twister, a volcano is coming too!
Counselor: You feel that your whole life is ruined and you can't stop it.

Results

This session lasted for an hour, at which point Emily was exhausted. She was able to calmly return to class and be successful for the rest of the day. How powerful a metaphor Emily had provided for her life, as it was indeed in ruins! She felt that a natural disaster had come into her life and turned everything upside down. Her disaster was something so powerful that it could not be controlled, and no area of her life was safe from the devastation.

Personal Reflection

As I looked at what used to be my neatly appointed room, I marveled at what had just transpired. Through the use of Child-Centered Play Therapy (Landreth, 1991), Emily was able to unleash her powerful and terrifying feelings. She was able to do so in an environment that provided limits to keep her and others safe. Emily was able to act out her feelings without aggression. She did not try to destroy objects or throw anything at me; she merely played out the twister and volcano that had entered into her life.

Rarely has a session been so powerful. I felt humbled by the sheer magnitude of Emily's emotions and grateful that I was able to help her to safely express her feelings through the use of Child-Centered Play Therapy (Landreth, 1991).

Emily's mom died the next day, and Emily did not return to school. I saw her one last time at the funeral. Emily moved away to live with relatives in another area.

Reference

Landreth, G. (1991). *Play therapy: The art of the relationship.* Muncie, IN: Acceler-
    ated Development.

Suggested Readings

Gil, E. (1991). *The healing power of play: Working with abused children.* New York:
    The Guilford Press.
Kottman, T. (2002). *Partners In Play: An Adlerian Approach to Play Therapy.* American
    Counseling Association.
Landreth, G. (2002). *Play therapy: The art of the relationship.* New York: Brunner-
    Routledge.
Fall, M. (1997). From stages to categories: A study of children's play in play therapy
    sessions. *International Journal of Play Therapy 69*(10), 1–21.

Biographical Statement

Linda Herschenfeld, LCSW, RPTS, is an elementary school counselor at Farrington School in Augusta, Maine. She has been an elementary school counselor for 12 years. Linda is a Registered Play Therapist-Supervisor with the Association for Play Therapy. You can reach her at lherschenfeld@augusta.k12.me.us.

4

I'm Not the Baby Anymore

Carol Hoheisel

Jared, a second grader, is not adjusting very well to his new baby brother. Carol Hoheisel uses a "new siblings" group to help him cope. Hoheisel provides a wonderful example of how group process works and practical ideas about selecting group members.

Many consider the birth of a baby to be one of the most joyous events in life. Although children usually feel excitement and love for their new brother or sister, they also may experience jealousy, sadness, or anger. Since their lives are often disrupted by the arrival of a new sibling, children may become anxious and frustrated over the changes that occur, which they can't control. In addition, older siblings may become confused since their emotions are not congruent with each other. If these feelings are not addressed, children's feelings could eventually lead to resentment toward the new baby. Children may regress in their behavior or become more demanding and difficult. Changes in children's conduct often stem from their insecurities and fears about how the baby will affect their lives. Children may be afraid that they won't be wanted or needed in the family anymore. In addition, they may feel ignored or pushed aside when adults focus on the new baby. Helping a child adjust to a new sibling does not have to be a complex process. Children often just need an opportunity to express their emotions and to receive one-on-one time with an adult. To meet the needs of my students who recently became older siblings, I decided to form a small counseling group for elementary students with new siblings.

The School

At the time, I was completing a doctoral internship in counseling at the elementary school where I conducted the new-sibling group. The school is located in a small rural town in Kansas with a population of less than 500 residents. The school enrolled approximately 75 students in kindergarten through fourth grade. In addition to this school, I also interned at a middle school for fifth through eighth graders. The middle school had approximately 90 students and was located in a nearby small community. Both schools are in the same school district. The schools' ethnic makeup was approximately 96% white and 4% Hispanic. Over 50% of these schools' students receive free or reduced lunch—above Kansas's state average of 39%. Agriculture plays a major economic role in both communities.

Student Need

The idea for the new-sibling group resulted from a teacher referral. One day, a second-grade teacher came to the counseling office and mentioned a concern about one of her students, named Jared. Jared's mother had just given birth and Jared refused to acknowledge his new brother. If questioned about the baby, Jared would get angry and withdraw from the conversation. Before the birth, Jared was an only child and was used to being the center of attention in his family. The teacher observed recent changes in Jared's behavior and asked if I would address this issue with Jared.

A few days later I was able to meet with Jared. During our first session, I met with him individually for 30 minutes. Since I had just started working at the school and didn't know Jared well, I decided to use an icebreaker activity in our first session. The teacher told me in advance that Jared loved to draw, so I decided to ask him if he would like to draw a picture of his family. I was curious to see if he would include his new brother in the drawing. While drawing his picture, Jared was very talkative and told me about his new brother, named Aaron. Surprisingly, he not only talked about Aaron but he also drew himself with him. Apparently, Jared's feelings about his brother had changed a little since the original teacher referral. However, Jared didn't draw his parents in the picture, so I asked him if anyone else lived with him. He said his parents also lived in his house and added, "I don't get to do anything with them anymore." He didn't want to expand on this comment and never drew his parents in the picture, which I found interesting. Although he was now willing to talk about his brother, he seemed to have some underlying issues that still needed to be discussed. I thought it was important to address the issues right away instead of waiting for Jared's behavior to get worse. After our session together, I consulted with my supervisor about Jared. Although I could have continued working with Jared on an individual basis, I decided to try a new idea and work with him in a group setting.

Goals and Strategies

I chose a group format for various reasons. Support offered by other students in a group can often be more potent to a student than support offered by a counselor in an individual session. In addition, more ideas, information, and insight can be shared in a group format. Group members also have opportunities to practice social skills such as listening, taking turns, developing self-control, and learning how to express themselves. In a group setting, students may learn that others share their problems and realize they are not alone. Finally, groups can offer a supportive and safe environment that provides children with a place to heal and grow. For these reasons, I believed participation in a group would be beneficial for Jared.

When I started developing the concept for the new-sibling group, I had no preexisting template to use as a reference. The only thing certain was that I wanted the group to consist of children who had new siblings. I had a rough idea of the overall goal of the group but not a detailed plan. My primary goal was to help children adjust to their new siblings and their new roles in their families. I was hoping to find ready-made materials to use but ended up not having time to locate them. Like many counselors, I brainstormed for topic ideas and created the activities I needed. I knew what I wanted to accomplish during the first meeting and decided that during the course of the group, the members would participate in a group project such as creating a book. Beyond those simple plans, I chose to pick activities for each meeting on a weekly basis, depending on the needs of the group members. Since I tend to be the type of counselor who likes to go with the flow of a group, I was not too concerned that I did not have a more detailed plan.

The next step in the process was selecting group members. My supervisor and I looked for students who would be appropriate for the group. In addition to Jared, we identified three other students who could possibly benefit from this group. Austin and Nicole, who were brother and sister, had a 1-month-old baby brother. Austin was a fourth grader and Nicole was a third grader. Austin was a very outgoing and active child, who demanded and received a lot of attention. He had a tendency to get into trouble both in and out of school. Nicole, on the other hand, was shy and often overshadowed by her older brother. Since she was well behaved, she did not receive a great deal of attention from her parents, who were busy dealing with Austin. We also considered Matthew, a third grader with a 1-year-old brother. Even though Matthew was not dealing with the birth of a new sibling, he was still facing adjustment and personal issues stemming from the addition of his brother. Furthermore, he struggled in the classroom because he had difficulty focusing on his work and using self-restraint. I thought that Matthew could be our "expert" in the group, providing the other group members with firsthand information about babies.

When making my final selections for the group, I chose Matthew and Nicole and decided against including Austin. Although I believed Austin could benefit from participation in the new-sibling group, I thought that Nicole needed more attention, which the group could provide her and which Austin could distract from. I also was concerned about the age difference between Jared and Austin, and questioned if it would be developmentally appropriate to place a second grader in the same group as a fourth grader. By coincidence, each child selected for the group was used to being the baby of his or her family, and each child had a new baby brother.

Although three students may not be the ideal size for a group, I believed the small number could work to our advantage. After observing Matthew and Jared in their classrooms, I recognized that they had a lot of energy and at times had difficulty staying on task. They required additional attention that would be easier to provide in a smaller group. I also thought Nicole would be more comfortable in a smaller group because she was shy.

Before we contacted the children about the group, we called their parents, described the new-sibling group, and asked permission for the children's participation. The parents liked and felt comfortable with the idea of the new-sibling group; the topic seemed not to threaten them. As a result, all of the parents gave consent for their children to participate. After getting the parent permissions, I then met with Jared, Nicole, and Matthew individually and described the new-sibling group to them. I asked the children individually if they would like to be a part of the group, and each child said yes. When I met with Matthew, I explained that he could be our group's "baby expert" because his brother was older. He liked the idea that he could help others and be perceived as knowledgeable about something. Underneath his cheerful exterior, Matthew had low self-esteem and needed positive attention. He seemed especially interested in the group and was excited to know when it would begin.

■ Process

I determined in advance that the group would meet for 30 minutes every Tuesday for approximately 8 weeks. Since children like consistency, the meetings were held at the same time every week: 1:30 P.M. A couple of days after making the initial contacts, the first meeting of the new-sibling group was held.

<u>Session 1.</u> At the beginning of the first meeting, I asked the children to introduce themselves by saying their name, the name of their baby brother, and their favorite activities outside of school. After the introductions, I briefly discussed the basics of the group: how long we would meet each week, how often we would meet, and when we would meet. I gave them an overview of what we would do in the group.

Next, we discussed the importance of having group rules. I asked them what would happen if there were no rules at school or home. I encouraged the members to make their own list of rules for the group. Since Nicole already knew that Matthew and Jared had a tendency to interrupt and speak while other people talked, she suggested that only one person should be allowed to speak at a time. Remembering a strategy that I used in a previous group, I suggested that the group could use a "speaking stone" to help them take turns talking. The speaking stone was just an ordinary stone that I had in my office; however, when someone held the stone in his or her hand, that person had permission to speak and everyone else had to listen. When members were through speaking, they would pass the stone to the next person who wanted to speak. Everyone liked the idea and started using the speaking stone right away. It appeared that they appreciated having a tangible and visible reminder of whose turn it was to speak.

Matthew suggested the rule that no one should make fun of what members said in the group. All agreed that it would not be nice if anyone laughed at what someone said. We talked about the concept of respect and how we could respect each other in the group. After these two rules were determined, the members were stuck and could not think of anything else to add. In previous groups, I have seen children make extensive and elaborate lists of rules. However, it didn't seem necessary for these members to create a long list. I decided that the concept of confidentiality also needed to be mentioned. I asked the members if they could tell me what *confidentiality* meant. Nicole offered the definition, "What we talk about in this room is private." Although I told her she gave an excellent example, I also wanted the members to know that this group was not about keeping secrets. It was OK if they talked with their parents about what *they* said in the group, but they shouldn't talk about anyone else in the group or what other people said. I asked all of them if they understood what I meant, and they said yes.

After we finished creating the group rules, we began discussing questions I had chosen in advance. The students seemed pretty comfortable with each other, so I jumped right in and started asking personal questions. Here is a sample of questions I included in our discussion:

1. How did you first feel when you heard you were going to have a new brother or sister?
2. What has changed in your life (good or bad) since your baby brother was born?
3. What is the best thing about being an older brother or sister?
4. What do you like best about your new brother?

I had several other questions prepared but decided to save them for other meetings. I was a little surprised that Jared did not seem too upset by the changes that had occurred in his life since the birth of his brother; however, Jared may not have been ready or able to verbalize his feelings at this point. I also thought the members might mention more negative things about the recent changes in their lives, but they were all fairly positive. One of my objectives for this group was to provide the members an opportunity to vent their emotions, but they did not want to discuss these feelings in greater detail. Looking back, I wonder if these questions were appropriate for our first meeting.

After our brief discussion, I asked the members if they would draw pictures of their families. Typically, when I ask children to draw the members of their family, I also request that the children label each person in the drawing if the children can write or spell. Although I am not trained in art therapy, I can gather a great deal of information about a child by simply asking the child to describe the drawing. Even though I rely primarily on the child's interpretation of the drawing, I also make my own cautious observations. For example, basic features such as how large the child draws him- or herself in relation to others, what facial expressions people have, and who is included in the drawing all can suggest subtle information that should be further explored with the child.

Most children enjoy drawing and tend to open up without effort while they draw. Drawing is a nonthreatening activity and a valuable tool in counseling. I quickly learned that Jared, Matthew, and Nicole all loved to draw, and they started drawing their families without further instruction. After Nicole was done, she described everyone in her picture, including her family pets. I found it interesting that she drew her brother Austin in the center of the page and bigger than anyone else in her family, including her parents. I wondered if she unconsciously realized the power Austin held in the family. I speculated that her drawing might reveal how she perceived the dynamics and power structure in her family. I also noticed that Nicole did not draw herself in her picture. Knowing Nicole's personality and background, I was not surprised by this discovery. Possibly Nicole did not receive a lot of attention in her family, and so felt she was not an important part of it. Instead of assuming this possibility, I asked Nicole, "Is there anyone else in your family that you would like to draw?" Nicole did not pick up on my cue right away. Instead, Matthew looked up from his own drawing and said bluntly, "Hey, you forgot to draw yourself." What was so obvious to Matthew was not immediately clear to Nicole. In response to Matthew's comment, Nicole just said, "Oops" and drew herself in the picture. Looking back, I wonder if I missed a valuable opportunity to explore Nicole's feelings about the role she played in her family.

Matthew drew his complete family and everyone had big smiles in his picture. Matthew gave a detailed description of what his baby brother, Nolan, was doing in the picture and seemed very proud when he shared with the group that Nolan had started walking. Jared's picture was similar to the one he drew in our first individual session. He spent a great deal of time drawing the furniture in his house, and once again drew only his brother and himself. I asked Jared if there was anyone else in his family that he wanted to draw, and he just replied, "My mom will really like that I made a picture for Aaron." He was satisfied with his drawing and I decided not to press him for more information. Just 2 weeks prior, Jared did not even want to acknowledge he had a brother, and now he was drawing a picture just for him.

As our first meeting drew to a close, I suggested to the students that they think of ideas for a group name. Everyone would have the chance to propose a name, and they could choose a group name during our next meeting. I thought the idea of giving a name to the group would help create a sense of identity for the group. At the end of the meeting, I realized that I had made the mistake of forgetting to tell the students at the beginning of the meeting exactly when our time would be over. Even though they had already met with me for 30 minutes, they were not ready to leave. I recognized that I would have to make a conscious effort each meeting to remind them of the exact time we would end, and I would give them a 5-minute warning before we ended.

<u>Session 2.</u> At the beginning of the second meeting, I made sure to point out that we had 30 minutes for our meeting and I would walk them back to their classrooms at 2:00 P.M. I have a large clock in my room so the students can monitor the time if they choose. After everyone settled in, we had an informal check-in time. I started by asking, "What is something special that your brother did this week?" Each member took turns answering my question and used the speaking stone. Jared still had a tendency to interrupt others; however, Nicole and Matthew would calmly remind him that he could speak only when he had the stone. I was pleased that they were demonstrating appropriate and assertive communication skills.

After check-in time, I read the book *When the New Baby Comes, I'm Moving Out* (Alexander, 1987) to them. When looking for a book on the Internet, I discovered several excellent books that had been published to help children deal with new siblings. In the end, I picked Alexander's book for two reasons: the book provided a good starting point for a group discussion, and our small school library possessed a copy of it. This short story focused on a young boy and his feelings about the arrival of his new sibling. The boy is angry and upset about the changes that will occur because of the new baby. At one point, the boy makes it clear that he is angry with his mother and will not let his new sibling use his old toys or crib. By the end of the story, he realizes how much his mother still loves him, and he embraces the idea of having a new sibling.

The group members enjoyed the book and its pictures. I began our discussion by asking basic, open-ended questions:

1. "How did you feel about the book?"
2. "Did you ever feel like the boy did in the story?"
3. "What did you not have in common with him?"
4. "How do you think he was feeling about having a new sibling at the beginning of the story?"
5. "How do you think he was feeling at the end of the story?"

I brought out my feelings poster to assist the children in identifying emotions. (Along with the feelings' words, such posters have pictures that depict a person expressing each feeling.) I did not want to assume that the children already knew the names for emotions. Jared looked at the chart and jumped right in by saying, "The boy was mad and sad." I asked Jared to explain why the boy might feel those emotions. He gave a short explanation, and I then asked him, "Did you ever feel mad or sad after your brother, Aaron, was born?" He just nodded and said in a strained voice, "I don't get to spend any time with my mom anymore. She always has to take care of Aaron. I never get to spend time with my dad because he works all day and then he has to take care of Aaron when my mom takes a nap. I just don't get any time with them."

Matthew joined in, stating, "I miss spending time with my mom too. I think my brother is cool, but I don't get time with my mom since he was born. Everyone is really busy doing stuff or are too tired, so I go to my room and watch TV a lot." I asked Matthew how he felt about not spending as much time with his mom, and he said he got sad sometimes. As a group, we made a list of things we could do when we feel sad. I tried to go back to Jared's comments about feeling sad and angry, but he did not want to discuss them anymore. Instead, he asked if they would have a chance to draw again. His response reminded me that sometimes children do not want to stay focused on one topic for an extended period of time.

Before I let the children draw, I reminded the members that they still needed to pick a group name. I asked them if they had thought of any names since our last meeting. Jared and Matthew could not think of any names; Nicole waited a moment and then finally suggested, "The Baby Brother Group." She explained that she chose this name because all of them had baby brothers. I told Nicole that she picked a great name and she seemed pleased with my comment. It quickly became apparent that Matthew and Jared really were not interested in picking a name, so I told the group that we could wait on making a final decision. By this time, we had only 5 minutes left before we were scheduled to end. I remembered to point out the time to the members and told them they could draw for the next few minutes. I discovered that drawing was a good closure activity; it helped them focus and settle down so that they could quietly transition back into their classes.

Session 3. Once again we started by having check-in time. I realized it was important to have this time at the beginning of each meeting because it provided the students an opportunity to transition from the classroom to the group. Also, it gave them a time to share personal information with the group. After check-in, I started our discussion by asking a modified version of the "miracle question." I asked them, "If a genie visited you tonight and promised to change anything in your life, how would you know the next morning if the genie granted your wish? Describe how things would be different in your life." This question led to an interesting discussion about things they would like to change. All members were in consensus when they said they wanted more time with their parents. Jared also said, "My brother can get really noisy at night and he wakes me up sometimes." Matthew reassured Jared by saying things would get better when his baby brother started to sleep through the night.

After our discussion, I gave the members two options for things we could do during this meeting. I could read them *The Berenstain Bears' New Baby* (Berenstain & Berenstain, 1974) or they could draw a picture. I am not sure if I should have given them the option to draw again because it did not promote group discussion as well as the books did. As it turned out, they ended up choosing to draw. To encourage conversation, I asked the members to draw a picture of what they would like to do with their baby brothers when their baby brothers reached their current age. They enjoyed this activity and focused on things they were going to teach their brothers as they grew older.

Each child discussed his or her picture with the group. Afterward, I told the group that we would begin making a project in our next meeting. I suggested that we could make a book for the library or a book to take home; however, I wanted the members to think of ideas before our next meeting. Without any prompts, Matthew stated that it was time to go back to class and I walked them back.

Session 4. After check-in time, we discussed ideas for our group project. Everyone liked the idea of making a book for other kids who have new siblings. After that decision, the members were stuck about how to begin making the book. I suggested that they could make an ABC book about babies. Each letter of the alphabet could stand for something about babies. Everyone agreed on this idea. Before we began making the list, I explained to the members the process of brainstorming. We would not critique or criticize any suggestion that was offered. Jared recommended that I should write down everyone's ideas. I made sure that I did not suggest any words because I wanted this book to be something they created on their own. On my sheet of paper, I wrote down every letter of the alphabet and recorded their random suggestions. Jared seemed fascinated with everything that was gross or messy about babies. Some of his more colorful suggestions included, "Absolutely Stinky" for *A*, "Empire of Stinkiness" for *E*, and "Vampire Baby" for *V*. Although Nicole and Matthew did not like some of Jared's ideas, I reminded them that we were still in the brainstorming process. Making the list took longer than I expected, and we were unable to finish by the end of the session.

Session 5. As usual, we started with check-in time. Jared was excited to share with the group that his brother was really strong and could now hold on to his finger. Everyone took turns sharing new things his or her new sibling could do. It was no longer necessary to use the speaking stone as they were much better at listening to others and did not interrupt each other as often. I found it enjoyable to hear the excitement in their voices as they spoke about their brothers. Briefly, I questioned in my mind if this group was actually necessary. It seemed like the members were adjusting to their new siblings very well. However, I had a gut feeling that the members were benefiting in other ways that I had not originally determined. I also believed they needed the extra attention, and all of them really looked forward to our group meetings.

After check-in time, we started working on our list again. Once they had words for each letter, the members voted on their favorite words. Jared voted for the more unusual words, but Matthew and Nicole told him to take things more seriously. Matthew was blunt and said, "Jared, we want this to be a nice book. Quit picking stupid words." Matthew and Nicole's comments indicated they were serious about this project and they took pride in their work. During the voting process, I tried hard to stay quiet so that I did not influence the outcome of the book. After the words were chosen, the group had to decide what would be the fairest way for picking letters to draw. Fairness and equality seemed very important to them—and to all elementary students!

Nicole found an old box in the room and suggested that they take turns drawing letters out of a box. The members wanted things to be fair and asked me to pick who would draw the first letter. I went back to an old standby and had them pick a number between 1 and 20 that I had in my mind. Nicole was the first member to draw a letter. Matthew had the next turn and finally Jared, who was a little impatient while he waited. Jared liked the letter he picked because it was *D* for "Dirty Diapers," which had been one of his colorful contributions. After the first couple of rounds, Jared picked a letter he did not want to draw. He wanted to slip the letter back into the box. Using their problem-solving skills, the group made a new rule that everyone could have the option of picking a new letter or switching letters with another member. The members drew pictures for the rest of the meeting. Although they were very focused on their task, they still had a long list of letters to draw during the next meeting.

Session 6. At the beginning of the meeting, the children seemed anxious to get through check-in time. They wanted to start working on the book right away. I was surprised by how task-oriented everyone was, including Jared. Even though our check-in time was brief, they had the opportunity to talk about their brothers while they drew. Since we had two more meetings remaining after this one, I thought it was important to begin preparing them for the conclusion of the group. Since I knew they had grown accustomed to meeting every week, I did not want to end the group abruptly. As it turned out, the members already assumed the group would end after the book was completed.

Once again, everyone worked hard on the book. Occasionally, Jared would act silly, but Matthew and Nicole reminded him to focus. Matthew got frustrated with Jared at times because he thought Jared was rushing through his drawings and was not doing a good job. I decided to stay out of this situation and let them resolve it. (I believe it is important for people to learn conflict-management skills at an early age.) By the end of the meeting, the members had made a lot of progress on the book, but it looked as if it would take at least one more session to complete it.

Session 7. During check-in time, Matthew was eager to share with the group that his brother was starting to talk. He said that his brother was trying to say his name. Jared said that he also thought his brother was already speaking even though he was only a couple of weeks old. I was glad that no one challenged Jared about whether or not his brother really was trying to say words. After check-in time, the members went to work. They realized that they did not have a lot of time left and wanted to complete the book. Because they were so focused on the book, they did not talk very much during this meeting. By the end of the meeting, they had finished all but five of the letters, which they could complete the next week. Before ending, I reminded them again that we had only one more meeting together.

Session 8. With only 2 weeks left of school, I decided to ask the members during check-in time what they were looking forward to doing that summer—a question that focused the members on themselves and not on their brothers. After a brief discussion, they were anxious to get to work on their book. When they finished drawing the five remaining letters, they asked me how we were going to put the book together. Instead of making the decision for them, I asked them how they thought the book should be constructed. It was interesting to observe them develop a plan of action. Jared did not give a lot of input, but Matthew and Nicole decided that the book needed a cover and a title. Nicole suggested that everyone should draw a cover and then they could vote on the best one. Nicole's simple cover was titled "The Baby Book." For his, Jared thought of the creative title "26 Things a Baby Does." Matthew liked Jared's idea so much that he decided to use it for his cover.

After they completed their covers, the members wanted me to pick the cover for the book. Once again, I placed the decision back into their hands. The group chose to vote on the best cover, and it was decided that Nicole's cover was the best and should be the cover for the book. Even though Matthew voted for Nicole's cover, he was a little disappointed that others did not choose his cover and said, "Nicole always gets picked for things." I told Matthew that he had drawn a very special cover and asked the group how we could include Matthew's cover. Nicole suggested that it could be the back cover of the book. Matthew seemed OK with that suggestion, and they proceeded to put the book together.

Once the book was assembled, Matthew asked where we should put the book. Nicole suggested that we place the book in the hallway by the water fountain so that everyone could see it. After a little problem solving together, we decided to punch a hole through the entire book and attach a string to it. We then stapled the string to the bulletin board in the hallway. Right after we attached the book, we noticed Matthew and Nicole's classmates coming down the hall. I was very surprised to see Nicole take the initiative and invite several of her classmates and her teacher to look at the book. The group members proudly stood by and pointed out their favorite parts of the book.

A few minutes before our meeting ended, we went back to my counseling office for final closure. I asked the group what they wanted to do with their book now that it was complete. They thought it would not be fair if one of them kept it, and they wanted me to have it. I mentioned that I could make photocopies of the book for everyone if they wanted a copy. Nicole and Matthew quickly responded that they each wanted one. Jared, on the other hand, decided that he did not need a copy since I would keep the original. Before we officially ended the group, they each took turns saying what they liked best about the group. Jared jumped right in and said, "I liked having time to draw." Nicole was next and declared, "I like that we made a cool book for other kids who have new baby brothers or sisters." Finally, Matthew gave a heartfelt statement and told me, "I like that you let me spend time with you and you are nice."

Results

As a rule, I conduct an informal assessment at the conclusion of groups. After I ended the new-sibling group, I asked myself what worked and what did not work in this group experience. Overall, I was pleased with the outcome of the group. The only activity that did not work very well was the naming of the group. I thought choosing a name would help promote cohesion among the group members. However, Matthew and Jared really were not interested in picking a name because it was not important to them. They did not seem to need a formal name to feel like they were part of the group. Besides this, I was happy with the outcome of the other activities and strategies used. The strategies I believe were most effective are:

1. *The Speaking Stone:* Using the speaking stone in the first few meetings helped develop a pattern for group conversations. The stone encouraged members to focus on the person speaking and reminded them not to interrupt others. In addition, I think it was a good experience for the holder of the stone, who had others listening to him or her. Being listened to can be a very powerful experience, especially if a person is not used to being heard.

2. *Check-in Time:* The check-in time helped the students transition from their classrooms to the group. Also, it provided them an opportunity to share special things about their lives.

3. *The Feelings Chart:* The feelings chart, an excellent tool, helped the students learn the names for emotions and assisted them in expressing their own feelings.

4. *Group Decision Making:* Encouraging the group members to make decisions enabled them to develop a sense of power and ownership of the group. They appreciated having the chance to make decisions because, at their ages, they may not have had such opportunities often.

5. *Time:* In the very first meeting, I was reminded that it is important to always point out at the beginning of each meeting the time the group would end. Students could then keep track of the time and know when they were expected to go back to their classrooms.

6. *Creating the Book:* Creating the book together turned out to be an effective activity. Students had the opportunity to develop their communication, cooperation, and conflict-resolution skills. In addition, completing the book was a good culminating activity that provided the group a sense of purpose and closure.

Looking back at this group experience, I realize that I needed to be flexible and willing to adjust my plans for each session. It was important that group members were allowed to delineate the direction of the meetings. Children will intuitively direct you where they need to go for healing. They know what hurts and what issues are important to them. If your agenda is too rigid, you may miss the subtle cues children give you during a session. Children are very perceptive, and I think counselors overlook this quality at times.

Two weeks after the group ended, I had an opportunity to meet Jared's mother and little brother—they came to the school to see Jared's spring program. When I arrived at Jared's classroom, I noticed that he was busy working on an art project. As soon as he looked up and saw me, he took a break from his work and rushed up to me. He wanted to introduce me to his brother, Aaron. You could hear in his voice the pride and love that he felt for his brother as he brought me over to Aaron. After a few minutes, Jared's attention jumped back to his artwork and he said good-bye. It was hard to believe that only a couple of months ago, Jared did not seem to even want to acknowledge his brother.

I also stopped by the third-grade classroom after the spring program. Right away, Matthew and Nicole ran up to me and gave me big hugs. I never would have guessed that Nicole used to be so quiet and reserved before we started the group. Nicole had really started to blossom and to reveal her wonderful sense of humor. According to her teacher, Nicole had become more assertive in the group and her class. She thrived in an environment that provided her attention and validation.

After he gave me his big hug, Matthew asked me, "Did you see that I waved to you during the program? I wanted to make sure you saw me." Yes, I definitely saw Matthew and realized what a special group member he had been. Looking back, I think Matthew may have needed the group more than anyone else. He needed to feel accepted, to make contributions, and to receive positive attention. Matthew's teacher even indicated that Matthew was demonstrating more self-control and was not interrupting others as often. I was really glad that I chose him to be part of the group.

■ Personal Reflection

As I worked with the children in the group, I recognized that the issue of "not being the baby anymore" really was not their main concern in the end. Eventually, most children learn to accept their new roles in their families as long as their basic needs are being met.

Working with children has taught me to be myself, to relax, and to laugh. Matthew assisted me in making an important observation about counseling children: He helped me realize I did not have to fill my office with the best toys or have elaborate counseling activities planned to be an effective counselor. Matthew's poignant comment, "I like that you let me spend time with you," said it all. I just need to give children what they want the most: *time* and *attention*. I rediscovered that the counseling relationship is the most important aspect of the counseling process. I believe that creating a strong counseling relationship facilitates the most personal growth for clients.

References

Alexander, M. (1987). *When the new baby comes, I'm moving out*. New York: Dial Books for Young Readers.

Berenstain, S., & Berenstain, J. (1974). *The Berenstain Bears' new baby*. New York: Random House.

Suggested Readings

Brigman, G., & Earley, B. (2001). *Group counseling for school counselors: A practical guide* (2nd ed.). Portland, ME: J. Weston Walch.

Gladding, S. T. (2005). *Counseling as an art: The creative arts in counseling* (3rd ed.). Alexandria, VA: American Counseling Association.

Means, D., & Thorne, B. (1999). *Person-centred counseling in action* (2nd ed.). London: Sage.

Biographical Statement

Carol B. Hoheisel, PhD, is a national certified counselor, a licensed K–12 school counselor, and a licensed professional counselor. She has worked with children and adolescents as a professional school counselor in Minnesota and South Dakota. Currently, Carol is an assistant professor of counselor education and school counseling program coodinator at North Dakota State University in Fargo, North Dakota. You may reach Carol at carolhoheisel@yahoo.com.

5

Rex and the Magic Dinosaur

Angie Hood and John M. Littrell

Most kids are attracted to dinosaurs. Seven-year-old Rex is *obsessed* with dinosaurs to the exclusion of everything else! His dinosaur fixation gets in the way of learning at school and aggravates his chaotic, blended family. Angie Hood, an elementary school counselor, uses brief counseling techniques that build on student strengths. Enter the Magic Dinosaur! The story is told in Hood's voice. John Littrell was her mentor and supervisor.

A

typical week for me, as the counselor at Smith, involves scheduling sessions with my 30 regular students who face problems such as divorce, friendship and social issues, incarcerated parents, poor study skills; behavior problems, abuse, and homelessness. Some receive outside counseling but most do not. In addition, I direct 4–5 small groups and teach 5 classroom lessons per week. I also juggle whatever else arises.

The School

Situated in southern Iowa, Smith Elementary houses 200 kindergarten through fourth-grade students. The children come from low- to middle-income homes; the population offers little racial or ethnic diversity.

Student Need

Rex, a 7-year-old first grader, can charm you with an outer innocence that tugs at your heart. That is, if you're not his teachers working with him in regular or special education classrooms for a total of 5 hours a day! Rex's special education teacher approached me for some guidance because Rex's growing fascination with dinosaurs was hindering his learning. As a first grader, Rex displayed extensive knowledge regarding dinosaurs. Dinosaur figures accompanied him virtually everywhere. He placed the figures on the corner of his desk while he worked, always ready to start an imaginary conversation that pulled him into a Peter Pan's Land of the Lost Boys.

Rex sported dinosaur T-shirts and, naturally, *Jurassic Park* ranked as his all-time favorite movie. More than once while working at my office desk, I would hear kissing noises and feel the hard rubber of the dinosaur's head on my neck. Rex's dinosaur loved to offer kisses. While Rex worked on his school assignments, he frequently uttered the squeaks of the raptor or the guttural sounds of the tyrannosaurus.

Rex's academics were strong. His part-time placement in the special education room derived from his lack of focus. And now his dinosaur fixation was proving to be detrimental. Rex needed some guidance and I was determined to help.

Rex's large, blended, disordered, and somewhat chaotic family was well known in our school. His family comprised step-, half-, and biological siblings. Rex was the third oldest. My initial contact was with Rex's stepmother. She did not raise any concerns when counseling for Rex was suggested. The dinosaur fixation was getting in the way at home. Rex's stepmother complained that despite numerous requests to complete chores, Rex "ignores me" because he is engrossed in his imagination. Rex's stepmother—his father was not present at any meetings—never contacted the special education teacher or me to inquire about Rex's progress. The school always initiated contact.

Goals and Strategies

Within the setting of the school, my overall goal for Rex centered on keeping him on task with his schoolwork. My basic theoretical orientation is brief counseling. In this situation, my instinct told me that brief counseling might not be so brief and might not fully extinguish these fixated behaviors. However, for the time being, I decided to stick with what I was trained in and what I knew well. Thus, brief counseling strategies and techniques served as my counseling foundation while working with Rex. With his solid academic ability and unique verbal range, the brief counseling approach provided for interesting sessions.

In brief counseling, the counselor utilizes the student's strengths to make changes. Often, the student is encouraged to do something different as a way of accomplishing the desired change. Rather than focusing on what does not work, the counselor assists the student to use personal strengths to find new solutions. Questions that emphasize the student's resources are prevalent.

Since brief counseling focuses on solutions and doing something different to achieve a desired behavior, I suspected this would work well with Rex. His creative mind and willingness to please matched up perfectly. With Rex, I would use his love of dinosaurs to help him make needed changes in his schoolwork such that the very source of his distraction, dinosaurs, would help him become more focused. One of Rex's favorite dinosaurs became the Magic Dinosaur. This one would stay on Rex's desk and would send warning signals to Rex that the dinosaur noises were coming. It was at these times that Rex would acknowledge the message and silently fight off the deceptive dinosaur intruders. If he were successful, the Magic Dinosaur would tell me later in the day. Of course, I would verify the Magic Dinosaur's report with the special education teacher, and if successful, Rex earned a prize or sticker. Dinosaurs, dinosaurs, and even more dinosaurs.

Over the course of our counseling, I consulted with Rex's special education teacher, and our frequent discussions elicited feelings ranging from frustration to wonderment regarding his unfathomable fascination with the dinosaurs.

Process

Session 1. Everyone knows Rex in our school, so our initial meeting neither required the formalities of introductions nor elicited the initial awkwardness that students sometimes feel. Rex communicates very easily with adults. At times, the adults at school would need to remind him to use a "normal" voice, as he loved to alter his voice. Rex had one good friend that he played with on a fairly regular basis. His stash of dinosaur toys brought positive attention from other first-grade boys. Yet, he did, I believe, stick out with adults and children as a bit odd. As is typical of the directness of first graders, Rex began our first session with some questions.

Rex: What am I doing in here? Can we talk about dinosaurs?
Counselor: Well, if that's what you would like to talk about.
Rex: Uh-huh, sure. Excuse me, did you know my raptor eats bugs?

Our first session was all about the vegetation and insects that dinosaurs eat. Curiously enough, in Rex's mind, dinosaurs did not eat meat. He told me that meat eating is too violent of a process. Because I am always searching for students' strengths, it didn't take me long to open my eyes to Rex's gentleness and good nature. My immediate response was identical to what many teachers had found themselves saying: "I wish I could take him home with me." Since I didn't know if bogs and jungle vines would prosper in my living room, I settled for meeting with Rex 3 days a week at school.

Session 2. After 3 minutes of brontosaurus talk, I turned the conversation toward his schoolwork. Getting Rex to discuss schoolwork was like trying to get a real tyrannosaurus to give up meat. I inquired if Rex was familiar with the Magic Dinosaur. He assured me he was not. Seeing his eyes wide, I knew he had been hooked.

Rex:	What does he do?
Counselor:	Well, he sits on your desk and he helps you stay on task and do your schoolwork.
Rex:	How can he do that?
Counselor:	Because the Magic Dinosaur is really special. He has a magic power that lets him talk to you. When you are doing your work, he tells you things like, "Great job, Rex. Keep it up. I'm so proud of you, Rex." But, if you get off task and start messing around with other things, the Magic Dinosaur will tell you, "Get back to work, Rex. Stay on task."
Rex:	How can I get that dinosaur?

I pulled out a collection of small dinosaurs and Rex eagerly went through them. I told him whichever dinosaur he wanted out of that bag could be the magic one. After several minutes of rummaging, it was obvious Rex was dissatisfied with my assortment. With a quirky look, he asked if I would like to go to his locker to see his dinosaurs and maybe one of them would become the magic one.

Rex's backpack housed substantially larger and brighter dinosaurs than my lame collection offered. He selected a 6-inch raptor that was bright yellow, black, red, and gray. Standing on its back feet, claws showing, and baring its teeth, this dinosaur didn't appear able to offer words of encouragement and simple praise.

Rex and I returned to my office to talk about the specifics of this new strategy. I told him the Magic Dinosaur would work only if it sat on the corner of Rex's desk and was undisturbed. The dinosaur's magic eyes would watch Rex, and at any time during the day, the dinosaur could mysteriously offer him praise or convince him to start working again. I further stated that the Magic Dinosaur would tell me about how Rex worked in class, but I would double-check with his teacher.

Rex:	Will he talk to me in a squeaky voice or a growling voice?
Counselor:	Any way you want him to. Shall we get started?

Rex proudly carried Magic Dinosaur back to his class, and I explained the procedure to his teacher. I left the special education room as Rex precisely placed the dinosaur on the corner of his desk. Rex took his seat, turned around, and gave me a calculating nod. As I quietly closed the door, I sure hoped this would work.

Session 3. I met with Rex the following morning. A check with his special education teacher indicated that the Magic Dinosaur might indeed be magical.

Counselor:	How did it go yesterday with your Magic Dinosaur?
Rex:	He talked to me a lot.
Counselor:	Tell me some of things he said to you.
Rex:	"Get back to work, Rex." "No more messing around. It's work time."
Counselor:	How did that help you in class?
Rex:	His magic helped because I stayed busy and got my work done. Can I go get him and play?
Counselor:	Let's finish talking about your day. You did great, huh? Tell me, though, how do you know it really worked?
Rex:	What do you mean?
Counselor:	I mean, how can you tell it worked? What was different?
Rex:	I got to go play at recess and Mrs. Smith told me I worked hard. My dinosaur talked a lot. My day was better.
Counselor:	Tell me what needs to happen today.
Rex:	Listen to my dinosaur.
Counselor:	You bet. You can do it again!

At this point, Rex and I exchanged a high five and turned the conversation back to his interests. Before Rex left my office, he was rewarded with a sticker from my treasure chest. Another session was scheduled for the next day. Could we make it 2 successful days in a row?

Session 4. A miracle happened! Toward the end of the school day, I visited with Rex's teacher. Rex's work performance registered high and the Magic Dinosaur was a hit. Through a crack in the door, I saw Rex working and, I admit, I beamed. Rex actually skipped to my room. Again, he opened the conversation with a question.

Rex:	Why do you think the dinosaurs died? Wait, I know. It was because of the volcanoes. BOOM! They all blew up at once and no more dinosaurs.
Counselor:	I hear there are no more dinosaur noises from you and you are a hard worker! That's so awesome! (High-five.) What good things happened to you today?
Rex:	Well, I got my work done.
Counselor:	Who do you think noticed a change?
Rex:	The Magic Dinosaur. He told me.
Counselor:	How about someone in your classroom?
Rex:	Mrs. Smith.
Counselor:	How do you know that? What did Mrs. Smith do differently because you changed your behavior?
Rex:	You know, she was nice. She told me she was happy.

Rex and I continued the conversation. I emphasized how his positive changes elicited positive changes in others. I allowed Rex to act out how his Magic Dinosaur was keeping him on task and to use the dinosaur's voice. Again, Rex left my office with a sticker and a smile. I was left wondering, how long will the kid keep it up?

Classroom Guidance Lesson. My next meeting with Rex occurred within the context of a classroom guidance lesson. I walked into Rex's general education classroom to teach my lesson and noticed Rex drawing pictures of dinosaurs. Rex looked forlorn and distant. I asked Rex to put away his paper. He slipped the paper into his desk but held on to it.

During the independent activity phase of the lesson, I slipped over to Rex and asked why he looked so glum. He said, "All the dinosaurs are up in heaven," and a single tear rolled down his cheek. I gave him a hug and sat quietly next to him for a minute. Then, without any prompting, he suggested that I help him with the lesson activity. In later counseling sessions I tried to explore the meaning of his comment, but to no avail. Rex would either change the subject or approached the circumstance with apparent maturity and acceptance. I wondered if I would ever find out what this was about.

Session 5. Rex told me, quite seriously, that he needed my help.

Rex: Can you help me, Mrs. Hood?
Counselor: Well, I'll try. What do you need help with?
Rex: I've got to find the missing ingredient for Chemical X. Can you help me?

Rex explained that to make his dinosaurs come back to life, Chemical X was required. He was missing a key ingredient to make the potion.

Rex: See, you have to lay your dinosaurs on the ground and surround them with dead brown leaves. Then, you have to pour Chemical X on the leaves and say a prayer. Then, the dinosaurs will come back to life.
Counselor: It sounds like the missing ingredient could be anything. Do you think we'll ever find it?
Rex: Nah, probably not, but we have to try.

Rex and I went through a zany list of possible ingredients: French fries, pencil shavings, orange juice, sunflower seeds, volcanic rock, palm leaves, and Pepsi. No luck.

Counselor: I'll think about this during the day and I'll let you know if I think of the possible answer. For now, Rex, can we talk about school?
Rex: If I figure it out I'll come and get you so we can have the ceremony.
Counselor: Sounds great. You know, you talked about Chemical X and all the ingredients that make it up. Let's think about your school behavior and school day. What are all the ingredients that make your school

	day a good one? (I took out a sheet of construction paper and drew a circle with "School Behavior" written in it.) Should we make up a chemical name for your school behavior?
Rex:	Yeah, Chemical Z.
Counselor:	Perfect. What are some behaviors you need at school? What makes Chemical Z work right?

As Rex listed behaviors, I wrote them on the construction paper. At the top, Rex wrote the words *Chemical Z*.

Counselor:	There, Chemical Z is done. All these things need to happen at school for Chemical Z to work, right? Let's look at them again and you tell me which ingredient is the most important.

We took turns reading the behaviors Rex had listed. Rex's ingredients were "listening," "getting my work done," "raising my hand," "not talking so much about dinosaurs," "listening to my Magic Dinosaur," "being a good friend," and "paying attention with eye contact."

Rex:	I think the most important thing is getting my work done.
Counselor:	Okay, I want you to put a star by that one. Can we work on that one today? Getting your work done?
Rex:	Sure. I can do that.
Counselor:	I think you need to remember the problem you had with Chemical X. You had a missing ingredient. What happened because one ingredient was missing?
Rex:	It didn't work.
Counselor:	Right. Same with Chemical Z. If you have one missing ingredient, say you don't pay attention, or you're not a good friend, what happens to your school day?
Rex:	It won't be good.

I asked him if he wanted to take the paper with him to class but he replied that Chemical Z needed to remain top secret. For me, this session illustrated how I could make use of a bizarre fixation such as Chemical X.

Session 6. I feared that a relapse might occur, and sure enough, Rex's Magic Dinosaur had become a distraction, and his special education teacher had to remove it from his desk.

Counselor:	Hey, Rex. I heard what happened to your Magic Dinosaur. Your teacher told me. Why don't you tell me your side of the story?
Rex:	Easy, my dinosaur just started talking too much and I started to play with him.
Counselor:	I thought the Magic Dinosaur had strong powers so he wouldn't play with you. He'd help you work.
Rex:	He changed his mind.

I thought, I love this kid because he keeps me smiling and guessing. Now what were we going to do? Rex didn't appear saddened by the dinosaur's removal. He decided that the Magic Dinosaur had really helped him but now the dinosaur wanted to play.

Counselor:	I don't know, Rex. I think we have a problem. You know, that dinosaur really helped you focus. You were being so successful. What do you think we should do?
Rex:	I can keep him in my pocket.
Counselor:	He's too big for your pocket.
Rex:	Oh, yeah. How about if I draw him? (A new solution!)
Counselor:	That's it! Let's draw him and post him on the side of your teacher's desk. Awesome plan! (High-five!)

Rex drew a near perfect rendition of his Magic Dinosaur. We waved our hands over the picture to give it the magic powers. Then I ceremoniously gave the dinosaur and Rex a round of applause. Then we tacked it on a bulletin board in his classroom.

Session 7. My faith in Rex was growing. This kid was succeeding in his schoolwork and doing great. I did not bring up Rex's home life until the seventh session because the dinosaur fixation seemed more manageable. Rex's family issues are something that I cannot change, but I knew there was hope with the dinosaur fixation. However, I knew that disruptions in family life can bring down school performance. When I prompted Rex to speak about his family, his squirming increased or he directly informed me the topic was not of interest. My limited knowledge of the family provided partial insight as to why Rex might be seeking to escape reality in the world of dinosaurs. If Rex could not find his place at home, he would, in the Adlerian sense, make a place for himself in imagination. The phrase "scrapper of a kid" came to mind. I admired his resiliency.

Rex's drawing continued to inspire him to outperform his previous classroom achievements.

Counselor:	How's it going with the poster, the magic poster?
Rex:	Cool. It's working. I mean, I'm working. I think the dinosaur's getting tired of telling me to work all the time.
Counselor:	How did you figure that out?
Rex:	He thinks I'm getting too smart for him. He doesn't think he needs to be in my room anymore.
Counselor:	Tell me what you think about that.
Rex:	I think he's right. I'm doing really good, right? I don't think he needs to stay much longer.
Counselor:	Uh-huh. What are you telling me? What do you want to change?
Rex:	I want the dinosaur to be quiet, but I think the drawing is really good. I like my friends to see it.
Counselor:	What if we left the poster up and had the dinosaur talk only under mysterious circumstances?

Rex:	What do you mean?
Counselor:	You know, the dinosaur will not utter a word unless mysteriously you start talking or not paying attention. Then, he'll only tell you once to stay on task, and if he talks more, you can take him down.

So, yet again, we struck a deal. I need to have as many counseling techniques in my repertoire as possible. Those new options come from my clients and sometimes from me.

The Park. It turned out to be a beautiful spring day and I decided to take Sam, my toddler, to the park. The park was not overcrowded and Sam and I headed to the huge wooden play structure. I heard a familiar voice calling, "Hey, Mrs. Hood, over here! I'm blasting aliens!" Coincidentally, Rex had appeared at the park, and I quickly realized my precious time with Sam would be difficult to keep private. Rex bounded over with his usual energy and quickly concluded that my son would be the perfect playmate.

Rex:	Is that your son?
Counselor:	Yes, this is Sam.
Rex:	Hi, Sam. Come over here with me and we'll blast the aliens. (Rex rubbed Sam's head gently and made laser-beam noises.)

My son was fascinated with the exaggerated sounds and looked eagerly at Rex. I reluctantly relinquished our mother–son time and walked Sam over to Rex's hideout in a far corner of the play structure. Rex had found a way to actually get underneath the play structure.

Rex:	Come on, Sam, jump down here.
Counselor:	Rex, I don't want Sam down there because he's too little. Why don't you play up here?
Rex:	Ohhhh, all right. But watch me, Sam. I'm going to blast the alien force field. They've captured the dinosaurs and I've got to free them. Watch out for the flying glass! There! The dinosaurs are free and I got all the aliens!

Engrossed in the action, my son followed Rex to the next area of play, the slide. While we were walking over, I noticed Rex's stepmom, sitting alone, smoking, apparently blasé. I tried to make eye contact and she made a halfhearted wave. I indulged Rex's need for a playmate for a few more minutes, and then announced that we had to leave.

Rex:	Ahh, come on, Mrs. Hood. Stay longer. I've got to teach Sam how to talk to the dinosaurs.
Counselor:	I know he would love that, Rex, but we need to get home. I'll talk with you at school tomorrow. Okay?
Rex:	Bye-bye, buddy.

As I placed my son in his car seat, I looked back over at the play structure. Rex was bent over, talking to himself, and alone. Not 15 feet from him, Rex's stepmom sat alone, smoking and looking in the other direction. My heart swelled with sorrow for

Rex. Seeing him in the park allowed me a glimpse of Rex's life outside of school. He needed not only my understanding, but also friends and a responsive family. Counseling alone, regardless of how long, would not fill these voids.

Session 8. True to my word, the next day I went to get Rex. I found him outside of class, trying to climb into his locker.

Counselor:	Hey, Rex. What are you doing?
Rex:	I've got to find an entrance for my dinosaurs. You know dinosaurs have to have a place to get through to this world. I have to find it for them. If I can't, they're stuck in their world.
Counselor:	(I jokingly, hopefully, not sarcastically, used his language.) Do you think you can find the entrance to my room? I need to talk to you for a few minutes?

Rex laughed and we headed to my office. When I inquired about his time in the park yesterday, Rex told me that he goes there often with his stepmom. He followed that up with an important news flash. The aliens were all blasted and dinosaurs have nothing more to fear.

Counselor:	Why were you in your locker? I mean, I know you told me why, but what made you think to find an entrance?
Rex:	I just know I have to do that. I think about the dinosaurs all the time and how to have them with me.
Counselor:	Are the dinosaurs staying away during your work time, though?
Rex:	Yeah, I'm doing good with that. Just when I'm not working I can do dinosaur stuff.
Counselor:	I think you've changed a lot, Rex. You are becoming such a hard worker and such a great listener. How do you know you've changed?
Rex:	I just know. My teacher knows. You know. Know what I want to do now? I want to draw my hiding place at the park.

■ Results

The more things change, the more they stay the same. Rex definitely experienced some positive behavior changes, yet his infatuation with dinosaurs remained. Given my limited time to work with him, I found this acceptable.

Using brief counseling techniques with Rex proved to be the key. My solution-focused questions allowed Rex to use his imagination at times but also remain focused on the issue. The changes, at first small, became solid with the invariable questions. Rex began to anticipate my questions and this forced him to think ahead with me and, I believe, while working in class.

Another component of brief counseling that I employed was the use of humor. Rex and I had fun. In fact, we had a lot of fun together. That fun forged a bond between us and built a solid bridge of trust. There is nothing better than to realize that a child totally trusts me. I work very hard to honor that trust. Rex knew that I valued our bond, and again, humor strengthened it at every step.

Rex experienced classroom success and I am confident that he will continue to experience success in the future. Focusing on the positive changes—not dwelling on negative behavior—remains the foremost reason I use brief counseling. Kids have so many personal obstacles to overcome. Why insist on talking about the things they already know don't work? The solution-focused approach immediately sparks children's interest and energizes them to seek out their true spirit, a spirit that might be lost without this simple recognition.

Personal Reflection

With Rex, I learned volumes. How delicate a child's emotions are. How fragile are a little boy's thoughts and feelings. How open is a young one's heart to understanding and love. How misunderstood many children are because negative behaviors mask their spirit.

I wish that Rex had been able to explain to me more fully his fascination with dinosaurs. My instinct tells me that understanding and helping Rex involve a combination of numerous factors, yet I long for definite answers. I know this is not possible; a definitive answer is an oxymoron in counseling.

Reflecting on my work with Rex, I wish I had worked with him all year because I wanted to know him better. I wanted our bond to remain intact. Fortunately, I will have the opportunity to continue with Rex in the coming school year. I will continue with my own personal style, which incorporates a brief counseling approach, because it served me well with Rex.

Suggested Readings

Berg, I. K., & Steiner, T. (2003). *Children's solution work*. New York: W. W. Norton.
Littrell, J. M. (1998). *Brief counseling in action*. New York: W. W. Norton.
Littrell, J. M., & Peterson, J. S. (2005). *Portrait and model of a school counselor*. Boston: Houghton Mifflin/Lahaska Press.
Littrell, J. M., & Zinck, K. (2004). Brief counseling with children and adolescents: Interactive, culturally responsive, and action-based. In A. Vernon (Ed.), *Counseling children and adolescents* (3rd ed., pp. 137–162). Denver, CO: Love.

Biographical Statement

Angie Hood, MA, is an elementary school counselor in Ankeny, IA. She has been a school counselor for 6 years and was an elementary teacher for 10 years. You can reach Angie at ahood@ankeny.k12.ia.us.

John M. Littrell, EdD, is professor and program coordinator of counseling and career development at Colorado State University in Fort Collins. His two books are *Brief Counseling in Action* (1998) and *Portrait and Model of a School Counselor* (with Peterson, 2005). The latter is an in-depth study of an exemplary elementary school counselor. John's e-mail is John.Littrell@colostate.edu.

6

What Happens When Mentors Don't Show Up?

Michael J. Karcher

Clayton is a fourth grader who, according to his teachers, is at risk for underachievement, for social alienation, and for developing an emotional or personality disorder. He skips classes and acts out a lot. At the time of this case study, Michael Karcher was a university researcher and coordinator of a mentoring program at Clayton's elementary school. Clayton connects quickly and well with Corissa, his mentor from high school. Karcher is faced with a problem when Corissa's attendance becomes sporadic. Karcher provides information about avoiding pitfalls in setting up a mentoring program.

I n response to the increasing feelings of disconnection of students, school-based mentoring programs have begun to flourish. Mentoring programs provide a student with an older person with whom to discuss concerns, experience attention and feelings of worth, and develop a significant bond. A mentor's job is not to teach, parent, or counsel the youth. Cross-age peer mentoring has become popular because it helps engage both an older and a younger student in developmentally appropriate structured activities; however, such programs are not without risk. Effectively monitoring and supporting relationships is a critically important role for school counselors or whoever manages such programs. This case describes a problem that emerged when a high school mentor could not participate regularly, and how I tried to ensure that the termination of this mentoring match provided enough closure to minimize the harm that could have resulted for the elementary school–aged mentee.

■ The School

In a school district with fewer than 2,500 students, where most families know each other's kids, it seems unlikely that disconnection would be a problem. Yet in this public school system, in a town of 15,000, people were confronting just this problem. The town is about an hour from the state capitol of a farm belt state, just far enough from the capitol for the students to feel isolated from the world they see on MTV. Most of the students are White, with about 10 Hispanic, 2 African American, and 1 Native American students in each grade. In any given year, about two or three families in the town are of Asian descent. The elementary school and middle school (Grades 7 and 8) are in the same building and are about three blocks from the high school.

■ Student Need

The present case study focuses on one mentee, Clayton. According to his teachers, he was at risk for underachievement, for social alienation from his peers, and perhaps even for developing an emotional or personality disorder. He often skipped classes, had a very difficult home life, and was unsuccessful both socially and academically. He acted out a lot. I was not sure he was appropriate for mentoring, but the principal insisted I include him. I worried for fear that his mentor would not be able to handle him.

■ Goals and Strategies

Given some of the positive reports about the use of mentoring to reduce fighting and substance use, as well as to increase school connectedness and hope toward the future (Grossman & Tierney, 1998; Karcher, Davis, & Powell, 2002), we decided to establish a cross-age mentoring program (Dennison, 2000; Noll, 1997), in which high school students would mentor elementary school students. I coordinated this program after school in the elementary school library, cafeteria, and gym. For this program, I recruited

30 high school students to work with 30 elementary school students for 2 hours twice a week. All the mentors were volunteers; the only other criterion was that their counselors could recommend them. Each high school student agreed to commit to work with one child for the full academic year. We involved a few middle school students (Grades 7 and 8) as protégés or substitute mentors, but generally there were 3 to 5 years' difference between the ages of the mentors and their mentees.

A graduate student from a local university, Jennifer, was hired using funds the district received from a 21st Century Community Learning Center grant to help coordinate the program. Jennifer ran the activities we planned for the mentors to engage their mentees. We divided the students into two 15-pair groups; one met after school on Mondays and Wednesdays, the other on Tuesdays and Thursdays. Typically, each day, we first met in the library and did structured activities selected from EQUIP (Gibbs, Potter, & Goldstein, 1995), Project Northland (Komo & Perry, 1996), and Life Skills (Botvin, 1989) curricula. Then the pairs each engaged in a structured activity. Following this would be a 20-minute group snack break in the cafeteria, and then we would conclude with interactive games with the whole group in the gym. This time was also used by mentors helping their mentees with their homework. Late buses took home the children whose parents could not pick them up at 5:00 P.M. Once a month we also conducted weekend events—"Super Saturdays"—in which we also involved the parents.

Not all of the mentees were at risk. Having read an article titled, "When Interventions Harm" (Dishion, McCord, & Poulin, 1999), I was aware of the negative effects of bringing a lot of high-risk students together in an after-school program. So, their teachers identified 15 mentees who had social, emotional, or academic deficits that the teachers alone could not address, and 15 mentees volunteered for the program just for fun.

The program was called developmental mentoring because we saw it as developmental for both the mentors and the mentees. Jennifer and I worked hard to include several safeguards to ensure that the high school student mentors were trained well enough to handle the responsibilities of being a mentor. We provided two 3-hour training sessions on communication, boundaries, and the history of mentoring. We worked with the mentors to ensure that their anticipated extracurricular activities would not conflict with or cause them to quit mentoring. Finally, we provided the series of structured activities for them to use.

Jennifer and I met with the mentors, in groups of 15, once a month during a lunch hour to discuss their mentor–mentee matches, to explain the curricula to be used in the coming month, and to brainstorm solutions to problems. Some of the mentors spent an additional 2 hours a month with Jennifer and me to help create the activities, organize the "Super Saturdays," and help with the grant-required program evaluation.

■ Process

There were many signs that Clayton and his mentor, Corissa, were going to be a great match. The way we matched mentors and mentees was, on a Saturday at the beginning, we held a day of fun activities to let the mentors and mentees meet and interact with each other. At the end of the day, both mentors and mentees were asked to list three people they were interested in working with as their mentor or mentee. Clayton and Corissa were both first on each other's list. So they were an easy match, and in the first few months, all appeared to be going quite well.

Clayton took to mentoring enthusiastically. He never missed a meeting. Every Tuesday and Thursday, he was the first one there. His teachers noticed improvements in his behavior. Each meeting he wanted to stay as long as possible and usually helped us clean up. Perhaps Clayton felt comfortable, like this was a place where he was accepted. Perhaps he just did not want to go home. Either way, he seemed to get restless and irritable as soon as he got on the bus to go home. He and the driver had confrontations because Clayton often fought with his sister on the way home. She, too, was in the mentoring program. I knew little about his family life. He was parented by his mother, who often appeared to be stressed and overwhelmed. She never came to the "Super Saturday" events. Sometimes she even showed up mid-Saturday morning to get Clayton, saying it was more convenient for her to get him after running her errands than to come back later. This seemed to embarrass Clayton, and it clearly gave us the impression that, at home, Clayton's needs did not come first.

With his mentor, Clayton seemed to have found a consistent source of attention, praise, and empathy. He liked Corissa very much. It had been suggested by a teacher that Clayton needed a male mentor, but we had few male volunteers—the ratio was 3 females to 1 male. Regardless, these two were drawn to each other, and from late September through early December, they worked well together.

In December, Corissa learned about tryouts for the high school play, and she really wanted to be involved. She had not anticipated wanting to be in the play, and beginning with the tryouts in December, she started to miss mentoring meetings. We had set up a system by which mentors could contact me by phone at the school and leave a message if for some reason they were not going to be able to attend. If a mentor got sick, had to leave for an emergency, was going to be late, or just got in trouble and was kept after school by the high school principal, that mentor could leave a message explaining this, and Jennifer or I would be sure to let their mentees know as soon as they arrived at the program. Because the mentor–mentee activities took place in a large-group format and we had substitute seventh- and eighth-grade protégés for absent mentors, no mentee was ever left totally alone when his or her mentor could not make it. Most mentees experienced this once or twice during the year—things came up and sometimes mentors missed a meeting or two. But beginning with the play tryouts in December, which ended with her earning a part in the school play, Corissa began missing more and more mentoring meetings.

Corissa was not negligent in an apathetic way; she just wanted to be in two places at once. She tried to work out a schedule with her drama teacher that allowed her to miss Tuesday rehearsals, but her drama teacher was not as flexible as she anticipated. Corissa would call, being very apologetic and assuring each time that she would make the next meeting. One day we realized Corissa had missed five of the seven mentoring meetings during December and January. What also caught our attention was that Clayton had started to misbehave.

Finding himself working with a different eighth-grade protégé each week, Clayton probably felt embarrassed and rejected when his mentor did not arrive. He began acting up. He started to pick fights with the other kids. He would defy his protégés by breaking supplies, running off, taking ice cream from the snack supplies, or pestering other mentors and mentees. His teachers also saw the return of the "Old Clayton" and began losing their faith in the reality of the "New Clayton" they had seen emerge in November and early December.

Corissa had begun to miss the monthly trainings, perhaps because she just could not face us or accept the responsibility for having to terminate her mentorship. We sought her out, met with her at the high school during her lunch hour, and explained the problem.

Our goal was to enlist Corissa in the process of terminating the mentoring relationship. Doing it any other way could surely leave Clayton with the enduring feeling that he was inherently bad, unlikable, and unimportant. Only through a one-on-one, honest talk with Corissa, in which she acknowledged how this must have hurt him, would he likely be able to move on to a successful mentoring relationship with someone else. I knew Clayton was too young to see how his feelings of being rejected and unlikable were causing him to act out toward the protégés or increasing his feelings of anger toward his sister, teachers, and bus driver. I needed to impress on Corissa how important it would be for her to acknowledge Clayton's complex feelings. That meant I needed to be extra clear with Corissa about how she likely had affected Clayton. At the same time, I needed to keep in mind that Corissa was young as well. I had to keep her developmental needs in mind and talk with her in a way that was realistic and honest, but empowering rather than shaming. We met during lunch and talked over some very odd-looking cafeteria pizza.

Counselor:	Corissa, I know you thought you were going to be able to do both mentoring and the school play, but that doesn't seem to be the reality of what is happening. We feel like we need to give Clayton a new mentor.
Corissa:	I know, but he and I work really well together, and if he could just wait a few more months, then I would be done with the play.
Counselor:	I know you did not mean for this to happen, but the way things worked out has left Clayton without a mentor for almost five straight weeks. Each week we told him that you promised us you would be back, but each week you didn't come. If you were not such a conscientious and sincere student, we would not have had such faith that you would return, and we might have tried to terminate the match earlier. But clearly you've tried to do both things, and the play won out. In the meantime, in your absence, I think each week Clayton has had to ask himself why you were not there.
Corissa:	He knows it is because of the play. He knows how important he is to me.
Counselor:	I think he is starting to question how important he is to you. But you know from your experience, in fact, to use your own words, "his

mother never puts Clayton's needs before her own." Well, I think in Clayton's mind, it's déjà vu all over again. After starting to trust and really depend on you, now I bet he is really questioning his worth.

Corissa: I know. I feel awful. That's another reason I don't go to mentoring sometimes. I just feel so bad for letting him down. I just figured, I guess I hoped, he would understand.

Counselor: Do you remember what we said might happen if the mentees were left without their mentor on a regular basis? When mentors are inconsistent and show up infrequently, it's not uncommon for them to feel bad and act out. That's what we are seeing with Clayton. Clearly he is out of control more and more in your absence. At this rate, at the end of the year when he completes the evaluation questionnaires, I'd be really surprised if he didn't report being more disruptive at school. I'd also bet that he will report feeling disconnected from school and lower self-esteem—he's already turning on us and his protégés each week, and he gets critical of himself very easily.

Corissa: I know, I'm sorry. What can I do?

Counselor: Well, I think we need to terminate the match. Like that Sting song says, "if you love someone set them free." If you care about him you've got to set him free to find another mentor. But, you'll also need to try to convey to him that your not showing up is not because you dislike him but because you chose to be in this play.

Corissa: I didn't choose the play over him. It's not like he's less important than the play. I was going to come back. I was going to work with him more.

I felt it was important that I help Corissa understand how her mentee probably felt. She needed to be shown how to step outside her own perspective and consider how Clayton felt, without feeling criticized or shamed.

Counselor: I know that is how you see it, but regardless of how you see it, I bet he simply sees that you chose the play over him. Maybe he won't be able to say it, but like he said about his mom, I have to bet that he feels you put your needs over his, and that his needs just aren't very important.

I told her how important it was that she acknowledge that this may be how he feels. Given one's goal as a mentor should be to provide empathy, praise, and attention, Corissa needed to show him she understood she hurt him (empathy) and tell him what she really liked about him (praise). She needed to attend to this situation by explaining that she wanted to keep working with him, but that she agreed with us that he deserved a mentor who could be more consistent. I also suggested she keep in mind that she likely was not the first person to let him down, and that experiencing these feelings again in another important relationship probably made it even harder for him not to feel like there was something bad, unlovable, or unimportant about him; that is, that he caused this. Here it seemed it was important for her to understand that was likely what he was feeling, even if he could not put it into words and even if he did not see that this was partly why he was acting up in mentoring and acting out with his protégés, sister, bus driver, and teachers. After hearing all of this, it was hard for her not to feel bad about stirring up these feelings in Clayton, but it helped her realize that she needed to meet with him to work toward closure.

Corissa:	Yeah. I get it. I feel awful. But I'll meet with him to talk it through.
Counselor:	I know you feel bad. In your mind, you were going to be able to do it all and now you have to face the consequences. I'm just glad that you are such a caring and concerned person that you are willing to take on this difficult task. It won't be easy. I really wanted to be honest with you about what I think is going on inside Clayton's head right now, because if you don't realize how powerfully this likely affects him, you might just go in there, say, "I'm sorry, Clayton, but I think you need a new mentor because I cannot make it anymore," and solely out of being defensive and hurt, he would say, "That's okay, I was wanting someone else anyway." Unless you are willing to sit with these hard facts and feelings, both of you will escape that meeting as soon as possible. Do you remember that scene in the movie *Good Will Hunting* when the psychologist has to say over and over, "Will, it's not your fault"? That's kind of what I mean here. You've got to help him feel like it is not his fault that you are leaving him. Now, don't just say that over and over—this isn't the movies— but just be aware that he won't want to acknowledge his feelings, so you may have to do it for him, and it won't be easy for either of you. But I really appreciate your willingness to tackle this head-on.

◼ Results

Clayton was assigned another mentor in January, a student-athlete, whose sport ended in December. Although Clayton was enthusiastic at the start of their relationship—this new mentor was perceived as "cool" in the other mentors' and mentees' eyes— Clayton never really opened up to his new mentor as he had with Corissa. Maybe he was protecting himself, which may have been a good thing: a new coping strategy. Maybe his experience with Corissa left him less trusting of mentoring relationships.

He did, however, return to participate in the program the second year. His involvement that second year was more with the program, though, than with his mentor. Clayton was eager to be a protégé. He regularly volunteered to assist with setup and cleanup. He was helpful with the younger mentees. He acted more like a peer or brother to his mentor that second year, who seemed just fine with that kind of relationship. By that second year, Clayton seemed to feel better about himself in relationship to others. Apparently he still saw the mentoring program as a place he wanted to be and a place where he felt appreciated or attended to.

In the third year, he became a protégé in the program, but midway through that year his family left the school district and Clayton enrolled in another school.

We did a full-scale evaluation of the program. After getting district and parental approval, we sought out volunteer elementary school children to be a comparison group. For participating, they were entered in a raffle for gift certificates, toys, and pens with different designs and sports team logos. These nonmentored children and the mentees completed surveys that measured their social skills, self-esteem, and connectedness. At the end of the year, we found that, compared to the nonmentees, the mentees as a group showed gains in connectedness to school, teachers, reading, and parents and increased their self-esteem.

We had also kept track of mentors' attendance. When we looked at the correlation between the mentees' changes and the number of times each mentee's mentor showed up, there was a strong relationship. We found that when the high school mentors skipped or missed mentoring, their mentees suffered. We found that those students whose mentors showed up infrequently demonstrated decreased social competence, feelings of attractiveness, and overall self-esteem (Karcher, 2005). This phenomenon was not unique to Clayton. We had worked hard to "do no harm" (Forester-Miller & Davis, n.d.) by mixing high- and low-risk youth, providing lots of training and support, and using structured activities to make it easier for the mentors. Nevertheless, it appeared that our program was having a negative effect on some students. We looked closer at the evaluation data to see if those mentors who were not showing up had the high-risk students—thinking these mentors may have been overwhelmed—but this was not the case. Not showing up seemed to have more do to do with the kind of mentor than the kind of mentee (Karcher & Lindwall, 2003): Whether the mentee was high or low risk was less important than was the mentor's attendance.

As for the mentors, our evaluation results suggested (Karcher & Linwall, 2003) that some mentors found working with their mentees challenging, perhaps even overwhelming. It is possible that these challenges promoted their growth and helped them develop more realistic goals as to the amount of impact they might have on at-risk children. As part of our study we had assessed their levels of social interest. Those mentors with high levels of social interest chose to work with the more challenging mentees and were most likely to return to the program the second year.

■ Personal Reflection

I have been interested for many years in the ways children work out their negative feelings through misbehavior and self-criticism. Often, school counselors are seen primarily helping to promote academic achievement, yet often they are the only or main advocates for the social and emotional development of students in schools. I have learned that when we create programs for kids, we need to be sure the programs do not inadvertently underscore students' prior dysfunctional or problematic family dynamics. It seems that despite our best efforts to ensure that a program goes well, a student can get hurt.

Many times the youth themselves replicate their own prior problems with new peers and adults, some say, to master the feelings they still carry with them from their experiences in their families of origin. Other times students are teased by peers, feel misunderstood, or perceive some discrimination that leaves them feeling worse about themselves after being with us.

If we want to take credit for the positive effects of our interventions, school coun-selors also need to acknowledge problems and make repairs when things do not go as planned. I learned early on that it is hard to acknowledge when I am unsuccessful in my school counseling efforts, and that I am unsuccessful more often than I would like to admit. That is why I think evaluating our efforts objectively is so important. Not only because it provides some concrete evidence of the usefulness of our program, but also so we can learn what aspects of the program need improvement.

In hindsight, I should have intervened more quickly in Clayton's situation. I saw Corissa as one of my more competent, caring, and mature mentors. Yet it was these same qualities that let her get in over her head and keep trying to do two things at once. Rather than thinking, "Oh, she'll get it figured out," I should have worked with the drama teacher to negotiate some workable schedule or to confirm the situation was unworkable. Seeing Corissa as mature, I left too much responsibility on her shoulders. When student mentors are absent, I have learned, we need to intervene quickly and decisively on behalf of the mentee.

The next year we did even more to ensure this did not happen. We asked our student mentors to sign an agreement that stated they did not anticipate participating in any conflicting after-school activities. We drew their attention to a new policy: If a mentor misses twice in a month or three times a semester, they will be replaced unless the parents of both the mentor and the mentee believe that the mentor can rectify the problem. We also developed a termination procedure and a training scenario for use by future mentors. By training mentors in these procedures for successfully terminating their relationships when attendance becomes a problem, we also underscored the importance of their consistency.

References

Botvin, G. J. (1989). *Life skills training teacher's manual*. New York: Smithfield.

Dennison, S. (2000). A win-win peer mentoring and tutoring program: A collaborative model. *The Journal of Primary Prevention, 20*(3), 161–174.

Dishion, T. J., McCord, J., & Poulin, F. (1999). When interventions harm: Peer groups and problem behavior. *American Psychologist, 54,* 755–764.

Forester-Miller, H., & Davis, T. (n.d.). *A practitioner's guide to ethical decision making.* Retrieved September 23, 2004, from http://www.counseling.org

Gibbs, J. C., Potter, G. B., & Goldstein, A. P. (1995). *The EQUIP program: Teaching youth to think and act responsibly through a peer-helping approach*. Champaign, IL: Research Press.

Grossman, J. B., & Tierney, J. P. (1998). Does mentoring work? An impact study of the Big Brothers Big Sisters Program. *Evaluation Review, 22*(3), 403–426.

Karcher, M. J. (2005). The effects of school-based developmental mentoring and mentors' attendance on mentees' self-esteem, behavior, and connectedness. *Psychology in the Schools, 42,* 65–77.

Karcher, M. J., Davis, C., & Powell, B. (2002). Developmental mentoring in the schools: Testing connectedness as a mediating variable in the promotion of academic achievement. *The School Community Journal, 12*(2), 36–52.

Karcher, M. J., & Lindwall, J. (2003). Social interest, connectedness, and challenging experiences. What makes high school mentors persist? *Journal of Individual Psychology, 59*(37), 293–315.

Komo, K. A., & Perry, C. L. (1996). Peer-planned activities for preventing alcohol use among young adolescents. *Journal of School Health, 66*(9), 328–334.

Noll, V. (1997). Cross-age mentoring program for social skills development. *The School Counselor, 44,* 239–242.

Suggested Readings

DuBois, D. L., & Karcher, M. J. (2005). Youth mentoring: Theory, research, and practice. In D. L. DuBois & M. J. Karcher (Eds.), *Handbook of youth mentoring* (pp. 2–11). Thousand Oaks, CA: Sage Publications.

DuBois, D. L., Holloway, B. E., Valentine, J. C., & Cooper, H. (2002). Effectiveness of mentoring programs for youth: A meta-analytic review. *American Journal of Community Psychology, 30,* 157–197.

Karcher, M. J. (2005). The effects of school-based developmental mentoring and mentors' attendance on mentees' self-esteem, behavior, and connectedness. *Psychology in the Schools, 42,* 65–77.

Karcher, M. J., Kupermine, G., Portwood, S., Sipe, C., & Taylor, A. (in press). Mentoring programs: A framework to inform program development, research, and evaluation. *Journal of Community Psychology.*

Rhodes, J. E. (2002). *Stand by me: The risks and rewards of mentoring today's youth.* Cambridge, MA: Harvard University Press.

Biographical Statement

At the time of the case study, Michael Karcher was a faculty member at the University of Wisconsin–Madison. He is now an associate professor in the counselor education program at the University of Texas at San Antonio. He has coordinated, run, and evaluated two cross-age mentoring programs and is the coeditor of *Handbook of Youth Mentoring* (Sage, 2005). You can reach Michael at michael.karcher@utsa.edu.

7

I'm Pure Evil

Patti Loewen

This case is set in a rural school in western Canada. Although it raised havoc with our spell-checker, we went with Patti Loewen's Canadian spelling, "counsellor."

Leading the life of a transient, Fran, a sixth-grade student and a member of the First Nation, uses bullying as a way to avoid developing closeness with others, including her counsellor. Loewen uses solution-focused techniques to help Fran make friends and elicit positive responses from peers.

Bullying is a big problem in schools. Helping a bully find better ways to relate to others is an especially good use of my time. If successful, I wind up helping a lot of people, not just the bully.

The School

Lantree Elementary School is a small rural school located in a fairly isolated area of western Canada. The area's economy is based on ranching and farming. Many families survive on a subsistence-level income. The student body is a mixture of Caucasian and First Nation students. While the school has only 80 students, Lantree is only one of seven schools that I serve as the student–family support counsellor. My caseload within the entire division would be about 125 students that I am responsible for working with directly or for assisting in programming for.

Student Need

Fran was an 11-year-old sixth-grade student at Lantree. Fran was one of the First Nation students at the school. Her family was living on income assistance and was very transient. She was referred by the principal/resource teacher for individual counseling because of inappropriate classroom and playground behavior. The behavior identified as most problematic was her verbal and physical bullying of both older and younger fellow students.

Goals and Strategies

Fran had been transient for most of her school life, not staying in one place long enough to form lasting relationships. Initially, I met with Fran to gather basic information and to establish rapport. The school staff's goals were to have her experience some positive interactions with her fellow students and to decrease the documented number of angry outbursts.

I used a solution-focused approach in an attempt to discover what her goals might be. Fran did not see her angry outbursts as a problem, but she did want to have friends at school. Her identification of her need for friends fit with the first goal identified by the school staff. I soon realized that working with her in isolation was not going to help me achieve this goal. I felt I needed to involve some of Fran's fellow students to act as role models and to provide a safe environment for Fran to attempt to establish friendships. I decided to work with all the girls from her grade, which in this small school amounted to six, a perfect number for doing some small group work. As a school team, we decided that this group would focus on interpersonal relationships.

Process

I met with Fran individually six times from November to June as well as on four occasions with the small group. I also met with Fran's mother twice, once near the beginning and again at the halfway point.

Individual Session 1. The school is physically small and there is no real counseling space, so our first meeting took place in the science room. Our meeting got off to a rocky start when the principal/resource teacher introduced me as a social worker and Fran immediately scowled and withdrew. This reaction was probably the result of her previous experience with social workers in the child welfare system.

I explained who I was and why I was there. Fran responded, "Don't talk to me. I don't want to talk to you." I told Fran that it was all right if she did not want to talk to me but that the principal expected us to spend some time together. I then asked if she would like to draw and gave her paper and felt markers. I told her that if she did not want to talk, she could draw or just sit until our time was up. I then told her I would use the time to do some paperwork, as I did not want to waste my time. Fran just sat watching me while I busied myself with my calendar. Fran wrote on the paper I had given her, "don't tack to me because I not going to anser." I wrote my response, and so began a 10-minute conversation without a word being spoken. The rest of the "conversation" went like this:

Counselor:	Okay, you can still draw if you want.
Fran:	You spellt my name rong it is like this.
Counselor:	5 more minutes and you can go but Mr. C. will want me to see you again next time I am here.
Fran:	than I will tell Mr. C. I don't have to come
Counselor:	Then you will need to show him how good you can be in class. (Fran felt she was there because she had been bad in class. She had stated this to the principal/resource teacher as we were introduced.)
Fran:	I cant be good I'm like prue evil.
Counselor:	No one is pure evil, everyone has one good thing.
Fran:	May be but no one can cang me but me hahaha
Counselor:	You're right I don't think I would want to change you or you wouldn't be Fran anymore. Fran, five minutes are up—you can go if you like—see you next time. Thank you for your time.

What would account for her awful spelling and grammar? Because her family was so transient, Fran missed a lot of school. When she enrolled in our school, Fran was placed in a multigrade classroom, Grade 6 to 8. However, her actual academic functioning tested out at Grade 2.5 to 3.2 in all subject areas. She could read at approximately a Grade 3 level, but her writing skills were at a mid to low Grade 2 level and her math was even lower, at a beginning Grade 2 level. However, because of her history of bullying in other schools, we felt that being with the younger students would be inappropriate.

Individual Session 2. Fran came with me very reluctantly; she wanted to know why I kept bothering her and told me that her mother wanted to talk to me. I replied that I would be happy to meet her mother. Fran said again that she was "pure evil" and that nothing I could do would change that. She stated she had been calling a boy in her room names and that she had gotten into trouble again. She also talked about how she was going to beat up this same boy as well as some of the other girls in her class. I attempted to engage her in some solution-focused dialogue to see what she saw needed changing. Fran was able to identify what everyone else would be doing, that is, being nicer to her and letting her play with them. However, she could not identify anything she would be doing differently as she felt there was no hope for her ever changing.

Parent Conference 1. Fran's mother, Mrs. Marnot (not her real name), stated that Fran was a hard child to manage and that Fran picked fights with her two older brothers, 14 and 16 years of age. The boys had been staying with relatives but had to return home after being charged with breaking, entering, theft, and assault with a weapon. Fran's father had no contact with his children and was in and out of jail. Mrs. Marnot had a boyfriend and they drank a good deal when he was around the house. Fran did not like this man and tried to avoid being in the house when he was there. Mrs. Marnot said that Fran would spend all her time at school if she could. It was my belief that Fran saw school as a safe place where she knew what to expect, as opposed to her chaotic home. Mrs. Marnot was quite open to my trying to work with Fran but did not want to work with me herself.

Individual Session 3. Fran finally began to open up and share some thoughts and feelings verbally.

Counsellor:	You look tired today, Fran.
Fran:	My brothers kept me awake last night playing loud music and watching videos.
Counsellor:	Did you tell your mom?
Fran:	Mom asked them to stop, but they wouldn't. Since mom's boyfriend moved in, she has no time for me.
Counsellor:	What would it be like to live at your house if things were better?
Fran:	My mom would have more time for me. I would not have to get myself up and make my own lunch. Now she is tired, cause the boys keep her awake too.
Counsellor:	What would you be doing that would be different when things were better?
Fran:	Nothing. I am pure evil and nothing will change. (I always provided Fran with paper and markers as she enjoyed doodling as we talked, and this statement was accompanied by a self-portrait showing Fran as a devil.)

Fran then shut down completely and refused to continue the conversation. Fran held no hope for herself or that anything would change in her world.

Individual Session 4. I decided to see if I could get more information about why Fran saw herself as "pure evil." I filled out a Self-Evaluation Scale from the book *Forms for Behavior Analysis with Children* (Cautela, Cautela, & Esonis, 1983). Because Fran read at only a Grade 3 level, the scale had to be done orally. This took all of the fourth session. The scale showed that Fran felt others had a very poor perception of her, that they did not like her or enjoy being around her. Her feelings of self-worth came out low. Fran's responses in the area of adaptive functioning were also very negative. Her perception of her body image was the only part of the scale that came out positive and strongly so. The only other positive responses revolved around her perception of her family relations. Fran's responses showed she felt loved and accepted by her family. The scale indicated that Fran did not believe she could learn or do well at school. Her responses indicated she recognized her interpersonal skills were poor. She responded to the questions "What I like best about myself is" and "What I like least about myself is" with the same word: "Nothing."

It was after this session that I decided to attempt to involve Fran in a group with the girls from her class. The class had only six girls, and all of the other five girls had tried to engage Fran at various times. According to their teacher, none of them had given up on her completely, and others still tried to include her.

Letters were sent home to all the girls' parents explaining the nature of the group. The girls were told that it was to be an experimental group in the school and that if it worked out well, I would be looking at working with other groups. They were not told that the group was being formed for Fran's benefit.

Individual Session 5. I had heard from the staff that Fran's brothers had been in court recently and it looked like they might have to spend time in the youth detention facility. Our meeting started with Fran coming into the room and tossing a wadded up ball of paper at me. When I uncrumpled the paper, it read, "I don't like you, leave me alone already." I acknowledged her note. Fran was obviously looking for a negative reaction; I just thanked her for being so up-front about how she was feeling. I then asked if she and her mother had received the letter about the group. Fran said, "I hate groups, they're dumb." I asked if she would at least try it and she agreed. I told her she and I would also continue to meet individually but not as regularly. This session ended early as Fran was taking part in a class activity.

Group Session 1. I adapted our group activities from the book *Thinking, Feeling, Behaving: An Emotional Education Curriculum for Children* (Vernon, 1989). The first topic was lifestyle choices. I had the girls cut pictures out of magazines and answer questions about that person's lifestyle. All six girls, including Fran, were able to do this exercise well. We then discussed their own lifestyles. Fran seemed to want to shock. For example, regarding recreation, she said, "I like to beat up people," and regarding family, "My brothers hate me and they beat on me all the time." There is no doubt in my mind that there was some truth in these statements. The other girls, to their credit, validated some of Fran's statements. They talked about times they fought with their siblings. They did their best to find some common ground with Fran.

Group Session 2. The object of this session was to discover that we can make wrong assumptions about people. The girls were invited to complete six "I am" statements to describe themselves. This was the first time I heard Fran make positive statements about herself. All the statements had something to do with her physical appearance or physical abilities, for example, "I am strong," "I am pretty," "I am good at wrestling." This was consistent with the Self-Evaluation Scale we had completed earlier. We then went on to discuss a time when someone had made a wrong assumption about us. Fran shared an incident at school where she had been blamed for something that someone else did. The girls in the group knew about this incident and agreed with Fran's side of the story. They had even told the principal that it had not been Fran. This interchange helped Fran feel that she was part of this group.

Individual Session 6. Fran and I met individually following the second group session. Fran was much more open this time. We talked about her strengths, "I beat my brother up when we were wrestling on the weekend," and "I can beat Sam racing." (Sam is a boy in her class.) I then identified strengths that I had learned about in our time together: her ability to cook for herself, to get herself up and to school on time, and her drawing. She did not understand that these were strengths. I then asked her if she would like to cook lunch with me at school sometime. She thought this would be good. We discussed when and what we might make and then Fran asked, "Can you make muffins?" I told her I could, and she asked, "Can we make muffins for the class?" We decided that the next time I came we would do this.

This was the first time Fran had made any attempt to do anything for anyone in the school. It also showed me she was willing to take a risk in sharing her talents with the class.

Individual Session 7. This session was taken up with baking muffins and sharing them with her class. While we were baking, Fran shared some of her family history with me. Fran did not want to take them to class herself. I believe she feared being rejected. I told her I would go with her, but then was called to the phone. When I came back she had gone ahead and served them herself and had been very well received. She came back beaming and asked if she could take the leftovers home to her family. This seemed to create a turning point for both Fran and the class and her behavior improved somewhat. The class was also more open to her involvement. This session was a turning point for everyone involved, students and staff.

Group Session 3. We looked at how and why people react to similar situations in very different ways. We looked at how people's behavior is influenced by their thoughts and feelings, past experiences, and assumptions or expectations. The girls worked in pairs to complete this exercise and then role-played their scenes. Fran was quite lively at acting out the scenes, and the other girls in the group wanted to partner with her.

Following this session, school staff noted that Fran seemed to be more open to involvement in classroom activities. There had been a decrease in her verbally and physically abusive behavior. Fran recognized a caring behavior of a classmate by adding a care note to the board the school kept as part of a friendship club.

Group Sessions 4 and 5. Fran was absent because her mother was having problems and Fran had been sent to live with an aunt. We were not sure she would be returning to the school. I continued the group with the other girls but will not spend time on these sessions, as my focus for this case study is Fran.

Parent Conference 2. I went to Fran's home to ask her mother if Fran would be back to school. The mother indicated that she had sent her to an aunt's home as Fran and her brothers were fighting. The boys had been ordered by the court to stay with their mother. Mrs. Marnot thought Fran would be back in a week or two, once the boys' court cases were settled. I explained how well Fran had been doing and expressed my hope that she would be back soon.

Group Session 6. The topic of this session was sensitivity to others. Fran was back for this session, but because she had been absent for 2 weeks, the closeness and continuity of the group was broken. The other girls welcomed her back but Fran was again making statements to shock the other girls. They ignored her inappropriate comments, and she was able to get back on track. We discussed how we wanted to end the group, and it was decided that we would have a pizza party.

Group Session Windup. The group had a pizza lunch together and we talked about what we had learned in our time together. Fran said she had learned, "These guys are okay, I like them. They let me do stuff now." All the girls felt that they knew more about why people acted certain ways and how things you say and do can be misunderstood.

At the end of the party, the girls gave me a small gift and a note. The teacher told me later that it had been Fran and one of the other girls who had instigated this. Fran had come a long way from our first meeting!

Fran and her family moved away shortly after this. Just prior to leaving, Fran was once again in trouble at school for physical aggression. Perhaps she was distancing herself from her classmates and the staff who had begun to become important to her.

Results

Was this intervention successful? In many ways I believe it was. Fran came to trust the girls in the group and me enough to take risks. Fran's verbal and physical aggression decreased somewhat. However, circumstances outside the school mitigated my intervention. Her brothers' involvement with the court system and the upheaval this caused near the end of the year set Fran's progress back considerably. At the end of the year, Fran basically disappeared. One day they were in their rented home; the next day they were gone. If Fran's family continues to move from place to place and Fran is not allowed to build any lasting relationships, I feel the long-term outcome for her will be poor. My only hope is that she will remember her small successes here and be able to build on them.

Personal Reflection

This was a good learning experience for me. The ability to include the target student in a group of average students was new. Previously, I had been locked into groups of only problem kids. This experience confirmed for me the desirability of groups composed of a cross section of the class.

In hindsight, I would have continued the group until the end of the year to maintain that accepting climate for Fran. For various reasons, including my own overburdened schedule, I had to stop sooner than later.

The other thing I would have done was to try and engage the mother more. I would have pushed the mother to allow Fran to be more involved in organized community activities such as skating and soccer. I did offer to arrange for Fran to attend camp during the summer, but the family disappeared before the application was completed. I would have liked to have spent more time helping Mrs. Marnot recognize the strengths Fran did have rather than always focusing on the negative aspects.

I have worked with lots of similar families in my previous job as a child welfare worker. This experience reinforced for me the devastating effects of a transient life. The child welfare system and the education system lack the resources needed to adequately support these families in their attempts to break free of this destructive lifestyle.

References

Cautela, J. R., Cautela, J., & Esonis, S. (1983). *Forms for behavior analysis with children.* Champaign, IL: Research Press.

Vernon, A. (1989). *Thinking, feeling, behaving: An emotional education curriculum for children Grades 1–6.* Champaign, IL: Research Press.

Suggested Readings

Crothers, L. M., & Levinson, E. M. (2004). Assessment of bullying: A review of methods and instruments. *Journal of Counseling & Development, 82*(4), 496–504.

Espelage, D. L., Bosworth, K., & Simon, T. R. (2000). Examining the social context of bullying behaviors in early adolescence. *Journal of Counseling and Development, 78*(3), 326–334.

Newman-Carlson, D., & Horne, A. M. (2004). Bully busters: A psychoeducational intervention for reducing bullying behavior in middle school students. *Journal of Counseling & Development, 82*(3), 259–268.

Smith, J. D., Schneider, B. H., Smith, P. K., & Ananiadou, K. (2004). The effectiveness of whole-school anti-bullying programs: A synthesis of evaluation research. *School Psychology Review, 33*(4), 547–561.

Biographical Statement

Patti Loewen, BSW, RSW, is the student–family counsellor for Pine Creek School Division in Gladstone, Manitoba, Canada. She has held this position for two years. Prior to this, she worked in the field of child welfare for 20 years. While in the field of child welfare, she worked with adolescents and their families, did after-hours emergency on-call, and worked as a child abuse investigator. You can reach Patti at ploewen@pinecreeksd.mb.ca.

Silent Sorrow

Shirley Redcay

    Bryan is a 7-year-old with hearing impairment whose baby brother has recently died. Shirley Redcay admits feeling apprehension about including him in a small counseling group she offers for children with bereavement issues. She learns to work with Bryan through an interpreter. Redcay also provides individual counseling and refers Bryan to summer programs for those with hearing impairment.

B

ryan (not his real name), aged 7, was a second grader in the program for students with impaired hearing. This student came to my attention through the school secretary. When Bryan's mother brought him to school, she told the secretary that his baby brother had died. The infant never came home from the hospital after being born, and had died in the hospital at 7 weeks of age.

■ The School

The school is in a large city in Florida. The student body of 670 represents a variety of nationalities and races: 60% Black, 19% White, 15% Hispanic, 4% multiracial, 1% Asian, and 1% Native American. Ninety percent of the students qualify for free or reduced lunch. Approximately 25 of them have hearing impairment.

■ Student Need

The mother wanted a counselor to explain to Bryan that the baby had died. Bryan had attended the funeral but did not understand that his brother was dead, because the mother did not know how to sign and was unable to communicate that information to him. She said he had had tears in his eyes at the funeral, but had not cried.

■ Goals and Strategies

Even though this child had a hearing impairment, I thought he could benefit from my Healing Hearts group for children at our school, which deals with death and bereavement issues. The group incorporates art therapy, which I thought could be a good technique for Bryan. I wanted first to meet him individually, so we could get to know each other and deal with the issue of his knowing his brother is dead.

■ Process

Individual Session 1. As I do not sign, an interpreter was needed, and the initial session with Bryan was scheduled so that he and the interpreter were both available. I went to their classroom to meet them. The interpreter would serve as our communication link by translating. I planned to keep my focus on Bryan and not get into conversation with the interpreter that would leave Bryan out. I explained that if Bryan wanted to share anything we discussed in counseling with others, it was fine for her to translate for him, but other than that, everything would remain confidential. Certified interpreters, not unlike counselors, follow a strict code of ethics that stresses confidentiality and clarifies interpreters' responsibilities as faithful translators of the communication occurring between their clients and others (Registry of Interpreters for the Deaf, n.d.). As we walked to my office, I asked the interpreter to explain to Bryan who I was and that we were going to my room to talk.

I learned from Bryan that he had held "Baby John" in the hospital. He believed John was asleep and that he would see him again. He displayed little expression as he relayed this information. I used the picture book *About Dying* (Stein, 1974), which explains the death of a bird, and then of a person, to teach the concept of death. The book shows pictures of a casket and graveyard. He responded by signing, "Like Baby John." When we talked about the funeral, he indicated that he felt sad during the funeral. His eyes teared slightly as we communicated. I explained that it was all right to cry and offered tissues, but he did not use them. I told him about the Healing Hearts group I would be starting soon and asked him if he would like to be in it. He agreed, and I gave him a form to secure his mother's permission for counseling. After this initial session, he walked calmly back to class.

I had followed through with his mother's request by seeing him and ensuring he knew his brother had died, but I knew Bryan needed more attention. At his developmental level, he might not understand the permanency of death. I knew having a child with a hearing impairment in my group would be a challenge for me, but because it could benefit him, I was willing.

Individual Session 2. The next week, I saw him again individually the day before the group began. I used the book *Goodbye Forever* (Boulden, 1994) to be sure he understood the difference between death and sleep. He talked about people in his family, including Baby John. He was more relaxed than he was the first time I worked with him. I made it a point to look at him and talk to him, not the interpreter as she signed to him and verbalized his signs to me. His communication was often in disjointed words and phrases. When discussing his brother, he would sign "baby" or "beautiful baby boy" and make a rocking motion with his arms rather than signing a sentence such as "I held my brother and rocked him." I had to ask careful questions to be sure I understood what he wanted to say. At times I summarized what I thought he meant and asked him if that was right. He expressed displeasure at having to go to work with a parent on an upcoming school holiday. When I asked him about that, he explained, "Dad types on a computer." By his facial expression I interpreted him to mean he would be bored.

Group Session 1. The next day, Bryan entered group counseling. I was apprehensive about how he would do in a group with students who did not have hearing impairments. I wanted him to experience being in a group with other students who had had someone they loved die. I hoped he could develop a connection with the other students. I was also concerned with whether I would be able to balance his communication needs with the needs of the other students and run an effective group.

There were eight children in the group. Bryan was the only second grader; the rest were in Grades 3 to 5. The deaths represented in the group varied: best friend, brother, mother, grandfather. Bryan was not the only one in the group whose brother had died.

Bryan was one of the last children I picked up as I went from class to class gathering the children for the group. Before I went to Bryan's classroom, I explained to the others that we would be picking up a child from one of the hearing-impaired classrooms and that an interpreter would be coming with him. Since many of the older students from the hearing-impaired program are mainstreamed part of the day, the children easily accepted the idea of Bryan being part of our group.

In my group area, the interpreter was positioned next to me, with Bryan across from us so he could see both of us at the same time. Once we were all seated, I began by explaining the reason for the group and teaching the concept of confidentiality. I explained how a cut heals, but that the heart heals differently. I taught confidentiality by saying each person could tell anything he or she wanted about what he or she said and did in the group, but not about what anyone else said or did, because that was each individual's private information. I also told them that each person in the group had been hurt very much, and that my room is a place where everyone will be kind to each other because no one needs any more hurt. (I model kindness even when I need to correct wrong behavior.) I stressed listening without interrupting so Bryan would be able to understand all the conversations. The group members agreed to these rules and did not add any others.

I gave each student a turn to tell his or her name and, if he or she wanted to, who had died. I was impressed with the way each one listened and was patient with Bryan when it was his turn. He had to be prompted by the interpreter to participate. I read the book *Sad Hug, Mad Hug, Happy Hug* (Bete, 1994) and discussed the story briefly. I watched the interpreter out of the corner of my eye as I read to be sure my pace was right for her. Bryan was attentive and interested.

The next activity was to create a cover for the memory book each would be making, a page each week. The cover has the words *In Memory of* with space to write the person's name and *By* with space for the child's name. The rest of the cover is blank. I do not attach the other pages until the second session; this makes the first session low risk and nonthreatening.

Bryan watched the others begin, then, with prompting from the interpreter, created his cover. He drew and labeled himself, his parents, and other family members. He then drew a coffin at the bottom, and drew John inside with a smiling expression. John was about one fourth the size of the coffin. I was very satisfied with Bryan's participation in the group.

Group Session 2. In the second group session, one of the other group members asked the interpreter if Bryan's brother died because he was sick. The interpreter directed the girl who had asked the question to touch Bryan's arm to get his attention, and to ask him the question, which she then interpreted to him. He answered the question, "His head was hurting bad. He went to sleep." The interpreter explained the answer to the group. At this point the group members seemed accepting of Bryan and the interpreter as participants. Bryan initiated little communication but answered when questioned.

After reading and discussing the book *About Dying* (Stein, 1974), which Bryan had already seen, the children began the "Family Portrait" page of their memory books. This page has a picture frame drawn around the edge. I encouraged the group members to include everyone in the picture, including people and pets that may have died, because they were still part of their family. The memory books now have the rest of their pages stapled to the cover made the previous week. The group was excited to see the rest of the pages and to know that they would take the book home after the last session. Between sessions, I keep the books for them so none are lost and I can review them. (If I identify any concerns from the books or group discussions that warrant individual follow-up, I meet one-on-one with that child a day or two after the session.)

So far, I was pleased with Bryan's progress. This mainstreaming experience seemed to help break down some of the isolation his hearing impairment had created. A few days after the first group session, I happened to be walking past Bryan's class as it was outside, and he greeted me with a smile. He seemed to be comfortable with me and accepting of my role.

Group Sessions 3–5. Unfortunately, Bryan was absent from the next three sessions due to illness and a class field trip. The rest of the group missed him, and I explained his absence. When group members return after an absence, I encourage them to go back and complete any missed pages after they complete the page that goes with the current week's story and discussion. The first memory book page Bryan missed was "My Physical Symptoms." This is a human outline to be colored in showing the pain the child experienced or is experiencing. (Some of the common responses drawn are a broken heart, a lump in the throat, upset thoughts in the brain, tears, frowns, etc. I am often amazed at the intensity of these drawings.) When Bryan completed this page, the most dramatic feature was a deep frown. He also drew lines around the hands, possibly because hands are an important part of his communication. He also used only a pencil, although crayons and markers were available.

The Session 4 page is titled "My Special Person liked . . ." I supply magazines, scissors, and glue sticks for creating a collage on this page. This page often reveals the personality of the individual who died and the relationship the child had with him or her. Group members usually end up helping each other find the pictures they want and initiating conversations about their loss with each other.

The Session 5 page is titled "I'd like to tell my special person . . ." This page can be a letter to the person, perhaps telling what has happened after his or her death. Younger children often draw a picture.

When I saw Bryan walking with his class on days when the group did not meet, he would wave or make an "ahhh" sound to get my attention. I let him know I missed him in group.

Group Session 6. Bryan returned for the final session. The goal for the session was to bring closure to the group. Bryan did complete all but two pages of the memory book. He finished the last page, which focuses on the theme "I'll Always Remember . . ." At times he sat without moving or communicating, seemingly not participating. He needed additional instruction and refocusing at those times to complete this task. At the end of the group, I gave group members glow-in-the-dark star stickers and let them each select a stuffed animal to keep. Bryan took his time in choosing his. His body language and facial expression demonstrated to me that he was satisfied with his choice.

Because Bryan had missed so many group sessions, I planned an additional individual session near the end of the school year to follow up.

Teacher Consultation. Before the third individual session, I checked with his teacher to find out how he was doing in class. She was concerned about his poor attendance due to sickness and weeks missed when his brother was born and when his brother died and stated, "When he is here, he seems to be constantly distracted and in his own little world. It is a daily struggle to get him to finish work or pay attention. I know he is not working to his potential. The behaviors he is displaying now remind me of many of the problems I had with him two years ago." I explained to her that this regression was not unusual after the death of a family member.

Individual Session 3. On his way to my office, Bryan signed, "My brother in heaven long time stay." Bryan associated coming to my office with talking about John. Once in my office, I read *Lifetimes: The Beautiful Way to Explain Death to Children* (Mellanie & Ingpen, 1983), one of the books he missed when he was absent from a group session. He was attentive, rubbing his eyes when they teared. I asked him to tell me about John's lifetime. He called his brother "beautiful baby boy" again and remembered holding him and kissing him. He smiled when he communicated this information. I offered him paper and markers to draw, hoping for a picture of himself with his brother. Instead, he chose to draw warrior figures from a computer game he plays. I perceived this as his way of transitioning from our conversation of the past back to the present. The faces he drew were angry, indicating power. When children do artwork, I often ask if they would like to keep their pictures or if they would like me to keep them. I signal nearing the end of the session by asking if there is anything else they would like to talk about or if they are ready to go back to class. When he finished, he indicated he would like to keep his picture and was ready to return to class. I walked back with him and the interpreter.

Referral. As the school year drew to a close, I believed Bryan could benefit from some summer follow-up, so I called the local office of the Deaf Service Bureau of West Central Florida (www.deafservicebureau.org) and found an individual who would work with him at no cost. I also found out about Sertoma Camp Endeavor for children with hearing impairment and learned the Deaf Service Bureau would also cover the costs for Bryan to go. This is a 1-week camp for children aged 7 and older with hearing loss that provides a team-challenge course, horseback riding, swimming, dance, basketball, and other activities. I passed this information on to his family. (I found out later he did not go to camp. Perhaps his family will consider sending him when he is a little older.)

Results

At the beginning of the next school year, I asked Bryan's teacher how he was doing. She indicated that he was participating in class more than last year. He was more cheerful and focused on academics. He also had had perfect attendance so far.

I also spoke with Bryan. When I saw him, he signed, "new pants" and "four pockets" with obvious pride in his new school clothes. When I asked about his summer, he signed, "Baby . . . beautiful baby. They had a box. That was sad. We prayed for the baby," as if remembering what we used to talk about. Then he smiled, made a motion showing a large stomach. "Mom pregnant . . . baby will be born . . . beautiful baby." I asked him how he felt when he thought of Baby John now. He signed, "Happy."

■ Personal Reflection

I am glad I was willing to get out of my comfort zone and invite Bryan to be a part of my group. After the first group session, I was no longer apprehensive about working with him in a group with students without hearing impairment. This experience left me more aware of the needs of our school's population of students with hearing impairment and interested in finding more ways to meet their counseling needs.

References

Bete, C. (1994). *Sad hug, mad hug, happy hug.* South Deerfield, MA: Channing L. Bete.

Boulden, J. (1994). *Goodbye forever.* Weaverville, CA: Boulden.

Mellanie, B., & Ingpen, R. (1983). *Lifetimes: The beautiful way to explain death to children.* New York: Bantam Books.

Registry of Interpreters for the Deaf. (n.d). *RID's code of ethics.* Retrieved August 13, 2004, from http://www.rid.org/coe.html

Stein, S. (1974). *About dying.* New York: Walker.

Suggested Reading

Lomas, G., & Van Reusen, A. (1999). Counseling services in Texas schools for students who are deaf. *Texas Counseling Association Journal, 27*(1), 15–22.

Biographical Statement

Shirley Redcay, MS, is a counselor at Cahoon Elementary School in Tampa, Florida. She has been an elementary school counselor for 13 years and has spent a total of 31 years in education. You can reach Shirley at sredcay@hotmail.com or Shirley.Redcay@sdhc.k12.fl.us.

9

The Boy Who Wanted to Call Me "Mom"

Catherine Somody

School counselor Catherine Somody receives a note from third grader Brian saying he wants to talk about friends. This was a tame start to a case that took some wild turns. Brian is the child of an alcoholic mother. A custody battle ensues between the mother and Brian's grandmother. Very few counselors want to get dragged into a legal conflict. This is one battle that Somody believes she must fight on the child's behalf.

am an elementary school counselor in San Antonio, Texas. This is a case about a child who was placed in jeopardy by his mother's alcoholism. Brian was probably lucky to have found me. I've had a lot of training in treating alcohol abuse, and I am a child of an alcoholic. This case was important to me.

The School

Our school has 520 students served by one full-time and one half-time counselor, making my caseload as the full-time counselor approximately 350 students. The majority of our students are white and live in affluent suburban neighborhoods, although there are a small number of students from very low socioeconomic families.

Student Need

I began working with Brian during his third-grade year. I received a note from him in my mail basket saying he wanted to talk to me about friends. I remembered Brian from classroom guidance as a good-looking, sturdily built boy with blond hair and bright blue eyes. I picked him up from his classroom, and we spent a few moments chatting in the hallway.

Counselor:	Hi, Brian, I got your note. Is this a good time for us to talk?
Brian:	Yes, we are doing math, and I hate math.
Counselor:	Oh, so I saved you from math today, huh? (Brian smiles.) Well, you may have to make up the work, will that be a problem?
Brian:	No, my grandma will help me if I need it.
Counselor:	Ah, grandmas can be very good for that.

Grandma? It is nice to have a helping grandmother in the picture, I thought, while wondering about his mom and dad. I didn't know it then, but Brian's grandmother was far more than a "helping grandparent."

By this time, we had arrived in my room. I have a very kid-friendly room, with lots of toys, art materials, gadgets, a trickling water fountain that I call the wishing well, a dollhouse, a large puppet theater, puppets, books, interesting rocks, games, and more. I always offer students a chance to look around and handle things when they first arrive, taking note of what they gravitate to, their attention to task, their enthusiasm or lack of it, and so forth. Brian glanced around very politely but declined the offer to play for a minute. He seemed very comfortable and ready to get down to business, so I jumped right in.

Counselor:	So, how can I help you, Brian?
Brian:	Well, some of the kids in my class are being teased a lot and I don't think it's right. I feel sorry for them.
Counselor:	Tell me more about that.

Is he really here out of concern for others? He readily gave several examples of two students in his class who are often picked on. We talked about ways Brian could be a friend and support these two students without bringing the teasing on himself. I also planned to schedule a class meeting to talk about teasing.

That afternoon, I talked to Brian's teacher. She said that she had some concerns about Brian and had planned to talk with me soon about him. She saw him as a very caring boy who was kind to all the students, and she really appreciated his social skills in the classroom. She did have concerns, however, about his attention to task, his work completion or lack thereof, and his miserable handwriting. Brian had come to us from out of state and he was struggling academically. We both agreed that he seemed very bright, especially in verbal skills. She said she had not had success with trying to schedule a parent conference with his mother and that his father was deceased but she did not know the circumstances. We agreed to monitor the situation and continue trying to schedule a parent conference, and we scheduled a class meeting to address the teasing problem. I also planned to send home a permission slip for counseling and continue to see Brian in an effort to identify any issues regarding his father's death or his academic problems and inattention.

I opened the class meeting by saying that it had come to my attention that some people were being teased in the class and asked the students if they would like to talk together about how to solve the problem. They were eager to let me know that there really was a problem. I was impressed with Brian's verbal and social skills during the class discussion. He was perceptive of feelings and articulate and avoided blaming anyone. He also made insightful suggestions while we were listing solutions. The class agreed on a plan of action, we wrote a class contract, and I scheduled time the following week to assess progress.

I received an unusual phone call from a man who gave his name and asked if I knew Brian. Of course, I could not divulge this information to a stranger on the phone, and I told him this. He said he understood, but he had some concerns about Brian that he thought I should know about. He said he had recently ended a relationship with Brian's mother, and he was concerned about Brian's welfare. He said Brian's mother had a drinking problem. He said Brian was a great kid and he hated to abandon him, but the relationship had ended and he wanted to be sure Brian and his sister were OK. He also asked me to keep his phone call confidential. I was careful to place my notes in a separate folder under the man's name, knowing that if I put it in Brian's file, it would become a part of his counseling record.

Later that week, I called Brian to my office again to offer counseling. I asked how he was doing in school, and he volunteered the information that math and writing were hard for him. I gave him positive feedback about his help in the class meeting and the fact that he brought the teasing to my attention. He beamed with pride. I asked if he would like to continue talking with me about his schoolwork, friendships, and any other concerns he might want to discuss. When he said he would like that, I gave him a parent permission form. He asked if his grandma could sign it. I explained that it really needed to be signed by his mother. I offered to call his mother and discuss it with her by phone. He said, "No, that's OK, you'd probably have trouble reaching her. I can ask her to sign it." I resisted the urge to question Brian further about his family situation and he did not offer any more information, so I ended the session.

The following week, Brian returned the permission slip with his mother's signature. At our next session, he began to open up about his family.

Counselor:	Tell me a little more about yourself, Brian. It sounds like you and your grandma are very close.
Brian:	Yeah, she takes care of us a lot. Right now she lives with us, but she has her own house, too. My dad is dead.
Counselor:	Oh, I'm sorry to hear that. That must be really tough for your whole family.
Brian:	Yeah, he died when I was three. But I remember him.
Counselor:	I bet you really miss him.
Brian:	Yeah.
Counselor:	Who else is in your family? Do you have any brothers or sisters?
Brian:	Yeah, my big sister. She's in ninth grade.
Counselor:	And you live with your mom, too?
Brian:	Yeah. But she's not doing too good.
Counselor:	What do you mean?
Brian:	She drinks too much. My sister and me and my grandma are getting tired of it.
Counselor:	That can be really tough for kids . . . I know because my dad used to drink too much.
Brian:	Did he go out to bars a lot?
Counselor:	Is that what your mom does?
Brian:	Yeah.
Counselor:	Brian, I'm glad you are telling me about these sad things because I think I can help you. Do you know what alcoholism is?
Brian:	Yeah, I guess my mom is an alcoholic but she doesn't think so.
Counselor:	Has your mom ever tried to get help?
Brian:	Yeah, but it never works.
Counselor:	What about you and your sister? Have you ever talked to a counselor before or anyone else that can help you?
Brian:	Just my grandma. She helps a lot, but it's hard for her, too. She is my mom's mom, and she doesn't know how to make her stop drinking, either.

I believe honest self-disclosure regarding the alcoholism in my family is helpful to children of alcoholics, allowing them to let go of shame and feel a sense of connectedness. And so the story unfolded. Brian and his sister had been struggling with their mother's alcoholism since the death of their father. It was unclear at this point if the drinking problem started before or after their father's death. I had many unanswered questions at this point.

Goals and Strategies

My strategy was to build a counseling relationship that would help Brian achieve the following goals: learn more about alcoholism and its effects on the family and learn some coping strategies, starting with the 4 Cs: I didn't Cause it, I can't Change it, I can't Control it, but I can Cope with it.

I would also schedule a parent conference with his mother to better assess the family history and current situation. I would try to get his mother to include his grandmother in the conference, and hopefully secure a release of information allowing me to talk directly with Brian's grandmother when appropriate. I would consult with Brian's teacher and share some strategies for helping Brian in the classroom.

Process

I started immediately with individual sessions for Brian. I asked his permission to share some of the information with his teacher, and Brian readily agreed to this, which was unusual for a child of an alcoholic. He did ask if she would keep it a secret, and I assured him that she would. Usually, the unspoken rule children of alcoholics (COAs) live by is Don't Talk, Don't Trust, and Don't Feel. Obviously Brian and his sister and his grandmother were able to talk openly about this problem, allowing Brian to feel more comfortable sharing the information with me. But as I began to educate Brian about alcoholism, it became obvious that he knew very little about the disease.

Brian grasped the 4 Cs like a drowning swimmer. I wrote them on an index card for him, and we talked about what they meant. He was able to recognize that he was trying to be the "perfect kid" so as not to upset his mom. He talked openly about pouring her booze down the drain and hiding the car keys. It was clear to him that he had not been able to prevent her drinking, and he was relieved when I told him that he could stop trying to control it.

We listed coping strategies. He could get involved in sports, listen to music, ride his bike, and play with friends. What *was* in his control? At the top of this list was schoolwork and homework. He admitted that much of his time in the classroom was spent thinking about home problems.

I scheduled a time to talk with Brian's teacher. In the meantime, she had finally succeeded in meeting with Brian's mother for a conference. She said his mother seemed very concerned and willing to do anything she could to help him. She had a college degree in business but was working part-time for a temporary agency and had not found a permanent job. His mother had asked if the teacher thought he might have an attention deficit. The teacher had shared that he did show some signs, but that we could not diagnose that at school. I explained to the teacher that I wanted to be very careful about the possibility of misdiagnosing him as having attention deficit/hyperactivity disorder (ADHD), because he was having a family situation that might be causing the poor attention. I believed she needed to know about the drinking problem that Brian was reporting. Luckily, this teacher was very well educated regarding alcoholism, and she immediately understood that this could very well be part of the reason for his academic problems. She did say she was surprised to hear this, because she had not picked up any clues from his mother, other than the missed appointments prior to their conference. She was supportive of his need for counseling, allowing much leeway for his counseling appointments. This was a lucky break, because usually it is very difficult to get teachers to allow time out of the classroom when a child is having academic problems. Brian asked to see me every day and his teacher and I were able to work out a plan where he came to see me briefly after completing a specified amount of academic work. If I was not in my office, he left a note.

In addition to the brief daily visits, Brian came for weekly individual and group sessions. The five other third-grade boys in the group had a combination of presenting problems, but all had some family dysfunction. We started each group session with "Sunshine–Cloud." We passed around a wooden token with a sun on one side and a cloud on the other. Each boy shared something happy and something sad when it was his turn to talk. Each of the boys set a classroom goal each week and discussed strategies for meeting his goal. We also had *fun*! Children of alcoholics need time and permission to have fun. We played therapeutic games as well as checkers, pick-up-sticks, Legos, and Nerf basketball. Brian was a good role model to the other boys in the group because he had such strong social skills.

Brian made some references to his home problems during group, but they were guarded, which I felt was appropriate. Once Brian said to me, "My grandma says I can tell you anything I want because it's against the law for you to tell anyone else." Wow!

Counselor:	That's true, Brian, unless I have your permission or if I think you or your sister is in danger. Then I have to get some help for you.
Brian:	We are not in danger, because my grandma stays with us. That's why she lives there. Before she lived with us we weren't very safe.
Counselor:	What do you mean?
Brian:	Well, my mom goes out to bars a lot and sometimes she doesn't even come home. My sister used to take care of us, but we got scared. Sometimes Mom would bring strange men home to sleep with her. We really didn't like that. Now my grandma won't let her do that. She won't let her come in the house if she has a man with her.

I set up a parent conference with Brian's mother. Mrs. Jameson did not invite the grandmother to attend, as I suggested. She was an attractive, intelligent, educated woman who very obviously had Brian's best interests at heart. It occurred to me once again how devastating alcoholism is. It causes such extensive denial. She talked about Brian's attention problems and asked if I thought he had ADHD. I had not yet decided how confrontational to be. I was intensely aware of the importance of not scaring her, resulting in denial of counseling services. She asked if I thought the death of his father could be a factor. I saw this as a perfect opportunity to recommend outside therapy. She said she had considered this but could not afford it. This surprised me, as they lived in a new house in an affluent neighborhood. She explained that since she was unemployed, they had no health insurance. They were living off an inheritance from Brian's father, which was dwindling.

I decided not to jeopardize the relationship and so I did not mention her drinking or its effects on Brian. Instead, I focused on ways she could help Brian with his organization, homework completion, and academics. The conference ended on a positive note and promises to stay closely in touch, a promise she was unable to keep although I think the desire was sincere.

The teacher and I pushed forward with a referral to our Level III CHILD committee for review. This was our prereferral process, involving other specialists on the campus, including our licensed specialist in school psychology (LSSP). I was feeling some pressure from the teacher to refer Brian for testing, and she believed he should see a doctor about his inattention. I continued to resist this, because Brian showed *no* signs of attention deficit while working with me in a group or individually. The committee decided that an academic/intellectual screening would be appropriate.

After her initial screening, the LSSP concluded that Brian showed signs of a learning disability in the area of written expression. She met with Brian's mother, who agreed to a referral for special education. His mother also scheduled an appointment with his pediatrician. The pediatrician prescribed a trial of Ritalin for Brian. Ritalin seemed to have some positive effects on his school performance, so the Admission, Review, and Dismissal (ARD) committee decided not to place Brian in special education, but he had access to a learning lab.

My first meeting with Brian's grandmother occurred around this time. (His mother had signed a release of information.) We had talked by phone on several occasions, and it was very obvious that she was the one monitoring Brian's school performance. She was already high on my own list of most admired people. She was a very grandmotherly figure, with snow-white hair. She thanked me for helping Brian so much. She told me that Brian's mom started her drinking problem prior to her marriage. She said she claimed she did not drink while pregnant, but Grandmother had doubts about that.

Brain's grandmother and her husband lived on their own rural property. Her husband was retired, and he was getting tired of her staying away from home every night to take care of the children. She said she went home every day while the children were at school but was sure to be back at their house by the time they returned from school. I was amazed at her dedication. How difficult it must be for her, away from home so much and watching her own daughter destroy herself with drink. She said her son also had a home on their property, and he and Brian were very close. Grandmother expressed concerns about Brian's medication because she did not believe Brian had ADHD. I asked his grandmother if she had considered Alateen for the children or Al-Anon for herself. She said the children did not want to go. I offered to pursue this idea with Brian. When I asked her how much longer she felt she could continue this lifestyle, she said, "As long as it takes. I would do anything for those children."

Brian finished third grade successfully.

Fourth Grade. Brian and I were happy to see each other after summer vacation. He excitedly told me about his baseball team and his adventures over the summer. When I asked how his mom was, he said, "Not good." When I saw his grandmother, she said, "He puts on a good front, but he is very clingy with his mother when he is around her. I can see his fears on his face, and there's nothing I can do to help." I said, "Yes, you are helping him more than you know. You are helping him live as normal a life as possible and you are keeping him safe."

I had hand selected Brian's fourth-grade teacher, a consistent, soft-spoken, caring teacher. She was also the best writing teacher in the school. I knew the state-mandated standardized writing test would be a challenge for Brian, and if anyone could get him through it, it was this teacher.

Brian no longer needed daily contact, and in fact, weeks would go by without his seeing me individually. I included Brian in an 8-week counseling group. All five of the children in the group had a family member with a drinking problem. There was a high level of trust in the group, and Brian was quite open about his situation, resulting in more self-disclosure from the other children in the group. It was helpful to have Brian in the group, with his highly developed emotional intelligence.

Fourth grade did bring some negative changes. Peer approval became very important to Brian, and he was no longer the champion for the underdog. In fact, he seemed to swing the other way. He often fought with his best friend. Both were guilty of putting the other down and we had many "mediation" sessions throughout the year. It was obvious when talking with Brian that he was striving for popularity and it was not "cool" to be nice to the unpopular kids.

Brian became acutely aware of his academic deficits and he resisted going to the learning lab, saying that it was too embarrassing. Luckily, he did not seem to be embarrassed about coming to see me. It usually isn't until fifth grade that some children begin to think counseling is not cool. He was also no longer taking his medication, probably for the same reason he did not want to go to learning lab; he wanted to be like the other kids. He did not seem to be struggling as much with academics.

After the eight group sessions, I saw Brian on an "as needed" basis. In the spring, one of our district substance abuse counselors came to my school to cofacilitate a group for children of alcoholics. The counselor, Suzanne Diou, was very experienced and well trained in working with these children. She had cowritten the curriculum we used for the group, called *Twelve Stepping Stones for Young Children of Alcoholics and Other Addictive-Drug Users* (1999). This was an ideal group for Brian.

One day, Brian came to tell me that his mother was bringing alcohol onto campus at lunchtime and he knew this was against the rules. In addition, our vice-principal had told me that she thought she smelled alcohol when his mother had attended a PTA meeting. Brian would ask his mother for a sip of "Coke." If it was just Coke, she gave him a sip. If she would not let him have a taste, he felt sure that it was alcohol. He said he also smelled it when she wasn't looking. Poor Brian, I thought, still trying to monitor his mother's drinking—but what 10-year-old wouldn't? He also said that he was embarrassed because his mother was coming to eat with him almost every day. Brian said he didn't want to tell his mom not to come because he felt sorry for her: "I think she gets lonely and doesn't have anyone else to be with." He wanted me to tell her not to come so often. I encouraged Brian to talk with his mother about this, with my assistance. I thought it was important for Brian to learn to verbalize his feelings directly to his mother, but he was adamant that he was not ready to do this.

That day at his lunchtime, I went to the cafeteria and, sure enough, his mother was at his table. Brian immediately jumped from his chair to intercept me, whispering that her drink was just Coke and that I didn't need to talk with her. I said, "Brian, trust me. I think I can help your mom understand without hurting her feelings." He agreed, and I asked his mother to come to my office after lunch.

Counselor:	I understand you have been coming to see Brian at lunch.
Mrs. Jameson:	Yes, I love to have lunch with him and his friends. He is such a support to me.
Counselor:	Mrs. Jameson, do you remember when you were in fourth grade? For most kids, this is the age when peer relationships are so important. He loves you very much, but honestly, he needs time alone with his friends. He would prefer it if you came only once a week. Would that be OK with you?
Mrs. Jameson:	I hadn't even thought of that. I'm glad you told me.
Counselor:	I know Brian is a great support to you, but you really can't rely on him to meet your personal needs for companionship. He needs you to be his mother. There's something else. He is worried that your drink sometimes contains alcohol when you come on campus. He is very worried about it because it's against the law.
Mrs. Jameson:	I would never do that! (Look of shock)
Counselor:	Good. Thank you for understanding.

At this point, I had to be straightforward and hope that she cared enough about Brian to permit him to stay in counseling with me. I made a point to check with Brian over the next few weeks, and he said things were much better. "She doesn't come as often, so it's OK now. She just comes once or twice a week. That's OK with me."

<u>Custody Case.</u> Toward the end of Brian's fourth-grade year, he came to my office, and as usual, he did not mince words: "We are going to go to court. My grandma is going to try and get custody of us. Will you help us?" I was careful to keep my face neutral, although an alarm went off in my head. Parents often try to drag school counselors and teachers into custody battles, and in most cases, it is something we try to avoid. But this case was different.

Brian:	My sister and I want to live with our grandma. Mom is getting worse, and we don't want to live with her anymore. She is getting mad at my grandma and says she doesn't want her to stay with us anymore. My grandma hired a lawyer and he said she has a good case.
Counselor:	How do you want me to help?
Brian:	Will you tell the judge about my mom? Will you tell him about how my grandma takes better care of us?
Counselor:	Brian, I can tell the judge about the things you have told me, but I want to be very sure that you want me to do that.
Brian:	Yes, I want you to do that. You have my permission to tell him anything you need to tell him.

There was no doubt in my mind that this would be in Brian's best interest. I called our director of guidance, Dr. Patricia Henderson. We reviewed the procedures.

I would need to receive a subpoena. I should take my notes to court to refer to but I should not turn over copies without a direct order from the judge to release them, and I hoped I could convince him otherwise.

I scheduled individual sessions with Brian so that I would have current information. Brian told me that he rarely saw his mother sober. He was very concerned about her drunk driving. I asked Brian what would happen if he told his mom that he did not want to ride with her when she was drinking. I could tell by the look on his face that he could not bring himself to do that.

I called Brian's grandmother and she verified the information Brian had given me. She said her lawyer specialized in family law and that he seemed caring and was very good with Brian and his sister. She had given my name to their lawyer and I would be receiving a subpoena. They hoped to keep the children from having to testify and planned to leave them at school on the day of court.

I knew it would be difficult to testify in front of Brian's mother about some of the things Brian had told me. I thought there was a possibility the judge would allow me to talk with him in private. When I arrived in the hall outside the courtroom, I was surprised to see how many people were there. Brian's grandmother was standing with a large group of people and when she saw me, she came and thanked me for being there. She attempted to include me in their large group, but I thought it was important that I not be a part of their group and, instead, stayed in "neutral" territory on a bench by myself. I was painfully aware of Brian's mother, alone with her lawyer. We had maintained occasional contact and my heart went out to her. They say some alcoholics have to hit rock bottom before getting help, and surely it couldn't get any rockier than this—facing the possibility of losing her two beautiful children, whom she loved deeply. I was relieved when Brian's sister's high school counselor arrived and we sat together.

Brian's lawyer came to introduce himself and talk to us. He thanked us for coming and said that things did not look good for Brian's mom. Her closest friend was here to testify against her. She had no witnesses in her defense. The two lawyers would be meeting with the judge to try and reach an agreement out of court. This meant we might not have to testify, but he wanted our recommendations to use in his negotiations. I said my immediate concern was the safety of the children and that Brian did not feel safe riding in the car with his mother. I suggested court-ordered treatment for Brian's mother and therapy for both children with someone who specialized in working with children of alcoholics. I also suggested a psychological evaluation for Brian.

The lawyers and Brian's mother and grandmother went behind closed doors. Several times during the negotiations, the lawyer came out to talk to us, asking our thoughts on different issues. Brian's mother was planning a trip with the children, and he asked if we thought that would be all right. I thought that was a bad idea. He also asked for the recommendation of a private practitioner. I gave several names of therapists and also suggested KidShare, an organization that worked with court-ordered cases. I was surprised that the lawyer had never heard of it. Before he and Brian's grandmother would agree to the final negotiation, he again asked our opinion of the arrangements. He said the judge was relying heavily on our recommendations. This was a very validating experience for me as a school counselor.

The final agreement was a trial period for Brian's mother to retain custody, allowing his grandmother to continue living with them. The court ordered treatment for Brain's mother and the children, and random urine tests for his mother. She would have to stay sober to keep her children, and she was forbidden to drive with them in the car. She was allowed to take them on the trip only if their grandmother would accompany them. The lawyer said this trial period was a necessary step before allowing Brian's grandmother to get custody. He seemed sure that Brian's mother would not be able to meet her side of the agreement, considering her history.

As I was leaving the courthouse, I saw Brian's mother sitting alone in the hallway. My heart went out to her, and I sat down next to her and said hello.

Mrs. Jameson: I have one more chance.
Counselor: Yes, I know.
Mrs. Jameson: I just can't lose my children.
Counselor: Will you get the help you need?
Mrs. Jameson: Yes, I have to.
Counselor: Will you go to a hospital?
Mrs. Jameson: No, I can't be away from my kids that long.
Counselor: It's your best chance for recovery. You wouldn't be away from them for long, and you would have the rest of your life to be with them if you stay sober.
Mrs. Jameson: No, I know I can't go to a hospital.
Counselor: What do you have in mind, then?
Mrs. Jameson: I don't know.
Counselor: Please, go see your doctor. Do whatever you have to do to get sober. Your children love you, and they need you. You have such wonderful children.
Mrs. Jameson: Yes, they are, aren't they? I must have done something right.
Counselor: Yes, you have done many things right. It's not too late to do this right, also. Call me if I can help you in any way.

She thanked me and actually reached out to give me a hug. I was very sad as I walked away, but I still felt a twinge of hope.

By the end of fourth grade, Brian's mother had lost custody of her children. They were living with their grandparents and their mother had supervised visitation rights.

Fifth Grade. I had again hand selected Brian's fifth-grade teacher and they were perfect for each other. Brian and his grandmother lived 30 minutes from school, and she drove him to school and picked him up every single day.

Again, I scheduled Brian in one of my groups. His peer relationships were better and he seemed more relaxed and confident. He still worried about his mother, but the lack of daily contact made it easier. There were times when she missed her visits and this was hard on him. He thrived on the consistent household procedures, chores, and dinnertimes that his grandmother provided. For the first time, Brian was living a relatively normal home life.

One day, his grandmother came for a conference. She told me that Brian calls me his "other mom." While this touched me, it also concerned me. Brian would be going to middle school in less than a year, and I began to think about how I could "wean" him. I suggested again that she take him for private counseling as his mother had not followed up on the court-ordered therapy. Unfortunately, the financial situation continued to be difficult, and they had no health insurance. His mother's child support was barely enough to buy groceries and essentials. The grandparents were living on retirement funds and the custody battle had been expensive.

Our school district had a received a grant for a federally funded counseling program. The licensed professional counselor (LPC) assigned to our school through the program was a man, and I realized this might be the perfect solution. What's more, this LPC would be able to follow Brian to middle school. The LPC took over Brian's counseling immediately. Brian could still see me as needed, but the frequency decreased dramatically.

■ Results

After Brian left for middle school, I never received a call or a visit, and I like to think that means I did my job well. I asked his LPC about him and he said Brian was doing fine and that Brian said to tell me hello. He never gave me any details and I decided that was good because I needed weaning, too.

I saw Brian and his sister one day in a bookstore almost a year later. He proudly told me that he was making all As and Bs. His sister had just been accepted to her first-choice college. I asked how his mother was doing, but he shook his head. They were still living with their grandmother.

■ Personal Reflection

I wonder what would have happened to Brian without his devoted grandmother. In retrospect, I would like to have had more time to explore possible grief issues regarding his father's death, although that was overshadowed by his mother's alcoholism. I believe much of the success of this case was due to my knowledge of alcoholism and its effects on the family. I have read books and attended training on counseling children of alcoholics. As I mentioned earlier, I, too, am a child of an alcoholic. I have a close family member who is very active in Alcoholics Anonymous, and the combination of my family experiences and my training was helpful. I hope Brian continues to get the help he needs, because the effects of living with an alcoholic mother can last a lifetime.

Reference

Diou, S., & Caldwell, L. (1999). *Twelve stepping stones for young children of alcoholics and other addictive-drug users*. Warminster, PA: Mar-Co Products.

Suggested Readings

Al-Anon Family Group. (1980). *Alateen: Hope for children of alcoholics.* Virginia Beach, VA: Al-Anon Family Group Headquarters.

Black. C. (1979). *My dad loves me, my dad has a disease.* Denver, CO: M.A.C. Printing.

Diou, S. & Caldwell, L. (1999). *Twelve stepping stones for young children of alcoholics and other addictive-drug users.* Warminster, PA: Mar-Co Products.

Typpo, M. H., & Hastings, J. M. (1984). *An elephant in the living room. The children's book.* Minneapolis, MN: Compcare Publications.

Biographical Statement

Catherine Somody, MEd, is currently a counselor at Leon Springs Elementary School in San Antonio, Texas. She has been a school counselor for 21 years, and she served on the Guidance Steering Committee of Northside ISD. She also serves as cluster leader for a group of elementary school counselors in her district. For six years prior to becoming a counselor, she was a classroom teacher and a special education teacher, working primarily with emotionally disturbed children. You can reach Cathy at CathySomody@nisd.net.

Bad as He Wanted to Be

Sheila Witherspoon

Jamal, an African American elementary student, is referred to his school counselor, Sheila Witherspoon, by his teacher due to defiant behavior toward authority. However, Witherspoon also recognizes that the teacher's disrespectful and racist comments contribute to Jamal's mistrust of authority as well as his disruptive behavior. Witherspoon uses Glasser's choice theory to help Jamal gain a sense of power and take responsibility for his own actions.

Jamal Stevens is part of my caseload. Excluding classroom guidance, I see about 45 students on a consistent basis and by referral.

The School

Rosa Parks Elementary School is located in a residential area of a moderately sized southern city. Of 500 students, grades K–6, 98% of the population is African American, 1% is Latino, and 1% is Caucasian. The majority of students reside in a housing project located within the residential community.

Student Need

Jamal Stevens is in the sixth grade. He is 12 years old. Jamal has recently returned to the south after a short relocation to Detroit. His teacher referred Jamal to me for constant and severe defiance in the form of verbal confrontations in class. The teacher described Jamal as his "nemesis," claiming that he had tried everything to work with him. One of the strategies was giving Jamal some leadership roles in the classroom (e.g., line leader, taking lunch request strips to the office).

Based on Jamal's own account, I knew that he had witnessed violence in his home, as well as in the projects of Detroit. He often mentioned the names of popular gangs. He was also distrustful of adults that he perceived were not respectful of who he was. However, he was respectful to adults he believed cared about him. For example, if you talked to him in a respectful tone or even chastised him in a respectful tone, he would respond in kind, especially when you allowed him to express himself loudly or forcefully. The school social worker and I worked with him simultaneously. Collaborating with the school social worker augmented our relationship with Jamal's family, providing additional services and resources that may not be as accessible to school counselors.

Goals and Strategies

Glasser's choice theory states that people strive to satisfy five basic needs—survival, love and belonging, power, freedom, and fun would best serve Jamal's needs. For Jamal, the need for power in a seemingly powerless situation with his teacher often resulted in disciplinary action. It was clear to me that Jamal believed his power, which he identified in many sessions as essential to his freedom and survival, was severely compromised by his teacher.

Of the 10 axioms of choice theory, the first tenet, "The only person whose behavior we can control is our own," helps counselees realize that they cannot control others. However inappropriate his teacher's comments were, Jamal was ultimately responsible for his own actions. This does not mean that I dismissed or invalidated his position. I believed it was important to allow to Jamal to talk and think through his actions and reactions. Without the opportunity to process, Jamal's behavior increased in intensity.

In time, I came to believe that Jamal's teacher was disrespectful of Jamal. Of course, I can't see inside someone else's head. Was he a racist? Was he ignorant about how to relate effectively with young Black males? I found lots of guidance from Pasteur and Toldson's *Roots of Soul: The Psychology of Black Expressiveness* (1982) and Sue, Arredondo, and McDavis's *Cross Cultural Competencies* (1992). I strongly recommend these two books to anyone who works with minority students.

Here were my strategies, from a practical point of view:

1. Begin weekly counseling sessions with Jamal.
2. Establish rapport by providing a comfortable and mutually respectful atmosphere wherein Jamal could "speak his mind" without repercussion of a discipline referral.
3. Empathize with Jamal by validating his point of view regardless of how "negative" it may appear to sound.
4. Collaborate and consult with administration, the teacher, Jamal's family, and our school social worker.
5. Help Jamal to understand his responsibility for his behavior as well as to learn how to verbally express his views in a more appropriate manner, without compromising his values.

■ Process

Session 1. I had known Jamal for quite some time. When he came to my office he was very pleasant and willing to talk to me. I use a checklist derived from Dr. Jawanza Kunjufu's book *To Be Popular or Smart* (1988). Dr. Kunjufu's research focus is manhood development of Black males, particularly in the area of education. He is concerned that Black students may believe that activities associated with academic achievement are perceived as "acting white." The checklist asks students to identify activities such as participating on a debate team, listening to rap music, and getting good grades as being "for me" or "not for me." After the student completes the checklist, the counselor encourages the student to discuss his or her choices.

Though Jamal identified with many positive activities, "getting good grades" was something he listed as "not for me."

Jamal:	It's not safe to be smart where we're from.
Counselor:	So it may not be a good idea for people to know that you get good grades.
Jamal:	Especially if you're a boy.
Counselor:	Really?
Jamal:	Yep. Like, I know I'm smart and I could do all the work in my class but . . . (voice trails off)
Counselor:	But . . .
Jamal:	You may have to fight a lot.
Counselor:	Are you telling me that you don't like to fight?

Jamal:	(adamant) I'll fight if I have to! You can't let nobody get you or your family! If people know you won't fight, they'll try to hurt you. I've seen a lot of people get beat up . . . man! And sometimes, it was bad!
Counselor:	Jamal, it appears to me that you really care about yourself and your family.
Jamal:	Yep! I'm the oldest so I have to look out!
Counselor:	You take pride in being a leader.
Jamal:	(incredulous) Who wouldn't!
Counselor:	I wonder if you understand how much influence you have on others.
Jamal:	(smiles, leans back in his chair, nonchalant) I do.
Counselor:	So I can see where you would make a good president.
Jamal:	I know!
Counselor:	Tell me some of the ways you could be a leader here at school.
Jamal:	Be good in school, listen to the teacher, get good grades, don't get in no trouble.
Counselor:	You know what to do! So what can we do to help you stay in class with your teacher and get along as best as possible?
Jamal:	I could ignore him but that don't mean I'm going to let him talk to me any kind of way!
Counselor:	Jamal, I can respect that. I don't like for people to speak to me in a disrespectful manner, either. However, sometimes, even here at school where I work, I speak my mind, but I have to do it in a professional manner.
Jamal:	'Cause you'll lose your job if you just get loud and go off on people.
Counselor:	Right!
Jamal:	Ms. Witherspoon, I know what you're saying, but that's hard and plus he be saying a lot of stuff I know he could get in trouble for.
Counselor:	The question is, what can you do if your teacher should happen to say something you don't like or feel is disrespecting you?
Jamal:	(raising his eyebrows) I could just write it down.
Counselor:	Would it be all right with you to set that as a goal for today to help you remain in class?
Jamal:	That'll work.
Counselor:	All right. I'm going to check up on you later!
Jamal:	(laughing) I know you will!

As I end all my sessions, I asked Jamal if he had any questions for me. Jamal asked when he could come back. I told him I would see him in my office again next week, but if he needed to see me sooner, he should ask his teacher.

Session 2. I positively acknowledged Jamal for that day last week when he came to my office and then got through the day without any incidents in class. But later in the week, Jamal was sent to In School Suspension (ISS) for 2 days for severe defiance to his teacher. I asked Jamal to discuss the events when he was sent to ISS.

Jamal:	He disrespected me! He's always talking about how his daughter can do better schoolwork than we can and she's in a lower grade. So I said, "Why don't you bring her to school and let her teach us then?" Then he told me to get out.
Counselor:	So you did not like that your teacher compared you to his daughter. I can understand why you would be angry.
Jamal:	See . . . he thinks we don't know he's prejudiced. But I know the deal.
Counselor:	What's the deal?
Jamal:	When y'all aren't around, he says a lot of things in class he's not supposed to. Difference is, I'm not afraid to call him out when he does.
Counselor:	You know there are a lot of great leaders that sacrificed their lives for what they believed in.
Jamal:	Like Malcolm X and Martin Luther King, Jr., right?
Counselor:	Yes, those are great examples. Tell me the difference between the two. How did they fight?
Jamal:	Well, Malcolm X believed you should defend yourself. Martin Luther King said you should just walk away and not fight back.
Counselor:	Which one makes sense to you?
Jamal:	They were both good. But Malcolm X makes more sense.
Counselor:	And you do have a right to defend yourself. But Malcolm X said that education is a way of defending yourself.
Jamal:	But how do you do that if people are constantly disrespecting you?
Counselor:	What did you do differently the day you went back to class and didn't get into any trouble?
Jamal:	I just ignored him. But he didn't say anything bad to me that day. But today, Ms. Witherspoon, he accused me of something I didn't even do. I tried to tell him but he always thinks it's me. That's why I embarrassed him.
Counselor:	How did you embarrass him?
Jamal:	I just got up and walked out on him when he was talking bad.
Counselor:	Oh! So you do know how to ignore him!
Jamal:	Yeah, when I get away from him. Then I don't have to hear him talking about how evil I am!
Counselor:	He called you evil?
Jamal:	(angry) Told you he says a bunch of stuff but y'all don't ever believe me!
Counselor:	He should not have called you evil.
Jamal:	True! True!
Counselor:	What do you believe would have happened today if you ignored him by staying in your seat and not talking back?
Jamal:	I would probably still be in class right now. But that doesn't mean he would've stopped messing with me.
Counselor:	True! True! (Jamal laughs) Can you control his behavior?

Jamal:	If I have to I will.
Counselor:	Meaning . . .
Jamal:	If he steps to me, I'll step to him right back!

Parent Conference. Jamal returned to ISS for the next two days. The teacher requested a conference with his parent, administration, and the counselor, which was scheduled for the following week. The conference was facilitated by our assistant principal and included the teacher; the school social worker; Jamal's mother, Ms. Karen Davis; Jamal's mother's boyfriend, Mr. Keith Tate; and me, the school counselor.

Assistant Principal:	Ms. Davis, we appreciate your meeting with us. We're really concerned about Jamal's behavior here in school.
Ms. Davis:	(angry) I'm concerned too! You see, Jamal tells me everything that goes on in this school with these teachers! This is the second teacher he has had this year, so I know that y'all got something against my son!
Mr. Tate:	(looks away and laughs, touches Ms. Davis on the shoulder) Karen, calm down and let the lady talk.
Teacher:	I appreciate your concern. That's why I called this conference. Jamal is a bright young man and could have an excellent future. But I will not tolerate his blatant disrespect in class. He has done everything from use profanity directed at me in a threatening manner to picking fights with the other kids.
Ms. Davis:	(rolling her eyes) So none of the other kids in your class do anything to him, huh! Why you always blaming Jamal for everything! And my son is NOT evil!
Assistant Principal:	I've discussed this incident with his teacher, who fully understands that his comment was totally inappropriate.
Teacher:	Yes, and I have since apologized to Jamal.
Ms. Davis:	So why are we here then?
Assistant Principal:	Well, Ms. Davis, within the past week, Jamal has spent more time out of the classroom than in due to his disrespectful behavior toward his teacher and his bullying of his classmates.
Mr. Tate:	She knows this! Look! He does this mess at home. He's sneaky, he lies, and he's manipulative, especially with his momma. But she don't want to believe anything anyone else has to say about how he acts. Then she wants to cry about how she can't control him. See, I don't take that mess off of him! He knows he can't get over on me!
Assistant Principal:	Ms. Davis and Mr. Tate, do you find that being firm with Jamal works to improve his behavior?
Ms. Davis:	I mean he knows how to act in class and all if the teacher would give him a chance!
Mr. Tate:	But see, Karen, that's your problem. You give him too many chances!

Ms. Davis:	But it's hard for Black boys out here. Police harass them all the time calling them . . . well, I'm not going to say the word in here but y'all know it starts with an "N."
Counselor:	Ms. Davis, I understand much of what you are talking about. Many Black boys have been unfairly treated. However, without you helping Jamal to understand that he is responsible for his behavior, regardless of how others treat him, his situation may become worse.
Ms. Davis:	Worse how?
Counselor:	Possibly suspension for the remainder of the year with homeschooling or an alternative school when he goes to junior high next year.
School Social Worker:	If Jamal is expelled, you will be responsible for finding alternate educational experiences for him. Also, you could be held liable if he is home unattended. If he is caught out in the street, not old enough to be declared an adult or not in school, the same harassment you talked about earlier could result in incarceration in the state's juvenile facility.
Mr. Tate:	I tried to TELL her that!
Ms. Davis:	I know . . . it's just hard for me to be mean to him. He's had enough meanness in his life.
Assistant Principal:	I'm a mother and I know how it is to become angry with your children, but it's more effective when you are firm.
Ms. Davis:	I understand. But that still doesn't give anyone the right to treat my son bad.
Assistant Principal:	Ms. Davis, please help us to understand what we can do to help Jamal.
Ms. Davis:	Just give him respect, even when he's wrong and you have to correct him.

The conference ended with me asking Jamal to come into my office. Ms. Davis and Mr. Tate told Jamal that he needed to respect his teachers. Mr. Tate added that consequences will ensue if his behavior didn't get better. Jamal's teacher agreed to send home weekly progress reports.

I continued to see Jamal to monitor progress in school, and the school social worker worked with Ms. Davis. The school social worker also saw Jamal to work on anger management.

◼ Results

Jamal was raised to protect himself at all costs, and it was difficult for him to refrain from talking back to his teacher. I knew that at least some of Jamal's complaints about this particular teacher were true. This teacher could be heard screaming at students throughout the hallway. During my classroom guidance lessons, just after I was finished, he would make subtle, covert racial comments, for example, "You people." Administration was also aware of his harshness with his students.

It became clear during parent conferences that Ms. Davis, Jamal's mother, would defend his negative behavior and blame school personnel for his actions. This only encouraged Jamal to be reactive. Further, she maintained a lenient parenting style that allowed Jamal full reign in the household.

I was worried about Ms. Davis's boyfriend, Mr. Tate, who appeared to receive respect from Jamal. Though I had no reason to suspect abuse, Jamal told me that Mr. Tate was "always hollering" at him. For many single-female-headed households in this community, boyfriends took the role of head of household, which included discipline of nonbiological fathered children. Regardless of how severe, some of the mothers sided with the boyfriend for purposes of maintaining the relationship, whether there was financial support or not.

Focusing on Jamal's strengths to form arguments and voice opinions, I tried to help him work toward a goal of entering into positive leadership positions.

A few weeks after our parent conference, his mother transferred Jamal back to Detroit to live with his grandmother. She admitted growing weary of trying to turn him around. Jamal lived with his grandmother in Detroit for a little over a month but then she sent him back to his mother because he wouldn't follow rules. Jamal attended another school in our district for about 3 months before spending his last month at Rosa Parks Elementary School. Then he was referred to our alternative school program for the remainder of his sixth-grade year.

■ Personal Reflection

When I was a child, my own father, while considered good enough to work at a suburban apartment complex, was not welcome to move his family there: "We don't rent to Negroes." My personal experience as an African American woman who was a daughter to a wonderful African American man, mentored spiritually and education-ally by African American men, has inspired me to be an advocate for African American males. My own students who are now adults tell me about how many times White women cross the street or clutch their purses when they walk by or enter into an elevator. Crossing the street, car door locks sound off in stressful cacophony. Friends, relatives, and colleagues blessed with advanced degrees and luxury cars continue to be suspect, pulled over by law enforcement for "Driving While Black." In fact, I have witnessed ill-natured treatment of Black male students by adminis-trators, teachers, and other school personnel, who many times have exhibited fear of or disgust with them.

The ability to understand Jamal's worldview through the eyes of a Black male helped me not to be so critical of Jamal's response to his teacher's behavior. I hope that I was a good advocate for Jamal.

One of the things I might have done differently was to confront the teacher regarding his comments. Often, principals choose to deal with teachers directly, especially if disciplinary action against a faculty member may have to be meted out. Given the chance, the teacher could have had the opportunity to explain his side to Jamal in a controlled environment with just me present to encourage an atmosphere of respect.

References

Kunjufu, J. (1988). *To be popular or smart: The Black peer group*. Chicago: African American Images.

Pasteur, A. B., & Toldson, I. L. (1982). *Roots of soul: The psychology of Black expressiveness.* Garden City, NY: Anchor Press/Doubleday.

Sue, D. W., Arredondo, P., & McDavis, R. J. (1992). Multicultural competencies and standards: A call to the profession. *Journal of Counseling and Development, 70,* 477–486.

Suggested Readings

Bradley, C. (2001). A counseling group for African American adolescent males. *Professional School Counseling, 4*(5), 370–373.

Davis, J. E., & Jordan, W. J. (1994). The effects of school context, structure, and experiences on African American males in middle and high school. *Journal of Negro Education, 63*(4), 570–587.

Kunjufu, J. (2002). *Black students/middle class teachers*. Chicago: African American Images.

Lee, C. C. (1995). *Counseling for diversity: A guide for school counselors and related professionals*. Boston: Allyn and Bacon.

Lee, C. C. (2003). *Empowering young Black males—III: A systematic modular training program for Black male children and adolescents*. Greensboro, NC: ERIC Clearinghouse on Counseling and Student Services.

Biographical Statement

Sheila Witherspoon, MEd, was an elementary school counselor for over three years. Sheila has worked with youth in various counseling capacities, such as pre-employment training counseling and college admissions counseling and recruitment, for 15 years. She is a candidate for a PhD in Counselor Education at the University of South Carolina. Her research interest is Black male issues in school counseling. You can reach Sheila at witherss@mailbox.sc.edu.

PART II

Middle School Cases

Healing Circles: Dealing with Separation or Divorce

Montserrat Casado-Kehoe

Parental separation and divorce often have significant behavioral and emotional consequences for children. Casado-Kehoe uses small group counseling to guide seventh-grade students through this painful loss. She helps group members express their feelings and develop coping skills. Casado-Kehoe provides details about setting up and running groups so that other counselors can establish their own groups.

W

hen I initiated the divorce group, I was working as a part-time mental health counselor in a rural middle school in the southeastern United States. There was also a full-time mental health counselor at the school.

The School

There were 420 students at our school, and I had a caseload of 20 to 30 students, whom I saw either for individual or group counseling. The ethnic composition of the school was 174 African American, 212 Caucasian, 26 Hispanic, and 8 Other; 138 received free lunch, 229 received reduced lunch, and 53 were full-pay.

Student Need

Students in my divorce group were seventh graders, ages 12 and 13, whose parents had separated or divorced that school year. Students in this group had been either self-referred or referred by a parent, teacher, counselor, or administrator. An initial needs assessment had been conducted in all classes in which the students selected various areas they would like to explore more in a group setting. Issues related to dealing with separation or divorce in the family were one of the categories listed in the assessment, as well as many other topics relevant to middle school students.

The majority of the students in this group had either expressed a concern either in terms of understanding the separation or divorce of their parents or in adaptation to the new family. Some were dealing with this family decision better than others were, but there was a general consensus that the separation or divorce of their parents had impacted them personally. An initial "Dealing with a Divorce in the Family" assessment form was used at the beginning of the group and during termination to assess if the students had changed any of their feelings, ideas, or attitudes as a result of participation in this group (Morganett, 1990).

Letters were sent home to parents about our Healing Circles: Dealing with Separation or Divorce groups. Nineteen students participated in the groups: 13 females and 6 males. Parental permission was required.

Goals and Strategies

The goals of the group were to help participants (a) explore how they felt about their parents' separation or divorce, (b) gain understanding of their feelings, (c) gain understanding of how their lives had changed, and (d) learn coping skills. The group created an opportunity for grieving the loss of the family unit the members knew prior to the separation or divorce. At the same time, the group format created a sense of universality, a circle of support, when members realized that they were not alone in dealing with issues related to the separation or divorce of their families, and an opportunity to develop empathy for others.

With the increase in the number of divorces in this country, it is predicted that one half of children under 18 will live in a family impacted by separation or divorce (Casado, Young, & Rasmus, 2002). The impact of separation or divorce can have a negative effect on adolescents if they do not have a clear understanding of what is happening in their families and the necessary coping skills to deal with such life adaptations.

Adapting to parents' separation or divorce can become an overwhelming experience, especially since one of the major tasks of adolescence is to develop an understanding of self in relation to one's family and to others such as peers. Thus, emotional and social support in how to deal with feelings related to parents' separation or divorce are essential to continue to strengthen the adolescent's growth at such a crucial developmental stage. The peer group provides a place in which the adolescent can continue to develop a sense of self and find a sense of belonging, as well as gain a sense of maturity.

The students were pulled from their third-period class once a week and met as a group in the School-Based Mental Health Counseling Office. The Healing Circles group met for eight sessions, each covering specific topics:

1. Getting to know each other: Sharing our family stories.
2. What is a family? Who is in your family? Redefining the new family.
3. Expressing feelings: Ideas and feelings about separation or divorce.
4. Understanding the cycle of loss.
5. Life brings challenges: Coping with separation or divorce.
6. Moving between houses: Learning ways to be in the family.
7. Feeling good about self and the new family.
8. Sharing learning and saying good-bye to the group.

The specific goals for each of the eight group sessions were:

1. To help the students understand their feelings about their parents' separation or divorce.
2. To redefine the meaning of family after parents' separation or divorce.
3. To develop a safe space in which the students could openly share how the separation or divorce had impacted them personally.
4. To create a sense of universality among the students.
5. To help the students identify their coping mechanisms as dealing with the restructuring of the family.
6. To assist the students in identifying strengths and challenges about their new family environment.

■ Process

The Healing Circles group that I will report on had 9 seventh-grade students, ages 12 and 13, with a mix of boys and girls.

Session 1. *Getting to know each other: Sharing our family stories.* I met with the group and went over introductions and described the goals of the group to the students. I then gave the group members a couple of minutes to complete the "Dealing with a Divorce in the Family" inventory as a pretest measurement (Morganett, 1990). Group members then introduced themselves and shared one thing they liked about themselves. After going around the circle and doing an icebreaker exercise to give each member an opportunity to remember each other's name, we discussed group rules. We brainstormed together as a group about what rules they needed to establish to feel safe enough to share personal experiences. The rules agreed on were:

1. What is said in group stays here.
2. Respecting one another.
3. Listening to one another.
4. No put-downs.
5. One may choose not to share.

I gave each member a small pad to use as a journal, and each member copied down the rules. As the group leader, I emphasized confidentiality and how important that is for people to feel safe to share their own personal feelings. I asked all members if they could agree to keep the group discussions confidential. They all agreed.

During that initial session, I gave each group member an opportunity to discuss briefly his or her family story. This gave each one a chance to talk openly about the separation or divorce of his or her parents. After each member had openly talked about his or her family situations, I talked about some of the common feelings one may experience while living in a family in which parents have separated or divorced. I explained that sometimes one feels like a yo-yo, with emotions going up and down, and unsure of what the future may hold. I also explained that separation or divorce is an adult decision that parents make on their own. As a result, the children feel a little out of control of their lives and may experience a wide range of emotions.

At the end of that session, we did a quick check-out. I asked each member to talk about something he or she had learned in group that day. A common theme seemed to be the realization that others were dealing with similar family situations. A couple of the members also commented on how they felt a little less nervous having had a chance to listen to other group members' stories.

Counselor:	I appreciate all of you coming today. I am aware you are going to be going back to class in the next five minutes and I would like to have some feedback from you. If you could share in one or two sentences, what did you learn from group today? Mark, why don't you start us off?
Mark:	Well . . . umm . . . I guess I learned that other kids have family situations too.
Counselor:	Thank you, Mark. What about you, Anna?
Anna:	This isn't as bad as I thought. I am not as nervous now.
Counselor:	And you, Jenna?
Jenna:	I feel like Mark, that other kids' parents get divorced, too.
Latanya:	Yeah, a lot of kids in our class have parents who aren't together anymore.

Counselor:	Anyone else?
Frank:	I don't know. I guess I understand more about my parents.
Miguel:	And I feel like it's not my fault.
John:	I like the group but I am still confused about my parents' separation.
Counselor:	Liz, what do you think?
Liz:	I'm still not comfortable talking about this right now.
Counselor:	Carol, would you like to share how you are feeling?
Carol:	(shakes her head no)
Counselor:	Okay, Carol. Maybe you can share with us next time.

Session 2. *What is a family? Who is in your family? Redefining the new family.* I did a quick check-in to see how everybody was feeling that day. After each person got a chance to talk, I asked the group how they would define "family." This developed into an interesting discussion because, for some of them, family meant people who lived together. It was interesting to hear some group members challenge that response because they felt that sometimes a family does not live together under the same roof, which is the case when parents separate or divorce. I gave each member a piece of paper, and asked him or her to draw all the people they would include in their immediate family since their parents' separation or divorce. This activity gave the children an opportunity to redefine who they felt was part of their families now.

This session provided the students with an opportunity to explore their new families, as well as feelings attached to the idea of their parents remarrying and their having a stepmom/stepdad, stepsiblings and half siblings, and other new family members. The session also allowed the students to discuss how they felt about having a family that lives in two separate households and has additional family members and what that meant for each of them. The general impressions at the time of check-out were the realization that families can have many forms and that sometimes one does not get along with all family members, whether they are biological or adopted. I emphasized that adjusting to a new family takes time and that for a while, one may feel like things are not the same as they used to be when Mom and Dad lived together.

Session 3. *Expressing feelings: Ideas and feelings about separation or divorce.* As usual, I did a check-in to see how the members were feeling that day. Since my session was going to focus on expressing feelings, I distributed a feeling chart handout to the members, and asked them to look at it. Then, as we went around the circle, each child described how he or she was feeling that day. After, I asked the group members if they could think back to the day they found out that their parents were separating or getting a divorce. I asked them to remember what feelings they had experienced when they heard the news about their parents' separation or divorce. I had them circle as many feelings as they could think they had experienced at the same time. Some talked about feeling sad, angry, confused, upset, nervous, scared, relieved, anxious, terrified, and miserable, among others. I emphasized that one can experience more than one feeling at a time. I then asked them to think of how they were feeling now toward their parents' separation or divorce as time had gone by a little. Some of them reported that with time, some of their feelings had changed and that they were a little bit more at ease, and yet, at times, they would still re-experience some of those initial reactions.

Session 4. *Understanding the cycle of loss.* During this session, I started group by saying that when parents separate or divorce, it feels almost like losing someone. I talked about death and loss and feelings associated with the cycle of loss. I gave them a handout that described what loss is and a list of examples of loss. At that point, I gave each member an opportunity to talk about what kind of loss he or she had each experienced with their parents' separation or divorce. Several got really sad during this discussion and actually broke into tears. I emphasized that tears are part of the healing process and that one needs to allow oneself to cry when one is sad. I asked how comfortable they felt crying, alone or in front of others, and what messages they had gotten at home. I did this intentionally to address gender issues in relation to expression of feelings. I know that guys do not feel as comfortable allowing themselves to cry and that most times, this comes from socialization.

After that discussion about loss, I gave them a handout that talked about the various stages of grief: denial, anger, bargaining, depression, and acceptance. I have used this model before with grief groups, and believe that adjusting to one's parents' separation or divorce involves going through stages of grief as the family readjusts. After discussing the stages, I asked the group members if they could identify which stage they were in. A couple of children commented that they felt like sometimes they went from one stage to the other. I emphasized that grief is not a linear process, and that one moves back and forth from one stage to another at various times. This helped normalize what some of them were experiencing as they moved through the stages of grief.

Before closing the group, I did a check-out, asking them to think of what had been the most difficult thing to adjust to as their parents separated or divorced. This was done in a brief manner, but I encouraged all to write about it in their journal in more detail. I also asked them to reflect on what had helped them deal with their grief.

Session 5. *Life brings challenges: Coping with separation or divorce.* I did a quick check-in to see how the students were feeling that day and asked if anybody had journaled after the last session. About half of them said they had actually written some in their journals. The rest had either forgotten about the assignment or felt that journaling was not for them.

Counselor:	I wonder if any of you took time to journal after our last meeting and would like to share what that experience was like for you.
Anna:	I did. And I actually started feeling really sad thinking about my dad having to move to another house. It brought back feelings of how I felt right after my parents told me they were separating. I also wrote about what had helped me deal with the situation. My older sister was very helpful. She would talk to me a lot and shared her feelings

too. But she always emphasized that no matter what, we would be all
right. She has really helped me through all this!

Counselor: It sounds like having someone to share your struggles with was very
helpful to you, Anna. I wonder if any others have felt that way, that
there was some person in their lives who helped them deal with the
situation. Anybody?

After this discussion, we talked about how all of us cope with difficult situations
in different ways. I told them that some people seem to reach out to others, while
others withdraw; and that some like to get their minds distracted so they do not have
to think so much about the events that make them feel uncomfortable. I emphasized
that we all have coping skills, but that sometimes it is good to expand our repertoire
of those when going through a difficult time. At that point, the students discussed
which coping skills they used the most and which ones they would consider adding to
their list and trying out. Before they left that day, I gave them an assignment for the
week. Their job was to notice what things they did when something would happen
during the week that was challenging. They were to write it in their journals and we
would discuss it during the following session.

Session 6. *Moving between houses: Learning ways to be in the family.* I started
group following up on last week's homework assignment. Several of the members
had tried out new coping skills and found that they were helpful. Some felt that their
most preferred ones were more helpful to them. This check-in gave the students an
opportunity to evaluate their personal ways of coping and also to learn how others
did it.

After this, I gave each group member a piece of paper and asked him or her to
draw a dotted line in the middle. I then asked the group members to write "Mom's
House" at the top of the left side and "Dad's House" at the top of the right side of the
page. They were to draw what happened in each house, who was there, and what
rules they had to follow. After they shared their drawings, we discussed how much
time they spent in each of those houses, how they felt as they transitioned from one
house to the other, the feelings that were evoked while being in an unfamiliar place,
and things they liked about having special time with each parent. This discussion
brought some very interesting feelings for many of them, but it normalized the
feelings that come up as one has to transition between two homes.

Session 7. *Feeling good about self and the new family.* I started group reminding everyone that we had two more sessions together, including this one. I wanted
the students to start preparing themselves for termination and feelings that this
would evoke. I then did a quick check-in to see how they felt about that.

I asked them what made them feel good about themselves despite their parents'
separation or divorce. They were to focus on things they like about themselves and
things that others seem to like about them. We went around the circle sharing those
ideas about self and how others viewed them. I then asked them to write all those in
their journal. After they finished with this activity, I asked each member to say one

positive thing they appreciated about each of the other group members. This exercise really seemed to boost their self-esteem.

I asked if they could think for one minute about positive things that the new family had brought for them. They all seemed quiet for a little bit and then started sharing. Some focused on the fact that they had more material things now from each parent, whereas others thought that finances were tighter at home. A couple mentioned that they enjoyed the quality time they had with each parent and the fact that they were no longer fighting. Some talked about the new family members that the divorce had brought into their lives and how they seemed to get along with these people. A couple still commented on the fact that they wished their parents had never separated and would still be together. Before the group ended that day, I processed the variety of feelings that each child was experiencing and reinforced that people are different and feelings sometimes change over time.

Session 8. *Sharing learning and saying good-bye to the group.* I started the group by reminding everybody that this was our last session together. Some expressed that they wished the group were not ending. At this point, it was clear they had bonded and had been in the working stage of group for a while. The check-in focused on how they felt about the group ending.

I went over some of the various topics we had discussed through the previous seven weeks. I asked the students if they would mind sharing what had been the most helpful to them during those times. Each seemed to bring up a different point and we added those to a big piece of paper entitled "Group Learnings." I emphasized that each had contributed something special to the group and that it takes team effort to make a group work.

The last part of that session was an activity to give them an opportunity to say good-bye to one another. I gave each one a circle and asked them to write their name in the center. They were supposed to pass the circle around and each person wrote something they liked about that person and something they would miss about that person. At the end of the activity, we processed how each felt and how difficult saying good-bye can be when we feel close to someone. I made the comparison that some of those feelings were similar to what they had experienced as they had had to say good-bye to their parents living together. Before letting them go, I gave them the postdivorce test inventory to see if their feelings had changed as a result of group. We then held hands as a group, and I reminded them that our Healing Circle had been a special time together, and that I wished them the best. I then gave each person an opportunity to wish something for the group if they wanted to. With this, I sent the students back to class and reminded them that if they needed to come and talk to me at any point, my door would always be open.

■ Results

Overall, most group members benefited from the group at various levels. The pre–post assessment inventories showed that they all developed a better understanding of the feelings involved when parents separate or divorce. When I asked the children what had been the most helpful about the group, many shared that the group normalized their personal experience and gave them a safe forum to talk about feelings.

Two of the children did not seem to benefit. One, in particular, being more shy than the others, did not feel comfortable sharing in a group. My impression was that he learned about others' experiences, which was probably helpful indirectly, but struggled in sharing his personal story in front of an audience. I referred him for individual counseling. Another student was still extremely upset about her parents' separation because her father had recently moved out of the home. Her grief was still too fresh to be resolved in the process of this 8-week group. I encouraged her to get individual counseling, also.

Group counseling impacts each adolescent differently, and much of the healing that takes place is related to individual readiness to face difficult situations and open up in front of peers. Although each student may share a different personal story, there are always common themes in the personal struggles the members present in group. For an adolescent, the thought that a peer may be able to relate to him or her can be therapeutic in its own way. Adolescence is a time of change: physically, emotionally, cognitively, and psychologically. It is a time to search for one's own identity and start separating from one's family. All of these tasks are hard to accomplish when one's family is also going through a personal crisis such as separation or divorce. Thus, peers can provide a great source of support group as adolescents face personal feelings related to their parents' separation that make them feel vulnerable and at risk academically and emotionally.

▣ Personal Reflection

I felt that this group really benefited the children. It reminded me how powerful groups are for adolescents. The group really was a "Healing Circle." As a marriage and family therapist, this group allowed me to see the effects of separation and divorce on children and how much counseling is needed for children to be able to adjust to such a difficult life transition. I learned that children can be very wise, resilient, and empathic, and how much power that has on other group members.

I also have a personal interest in the effect of family changes on children. Although my biological parents never divorced, my mother did remarry after my father's death when I was 9 years old. I remember struggling with adapting to a new family and also dealing with my grief over my father's death. There were many feelings that I did not understand. As an adult, I remember all the adjustments my family made when my twin sister divorced after 11 years of marriage. What surprised me the most was that her divorce impacted not only the nuclear family, but also other subsystems of the family. As a member of the family, one of my primary concerns was how her two children were going to deal with it.

As a counselor, I try to share with parents that divorce is a parental decision and, as such, one that the children may not agree with or understand. Therefore, it is the parents' responsibility to help their children understand this adult decision and to help their children express their feelings. In situations where parents are able to remain amicable and respectful to one another while going through the separation, children are able to adjust better. If they don't have the resources to manage this themselves, parents can turn to a counselor and group counseling experience for their children.

References

Casado, M., Young, M. E., & Rasmus, S. D. (2002). *Exercises in family therapy.* Upper Saddle River, NJ: Merrill/Prentice Hall.

Morganett, R. S. (1990). *Skills for living: Group counseling activities for young adolescents.* Champaign, IL: Research Press.

Suggested Readings

Ahrons, C. (1998) *The good divorce.* New York: HarperPerennial.

Chen, M., & Rybak, C. J. (2004). *Group leadership skills: Interpersonal process in group counseling and therapy.* Belmont, CA: Thomson Learning.

Corey, G., Corey, M., Callanan, P., & Russell, J. M. (2004). *Group techniques.* Belmont, CA: Thomson Learning.

Biographical Statement

Montserrat Casado-Kehoe, PhD, is an assistant professor in Counselor Education and play therapy certificate coordinator in the Department of Child, Family and Community Sciences at the University of Central Florida, Orlando. She was a school-based mental-health counselor at the time of this group. Montse is a licensed marriage and family therapist, a certified family therapist, and a registered play therapist. She coauthored *Exercises in Family Therapy* (Merrill/Prentice Hall, 2002) and *Instructor's Manual to Accompany Family Therapy: History, Theory, and Practice,* 2nd ed. (Merrill/Prentice Hall, 2002). Recent publications also include a chapter, "Living Between Two Worlds," in L. B. Golden (2003), *Case Studies in Marriage and Family Therapy.* You can reach Montse at mcasado@mail.ucf.edu.

Trusting the Process: Clinical Supervision of a Group Counselor

Katrina Cook and Courtney Storment

The focus of this case study is on the supervisory relationship. After observing her supervisor, Katrina Cook, leading a group, it is Courtney Storment's turn to put her soul on the line. Storment could play it safe and run a structured group for, let's say, enhancing study skills. Instead, Storment sets up a group of sixth-grade emotionally disturbed boys, all on medication for ADHD, all having been accused of bullying. I can only imagine the temptation to structure such a group with lots and lots of activities. Storment's desire, however, is to trust the group process. The writers use italics to make it easy to compare supervisor and supervisee perspectives on the same incident.

O ur case study is about group counseling with emotionally disturbed children. Even more, it is about a supervisory relationship.

The Schools

As the Safe and Drug-Free Schools and Communities Counselor (SDFSCC), I provided prevention, intervention, and staff development services for approximately 20 campuses. Part of that responsibility was to work individually with counselors and provide clinical supervision to help them refine their group counseling skills. Counselors who wanted my help could volunteer for this supervised experience.

Supervisee Need

All counselors in our district are expected to provide small group counseling for students. Courtney Storment was beginning her second year as a middle school counselor. Highly motivated, she was eager to improve her group counseling skills and requested clinical supervision from me.

Throughout, we've used italics to highlight Courtney's perspective of the supervision process.

Courtney's Perspective *I had run a few eighth-grade groups in my first year but felt that I needed more help in finding my own style as a group facilitator. I also knew that once I found my style, I needed help trusting it. One particularly appealing part of the supervision process was the opportunity to observe Katrina's group. I had never worked on a high school campus and the thought of observing freshman through senior boys in a drug-and-alcohol group was exciting and also nonthreatening because I could just observe. I also knew that there are students on my middle school campus with drug and alcohol problems. I expected to learn how to run such a group on my campus.*

The part I was a bit nervous about was having someone observe me. What if Katrina thought I was completely incompetent? What if my idea of running a group was way off? What if I failed in front of her?

Goals and Strategies

I ask counselors to observe me conducting six sessions of a group on a high school campus. Time is allotted before and after each session for debriefing. Next, I observe the counselor facilitating six group-counseling sessions. Before each session, I meet with the counselor and she tells me how she'd like me to focus my attention. I tailor my feedback to the expressed needs of the counselor. This supervision is not part of their performance evaluation and so is relatively nonthreatening.

Courtney observed six sessions of one of my groups. Although my groups have been observed many times, I still get self-conscious. While I want to "Wow" my observers with flawless and effortless group facilitation, I am painfully aware of all the things I meant to say or do but didn't. Fortunately, observers learn from the mistakes I make. New counselors seem to think they have to be perfect group leaders before they can conduct group. This desire for perfection keeps many counselors from even trying. If a counselor leaves my group saying, "You know, I think I can do that," I feel that the observation has been successful.

■ Process

Courtney arranged her schedule so she could leave her campus once a week to come to my school and observe me facilitating group. She wanted to learn to facilitate similar groups with her middle school students. Courtney was especially interested in how the group members interacted with each other. She liked how they supported and confronted each other rather than relying on me to provide activities for discussion.

Courtney's Perspective *What impressed me most was that this was a "student-directed" group. I am a firm believer in the group process and I sometimes feel that we are taught to use too many activities and lessons rather than allow the group to fully develop through interaction. Katrina's group fit this style. One thing that really stuck with me is when a student had begun using drugs again. Katrina didn't need to say anything. The other students began confronting him and reminded him of the reasons he had given for stopping. The relationships would not have developed enough for this to occur had Katrina treated each session as a class, filling it with lessons and activities. This is when I fully realized the power of the group process as well as the influence students can have on one another when given the chance. But could I do this with sixth graders?*

Someone's Watching. Because being observed can be stressful, I have found that many counselors prefer to play it safe and select students who are not likely to drop any surprises and who will be models of perfect group behavior. They'll rely on activities and techniques that they are already comfortable with. While this strategy might limit the possibility for the counselor to experience embarrassment, it could also limit the opportunities for professional growth and development. Just as I want my students to feel safe enough with me to explore and take risks, I want the counselors I supervise to also stretch their skills.

The Group Members. Far from playing it safe, I was worried that Courtney might be setting herself up for failure. She proposed to facilitate a group of 5 sixth-grade boys. Each of these boys was considered emotionally disturbed. They were all on medication for ADHD. They had been referred by teachers and parents because they had difficulty in problem solving and communicating. Each of them had individually told Courtney about feeling bullied by others. However, each of them had also been accused of bullying through name-calling and verbal threats.

After suppressing my initial reaction of wanting to scream, "What? Are you crazy? Why would anyone choose to work with such a difficult group?" I calmly asked, "Are you sure this is the group you'd like me to observe? Are all of these students suitable for group? Many experienced counselors would not tackle a group such as this. Are you really sure you want to do this? What safeguards are in place to ensure that no harm is done? How can you guarantee this is a safe place for these students?"

I didn't want to squelch or discourage Courtney's enthusiasm, but this group seemed extremely challenging.

Courtney's Perspective *The main reason I chose this group for supervision was that I wanted feedback and support in working with this population. Simon, Tim, Steven, Joey, and Robert had very few social skills and often found themselves angry and alone. At the middle school level, we do not have a specific special education counselor and emotionally disturbed students often get overlooked. Two of the group members we worked with, Steven and Joey, spent most of their day in the Behavior Management Center (BMC), which is a self-contained classroom for children with severe emotional disabilities, so they were not in the mainstream population. I wanted them to learn how to interact. I wanted to provide them a safe place where they could gain feedback on and learn to self-monitor their behavior. One of my main concerns was the volatile nature of the students. Simon, Tim, Steven, and Joey had been known to be violent when provoked. Could students who normally require great amounts of structure thrive in a group that focused not on structured activities, but on interactions with each other?*

Courtney assured me that she had followed these students closely and had built strong relationships with each of them. All of them had shown more stability this school year than they had in previous years. Her objectives were realistic in that she knew she wasn't going to "fix" these kids. She knew this was a risky group for her, but that was exactly why she wanted me to observe. I was still worried but Courtney's enthusiasm challenged me to temper my experienced cautiousness with her fresh excitement about the possibilities of group counseling.

Structure Versus Nonstructure. We met to plan the group sessions. Courtney's goal was to not let her plans dominate but, instead, to trust the process. So, I was surprised when she described the plans for her first session. In one 45-minute session, she had scheduled an icebreaker, discussion of group rules, a team-building activity, a balancing trust activity, and closure. She also had a few backup activities, just in case she had extra time left over with nothing to do. It had been a long time since I had worked with middle school students and I knew they would probably need more structure than high school students. All the activities Courtney proposed can be effective, but this seemed overkill.

Courtney's Perspective *My goal for supervision was to have a more interactive, nonstructured group. However, without realizing it, I had planned just the opposite. I armed myself with a lesson plan to protect myself from the unexpected. I had even scheduled how much time each activity would take. There was no room* *for mistakes. My fear was that Katrina would see chaos or lack of control. I wanted her to view me as a counselor who was prepared, knowledgeable, and fully capable of controlling such an unpredictable group of students.*

<u>Rush Hour.</u> As I observed Courtney lead this first session, I was struck with how she seemed to be rushing from one activity to another without really processing. Courtney seemed to work at being one step ahead of the students. She worked harder at the group than the students did. The group had a frenetic energy about it. A phrase that Courtney repeated several times was, "OK, next thing we're going to do is. . . ."

When she did process the activities, she demonstrated sensitivity and insight. She asked open-ended questions such as "Tell me a little about what that was like." and "What did you do to get rid of the frustration?" Of course, sometimes even open-ended questions fail to open things up. For example, when she asked, "What did you learn from that?" Robert responded, "Nothing." We've all been there!

A word that kept coming into my mind was *linger.* I wanted her to slow down and allow connections to deepen rather than rush off to the next distraction. I could see that Courtney had the potential to be more present to the immediacy of the group, but she didn't seem to know that herself yet.

Courtney's Perspective *I became susceptible to the students' nervous energy and was not centered and confident. I trusted the activities more than my own abilities. I worked so hard to keep the group going that I was exhausted when it was over. I was disappointed in how the group went. I maintained overt control of the group, but was that really my goal?*

<u>Session 3—Atomic FireBalls from Hell.</u> *One of the rituals I planned was to end each session by giving each student a piece of candy. The candy was meant to serve as a springboard into discussion about a particular prompt. For example, during the first session, I gave each student some Tic Tacs and asked, "What really 'ticks' you off?" During the second session, I gave each student a Life Saver and asked, "Who has been a 'lifesaver' to you?" The third session involved Atomic FireBalls. Each student received an Atomic FireBall and was asked, "What makes you really angry?"*

Actually, I am not a big fan of candy or food in group but I also do not want to impose my preferences on the counselors I supervise. Courtney used these activities as closure for each of the first three sessions and they generated some deeper-level discussion, but because it came at the end of the group, there wasn't enough time to process. For example, when students shared about feeling "ticked" when someone bullies them, Courtney said, "That would be a good group topic." She made sure to follow up on this topic during the next session, but the immediacy was lost. Also, while the topics of the candy closures did provide rich material for discussion, they did not always seem connected with the topic of the rest of the session. If Courtney had opened with this activity, it could easily have been the focus of an entire session.

Courtney's Perspective *The Tic Tacs generated some good discussion. Each of the students responded that he gets "ticked off" when others make fun of him or* *push him around. They saw that they had something in common. The Life Savers also generated some valuable conversation. They each named someone who has stood up for them as their "lifesaver." From there, the students discussed whom they had been "lifesavers" for.*

Robert:	Even a kid nobody likes can be a lifesaver.
Counselor:	Talk about a time when you've been a lifesaver for someone.
Robert:	Once a kid I didn't know was being picked on by one of my friends. I told him to cut it out and he did. I stuck up for that other kid.

Courtney's Perspective *Atomic FireBalls are very hot candy and the boys complained that they needed to get a drink of water. Some of them spit the candy out. I intended to use the candy as a metaphor for anger, but the FireBalls were the downfall of the third session. Next, I moved onto an activity where students went outside to shake and open a soda can to demonstrate what happens when they let their anger build up. When we came back inside, the boys were out of control. They began putting each other down. I closed the group by asking the boys how they would rate that day's group experience on a scale of 1 to 10.*

Tim:	Mine was a zero.
Counselor:	You didn't get anything out of group today?
Tim:	No.
Counselor:	Why is that?
Tim:	Because no one took it seriously.

Courtney's Perspective *We had moved into so many activities that the boys were not focused. Plus, it was the day before Christmas break. Without that focus, they put each other down and almost treated the group as a free-for-all. Although Tim had been right in the middle of the disruptive behavior and put-downs, he was disappointed that group was not more serious. That opened my eyes. I chose not to use candy after that session.*

The session previous to the infamous Atomic FireBall session had been successful. The students shared at a deeper level and Courtney was moving away from so much reliance on activities. I have found that after a moving group session, the next session is often superficial. It's as if the students need to spring back from the vulnerability they touched and bring protective behaviors into play. This flow can be very discouraging for counselors who aren't familiar with it. The counselor feels successful and encouraged from the previous session and then the bottom falls out. In addition, this group was held the day before winter holidays. There was a festive mood on the campus and lots of distractions, which can be difficult for ADHD students to handle.

Courtney was very discouraged after the FireBall group. The first thing she said to me after group was over was, "That was horrible!"

Courtney's Perspective *I felt that this group was unsuccessful because the students did not feel safe. Safety and trust make up the foundation of a successful* *group, and neither existed when this session ended. I felt embarrassed that Katrina had witnessed what I considered a failure on my part. Would she think I was incompetent?*

It's OK to Stop Group Early. Courtney decided to start the next session by talking about what had happened. By throwing it out to the students, Courtney could accomplish several objectives. First, she would let them know that the put-downs and disruptive behavior were unacceptable. She would discover what they thought about the chaotic group. She could let Tim know she heard him when he said group was a "zero" and elicit his support as a leader in group. She would also be setting the boundary for safety in the group, which is her responsibility as the counselor. Interestingly, when Courtney asked the students what would make group a safer place for all of them, Robert responded, "No more candy!"

Courtney's Perspective *In this fourth session, we began by processing the previous miserable group.*

Counselor:	I was very disappointed in how the last group went. I felt like many of the group rules you had made at the beginning of group were broken, and the group wasn't safe. Tim rated the group experience a zero. Why is that?
Tim:	Because nobody took it seriously.
Counselor:	How did that make you feel?
Tim:	Angry.
Counselor:	What do you want from the group?
Tim:	I want them to take group more seriously.
Counselor:	What would that look like? How would everyone behave differently from how they behaved last week?
Tim:	They wouldn't put each other down.

Following this dialogue, I had the boys watch a video on anger management, during which they had a hard time sitting still. At this point, I thought they needed more concrete information about anger. As we began discussing the video, the boys started putting each other down and acting silly.

Robert:	I've been in that situation before.
Simon:	That's stupid.

Tim said that he had a secret to share but changed his mind about telling the group. He said that he didn't feel safe in the group. I told the students that we would be ending group early that day because the group was not safe. They were argumentative and asked for another chance. I told them that the rules had been reiterated earlier and that we would not continue that day. I hoped they could come back the following week and make the group a safe place to be. I finally felt like I had taken control. It was a turning point for me. Instead of continually attempting to combat the name-calling, I simply ended group. I felt good about the group and that boundaries were clearly defined and I knew these boundaries are what make the group safe. They now knew that maintaining emotional safety in the group was nonnegotiable.

Ending group early took a lot of courage from Courtney. In reality, the group ended only about 5 minutes early, but the students definitely felt the impact. Courtney wasn't punitive or critical. However, she very clearly established a boundary. She gained credibility with the students. They knew that group safety was important to her, and she was not going to accept put-downs.

Session 5—But I Don't Have Enough Activities! **Courtney's Perspective** *The following week, I was frantic. I had a rough morning already and felt unprepared for group. Although I felt good about ending group early the previous week, I was scared about what this session would entail. I didn't feel that I had enough planned, and I was anxious.*

When I arrived on campus and met Courtney before this session, she seemed panicked. I actually thought something tragic must have happened.

Courtney exclaimed, "I'm not prepared. I even thought about canceling it but it was too late to call you! I can't find the 'Feelings' bingo game!"

Supervisor:	What would happen if you didn't have activities?
Counselor:	Nothing will be happening. They'll just sit there and be quiet.
Supervisor:	What would happen if they sat and were quiet?
Counselor:	We won't make progress. Actually, I think I will feel uncomfortable. I feel so responsible for the group and keeping it going.
Supervisor:	What if you let go of some of that pressure and responsibility?
Counselor:	This is sort of confusing for me because I actually really do believe in the power of silence in group and have allowed silence to linger in other groups. However, I worry about this group. I don't know if they can handle silence.

I saw this as an opportunity for Courtney to let go of her activity crutch and step into her personal power as a group counselor.

Courtney's Perspective *Going into the group, I was still nervous about what their reaction to silence might be. Still, if silence is productive with other groups, why couldn't it be productive for this group? I began to realize it was less about them and more about me and how I would respond to situations like silence.*

At one point in the group, there was silence. Instead of starting an activity, we all sat with the silence.

Simon:	It's too quiet. I don't like it.
Counselor:	How do you feel when it gets quiet in group?
Simon:	Lonely. When are we going to do an activity?

That week, I didn't fill the silence with an activity. We continued to process and the group became closer as a result. My ability to stay calm and centered influenced them, instead of their nervous energy influencing me. I saw what effect my calmness and confidence had on them. They followed my lead, and the result was a rich, thoughtful, intimate discussion between the group members.

<u>Trusting Myself.</u>   **Courtney's Perspective** *I felt encouraged going into the last session. I felt much more confident in my ability to lead the group. As we started the group, it was obvious that Simon was visibly upset with Steven. His fists were clenched and his brow was furrowed as he glared across the group at Steven.*

Counselor:	I'm sensing some anger right now.
Simon:	Steven talked about us outside of group.
Counselor:	Look at him and tell him that.
Simon:	I'm angry at you that you talked about group.

Courtney's Perspective *Steven's typical response to any confrontation was to react violently. He had even been known to throw chairs in the classroom.*

Counselor:	Steven, what's your reaction to what Simon just said?
Steven:	I want to hit him. I know dogs that are smarter than him.
Counselor:	Steven, what do you feel?
Steven:	Nothing.

Courtney's Perspecitve *Simon began squirming and getting very angry. I was concerned about a fight breaking out. But they had controlled themselves up to this point.*

Counselor:	Do you think we could continue this conversation without a fight? Can you contract with me that you will use words and speak respect-fully to one another? (They all nodded in the affirmative.)
Steven:	My dad deals with anger by yelling and putting me down. But I know another way. I go to a room by myself and meditate.
Robert:	What's meditate?

Courtney's Perspective *At this point, Steven showed the rest of the group how to meditate. When we were finished, it was time to wrap things up and end our last group. The boys asked if we could continue group for a few more weeks, although they knew it was time to terminate.*

As an observer, I'm supposed to be writing down everything that happens in a session. However, this last session was so moving for me that I had to put down my pen. When tension filled the room, Courtney guided the boys through the difficult moment. The boys expressed anger without resorting to violence. Steven had the great experience of being a leader and sharing his knowledge.

■ Results

Courtney's Perspective *What struck me most is that during that last session, for the first time, they didn't ask for an activity. Their interaction with one another was the activity. I was privileged to experience the power of the process. Since this group*

I have facilitated seventh-grade boys' and girls' divorce and anger management groups as well as an eighth-grade substance abuse group for girls. The more I free myself from the lesson plan, the more I enjoy facilitating and the more my students get out of it.

Courtney always had the skills she needed to lead this group; she just didn't know it. As a result of this successful experience, Courtney and I cofacilitated an eighth-grade girls' group for students who were using drugs and alcohol.

■ Personal Reflection

Courtney's Perspective *I thought they might not be able to handle a more unstructured group. However, it wasn't really about their discomfort but about mine. It's hard to look at my own fears and see how they might stunt the growth of the group. It's even harder to do it in front of a supervisor. Katrina created a supervisory relationship that made it safe to examine the areas in which I felt most vulnerable.*

I remember feeling some dismay when I realized I would be providing supervision for other counselors. I knew it would be difficult for me to watch and not jump in and rescue. An even bigger fear was what if they discovered that I don't really know that much after all?

I struggled with how to give Courtney constructive, honest feedback without discouraging her. I also didn't want to impose my style on her. There were a few times I had to refrain from the impulse to rescue her. I had to let Courtney discover her strengths through her experience. Telling her that I thought she was an effective counselor would seem irrelevant unless she experienced it. I realized through the privilege of working with Courtney that I enjoy providing supervision for group counseling as much as I enjoy facilitating group myself. Courtney's excitement about group was contagious. Further, it is gratifying to know that many more students will receive effective group counseling experiences because of this time that Courtney and I shared together. I admire Courtney for the courage she demonstrated by asking me to observe her. She allowed herself to be vulnerable and to expose her self-doubts with another professional.

One more thing, if you would like more information about the clinical supervision model I used for this supervision experience, check out the book *Leading and Managing Your School Guidance Program* (1998), by Patricia Henderson and Norm Gysbers, published by the American Counseling Association.

Suggested Readings

Corey, G. (2004). *Theory and practice of group counseling* (6th ed.). Belmont, CA: Wadsworth.

Corey, G., Corey, M. S., Callanan, P., & Russell, J. (2004). *Group techniques* (3rd ed.). Belmont, CA: Wadsworth.

Henderson, P., & Gysbers, N. C. (1998). *Leading and managing your school guidance program staff.* Alexandria, VA: American Counseling Association.

Jacobs, E. E., Masson, L. L., & Harvill, R. L. (2001). *Group counseling strategies and skills* (4th ed.). Belmont, CA: Wadsworth.

Yalom, I. D. (1995). *The theory and practice of group psychotherapy* (4th ed.). New York: Basic Books.

Biographical Statement

Katrina Cook, LPC, LMFT, is a doctoral student in counseling at the University of Texas at San Antonio. At the time of this case study, she was an SDFSCC for both Taft and Warren High Schools in Northside Independent School District in San Antonio. Katrina has been a counselor for 19 years and a clinical supervisor for 3 years. You can reach Katrina at katrina.cook@utsa.edu.

Courtney Storment, LPC, is in her third year as a counselor at Jordan Middle School in San Antonio. Before becoming a counselor, she taught seventh grade for three years. You can reach Courtney at cnstorment@grandecom.net.

Conducting an Eighth-Grade Girls' Group: Who Is in Charge?

Terrie J. House

Terrie House is a counseling intern at a rural middle school serving a predominantly Latino population. The school faces increases in students' use of tobacco, alcohol, and drugs and a rise in teen pregnancies. House and another intern offer small group counseling for eighth-grade girls with the goal of enhancing self-respect and responsible decision making. House describes her experiences in getting permission from administrators and recruiting participants for the group, and she gives us an intimate view of the 10 sessions.

T his case study illustrates how I, as an intern in a master's degree program, along with another intern (Diane), developed and ran groups for eighth-grade Latinas. The chair of our university department invited a group of us to participate in an ongoing partnership between our university, "Lemongrass" (CA) school district, and Healthy Start—a government-funded element of the community's Family Services Center. The family services agency had collaborated with the school district to create programs for at-risk students. The program we participated in provided individual and group counseling services through Healthy Start.

The School

Diane and I were assigned to the middle school. The school serves students from a small, rural town as well as nearby ranches and farms. The local economy is agriculturally based. The student population mix at the time was 93.2% Latino, 3.6% Filipino, 2.7% White, .3% Pacific Islander, and .3% African American. The school district employs one school counselor to serve all of the schools in the district.

Student Need

Linda, the head of Healthy Start, and the school administration outlined many of the students' needs. There was considerable concern over the alarming increase in middle and high school students' use of drugs, tobacco, and alcohol and teen pregnancy. The middle school had one student on campus that was six months pregnant. This was causing great controversy in the school because the administration wanted her to leave, but her parents insisted she stay in school. Many of the students were confused about the pregnancy and had many unanswered questions. Further, there was concern for the eighth-grade students, especially the females. The high school that they would attend is about a half hour away from Lemongrass, in a much larger town. The administration was finding that after leaving middle school and starting high school, many of the Lemongrass females were dropping out of school. I was overwhelmed with all of the issues the students were facing and wondered how I could make any difference. After several meetings among the agency and school administration and Diane and I, it was decided that we would provide small group counseling for eighth-grade Latinas.

Goals and Strategies

We came up with four goals for the members of our groups:

1. To grow in self-acceptance and self-respect
2. To learn to live with struggles, and how to make one's own decisions and accept the consequences of those choices

3. To learn ways of applying what is learned in the group to everyday situations
4. To develop sufficient trust within the group to allow for an honest sharing of attitudes and feelings

In developing the group, we used an eclectic framework, borrowing techniques from a variety of therapeutic models to help us meet our goals. At this point in both Diane's and my young counseling careers, our philosophical orientation was strongly shaped by the existential approach. This approach emphasizes that through the counselor/student relationship, constructive change can take place. We believed in paying close attention to the quality of our relationships with each of the members of the group.

We also believed that students are responsible for their behavior, and counselors and students share a collaborative partnership. Through positive experiences and discussions, we hoped the members of our group would develop an understanding of themselves as well as realize that they have the power to make choices in their lives.

Our group was designed to be action oriented. This approach allows group members to bring feelings and thoughts together by applying them to real-life situations. We also used aspects of the person-centered approach. We valued listening with understanding, and encouraging members to put into words what they were feeling at the moment. In addressing these goals, we used the following activities in our sessions.

Activities that explored identity issues ("Who am I?")

1. Biographical Poem
2. "Positive Comments About Me"
3. Valentine's Day—Cookie decorating/Gift for self, gift for someone special
4. Makeup and hair demonstration
5. Knot Game (Devencenzi & Pendergast, 1988)—Cooperation skills and team building
6. Web Game (Devencenzi & Pendergast, 1988)—Group cohesion and team building

Speakers that explored issues of sexuality, intimacy, and choices

1. School nurse spoke about birth control, pregnancy, and resources available.
2. School counselor spoke about resources available to group members.
3. She focused on issues of domestic violence, rape, and health issues.

Discussions that explored issues raised by group members

1. Learning to cope with feelings revealed in the biographical poems (e.g., loneliness, anger, fear, rejection, hostility)
2. Discussing love, sex, and intimacy
3. Personal responsibility for choices and actions
4. Exploring conflicts related to school and moving on to high school
5. Discussing friendship and what friendship means
6. Communication skills
7. Self-esteem and image issues

■ Process

I will start at the very beginning of my experience and walk through the entire process
from our very first planning meeting to our group's final session. Several planning meetings were held with Linda, the head of Healthy Start, and with the school principal.

First Planning Meeting. Linda was excited about having interns work at the
schools in this small rural school district. She emphasized that having interns in the
agency was new, and that we would have the opportunity to choose what we wanted
to do. She gave us information about the demographics of the town, and we toured
each of the schools—two elementary and one middle.

Second Planning Meeting. We met with Linda for about 2 hours. She provided us
with a large folder that was filled with a variety of information. It contained data on
Healthy Start, the school district, and other community agencies and resources. She
reviewed the programs and suggested multiple options for where she would like to
place us and what projects we could undertake. The list of options was overwhelming. It seemed like she wanted us to work on five projects at once. Her expectations
were rather expansive for our one-day-a-week internship commitment. This is where
our frustrations began. We left feeling very confused, without any clear idea of what
we would be doing.

Third Planning Meeting. Linda decided she wanted us to work at the middle school
with the students that the administration identified as at-risk, which we later learned
were all of them. It struck me that it was up to us to create this program. At first I was
scared. Whom should we target? What format should we use? After talking with several
people, we decided the best way to reach as many students as possible would be to run
a group. This was intimidating to me because I had only just completed my group
counseling class. Linda expressed concern that she did not know if student interns
could handle the students. This lack of trust in our abilities did not help our confidence level. She portrayed some of the students as dangerous, and this concerned me
greatly. Because of this concern over the self-control of the students, it was decided
that Diane and I would cofacilitate two groups rather than each of us having our own.

Linda had arranged a meeting with the principal of the middle school so we
could discuss our ideas with her and obtain the information we needed to get started.
Our meeting, which was scheduled for half an hour, consisted of 10 very rushed
minutes, and we knew little more when we left than when we arrived.

Fourth Planning Meeting. Another appointment with the principal was set for the
next week, since our first engagement was cut short and was unproductive. We called
in advance to confirm that she would be available. She explained that the previous
week she had not been given any prior notice that we were going to be on campus, so
she had not expected us.

Prior to this second meeting, Diane and I discussed our frustrations and
decided to approach Linda with our feelings. We were excited to start on our projects,

but we were not receiving any form of direction, and no one seemed to have time to answer our questions. Linda suggested that she attend our meeting with the principal so we could get clear details. Both Linda and the principal seemed to have aggressive personalities and Diane and I—as students—felt uncomfortable confronting either of them.

During the meeting, Linda helped us a great deal. I discussed my plans for a lunchtime program that would target eighth-grade girls. By the end of the discussion, it was decided that Diane and I would lead such groups. Since there was one known pregnant girl on campus, we assumed that others were also sexually active. As well, the girls were facing different issues dealing with the transition to high school. We all felt this was a good group to target.

We decided that for girls to participate, they had only to volunteer. In other words, there would be no prerequisites, for example, high GPA, good school records, no referrals, and so forth. The principal felt that each of the girls had some risk factors and therefore she did not want to be responsible for selecting the members. She suggested that we set up a table in the cafeteria immediately to identify interested students. (It was a rainy day and the students had to spend their lunch period in the cafeteria, making them more apt to want to know what we were offering.) We frantically typed a sign-up sheet that requested their names, teachers, and areas of interest. We also decided to name the group beforehand so that it did not start with any stigma related to it. We called it the "University's Eighth Grade Girl's Group." We felt it was important to affiliate our university with the group, giving the girls a connection with the university.

We set up our table in the cafeteria with our sign. I felt a little silly, thinking back to my middle school days. I thought, "None of these students are going to approach two total strangers." I could not have been more wrong. The sign-up process was crazy. Students—all students, not just the girls—bombarded us. They asked questions from all directions. We were surrounded. We had so much interest from the seventh grade that we began a sign-up sheet for them as well, but we told them they would probably have to wait until next year. By the end of lunch, we had 28 eighth-grade girls on our list. We were ecstatic! We had hoped for about 10 students to join our group, but I guess we did not realize the need for care and attention these students had.

We reported our results to the principal and gave her the list of students and their teachers. We also drafted a parent permission slip. The principal offered to finalize the permission slip and get it to each of the girls to take home. We were finally on our way and starting to feel we might accomplish something!

Diane and I met to go over the sign-up sheets and to discuss what we wanted to do in the groups. The girls had listed their interests as sports, makeup, boys, cooking, hairstyling, pregnancy, music, art, and entertainment. As we planned our groups, we tried to incorporate all of their interests into our sessions.

Fifth Planning Meeting. We met with the principal to ask her about the logistics for the group, that is, where we were going to meet, when, how long, et cetera. She gave us some answers and then suddenly decided we were going to have our first meeting that day at lunch. We were not prepared for this at all!

Session 1. Later that day, the group members were told to meet in the library. Twenty-eight of them came! Both Diane and I realized that this would not work for one group. We could not manage a group with 28 members. They were all talking, and it seemed to take forever to get them quiet. We introduced ourselves as beginning counselors at the local university. We also told them about our plans for the group and filled them in on all of the logistics, including confidentiality. We then asked the girls if they had any questions. They kept referring to us as teachers, and we kept correcting them, saying we were counselors. What we neglected to realize at the time was that in Latino culture, problems are dealt with in the family; it is not seen as appropriate to go outside the family for counseling with personal problems. Calling us teachers seemed to be a solution to the cultural issue, and once we became aware of it, what they called us was no longer important. To alleviate this issue, we had the group members call us by our first names.

In the beginning, the girls were curious about us.

Michelle:	How old are you two?
Counselors:	(We each told them our ages.)
Lisa (to me):	Are you married?
Terrie:	Yes.
Lisa:	Is he White? What color hair and eyes does he have?
Terrie:	Yes, he is White, with blond hair and brown eyes.
Lisa (to Diane):	Are you married?
Diane:	No.
Lisa:	Do you have a boyfriend?
Diane:	Yes.
Lisa:	What race is he?
Diane:	White.

We attributed this question to Diane to the fact that the girls assumed her boyfriend would be Latino because she has features similar to those of the girls in the group. (Diane is Portuguese, with dark hair and brown eyes.) All of a sudden we looked at each other and realized that our ethnicity made a difference to this group. (I am White, with blond hair and blue eyes.) Earlier, we had wondered if our ethnicity would be an issue. It was. I was the first White person other than teachers that many of the girls had dealt with.

Stephanie (to me):	How much are you being paid to be here?
Terrie:	I am not being paid. I am here because I want to work with all of you and look forward to our time together.
Stephanie:	No White people come out here unless they're paid. No one ever does anything for us because we are just a bunch of Mexican throwbacks.

I was taken aback by this statement! I told the group that I cared about them as people and that I did not view the group as Stephanie had described. They discussed with us how they felt as Latinas. They seemed to believe that they were less valued because of the color of their skin. This was the start of our trust building. After we addressed the issue of race and answered their questions, the entire room seemed more relaxed, like they were okay with us. Several of the girls asked if they could touch my hair and look into my eyes. I said, "Of course," and this was the beginning of our group journey together.

Session 2. Chaos struck as soon as we entered the school. The girls ran into the library, handing us permission slips; some had forgotten, so we gave them an extra week. Prior to the second meeting, the principal was to have divided the girls into two groups that would run back to back. She had not done this, so the start of our second meeting consisted of the principal telling half the girls they had to leave and come back at a different time. Several were very unhappy to be split from certain friends, but Diane and I had no control over the situation.

Group 1. Because of all the confusion, Group 1 started late and was very disorganized, even though we had planned activities. Diane had created an agenda, but we did not get a good response from the girls. It was also Valentine's Day, so there was extra excitement in the air. We added to the commotion by handing out candy and stickers. There were 13 girls in the first group, and they were very talkative and wanted to be social. We had planned what we thought would be a good way for us to get to know the girls better and for them to know us. We were going to have them create a biographical poem. We handed out a format for these poems, and we had two girls read ones we had written as examples. After hearing ours, they started working on theirs, but their attention span was short and only two girls completed their poems during this session. I offered to type the poems and print them on colored or decorative paper. The girls were excited to choose how they wanted their finished poems to look.

Group 2. This group was less chaotic, but seemed like it was going to be more challenging. There were 8 girls in this group. One of the girls had just returned to school after being on suspension for stalking and assaulting another student. One student sat at a table by herself, and two students spoke little English. We did not want to make the same mistake twice: We let the first group sit at tables and did not have them get into a circle. We had all the Group 2 girls move into a circle. This group was initially not responsive to the biographical poem; they kind of stared at us and were not motivated to work on the poem. Once a few finally started with our help, the others followed, and they seemed to enjoy it. Two of the girls wrote in Spanish, but one asked for assistance in writing hers in English. All of the girls completed their poems. They left with a much different attitude; they were a lot friendlier to us and they were smiling and talking to each other and us. This felt rewarding.

Below are two examples of the poems.

Susan Smith
Friendly, active, funny, understanding
Oldest child of Monica and Bob
Lover of music, volleyball, and family and friends

Who feels tired after doing homework, hyper after eating lunch and
    happy after finishing something
Who fears being rejected, put down, and not trying my best.
Who would love to see myself graduate, have a good job, and see my
    family live a good and happy life
Resident of Small town in California, Oak Street

Laura Davis
Funny, lazy, lonely, noisy
Oldest child of Greg
Lover of cats, dogs, birds, and the earth.
Who feels good with my family, tired when school is over, and happy on
    Friday afternoon.
Who fears my mom with a belt in her hand, of cars on the road and
    unknown dogs,
Who would like to see my brother graduate, Magic Mountain, and Las Vegas.
Resident of Small town in California, Maple Street

Session 3. The activity we had planned for this session was to do a "Positive
Comments About Me" exercise. Each group member had a piece of paper taped to
her back. The other members had to write something positive on each member's
piece of paper. With the paper on our backs, we would not know who wrote what
comment. This anonymity provides the students an opportunity to be open with
compliments they might otherwise never say. We invited the girls to volunteer to read
their comment sheets and express if they agreed or disagreed with the way others
viewed them. Many of the girls were shocked to realize that people actually saw positive attributes in them.

Group 1. Again, the group was disruptive. We noticed that it was fostered by a
group of about five girls who dominated the entire group, and we could not seem to
get any of the other girls involved. This discussion was disorganized, but the topic of
high school did come up. Members of the subgroup voiced fear of losing some of
their friends once they entered high school, along with anxiety over being "beat up"
because they were from Lemongrass.

Group 2. Two girls in Group 2 talked and giggled a lot. Diane and I were also bothered by some of the girls that we knew spoke English but would only speak to each
other in Spanish. We did not know if they were testing us, but we assumed they were.
During our discussion time, the group did not seem to want to discuss anything. Then
one student said, "Let's talk about boys." After some struggle, this member talked about
her experience over the weekend. What finally came out is that she had attended
a party, gotten drunk, had sex, and now she worried that she was pregnant.

Wendy: Can you get pregnant from kissing?
Counselor: No, not from kissing.

Wendy:	Can you get pregnant from just touching?
Counselor:	Can you be more specific about the touching? It depends on what is touching what.
Wendy:	How do I find out if I am pregnant?
Counselor:	There are several ways. One is a urine test and the other a blood test. Wendy, why don't you stay after the group and we can talk more about resources for you and where you can go.
Wendy:	Okay.

I confess I was not prepared for this type of self-disclosure. At this point, Diane and I realized that it would be good for the school nurse to come in and address this issue. We also had to check with the principal about what specific information we could discuss in the group concerning sex and pregnancy. Again, we did not get clear answers. We took the situation to Linda, and she called the school nurse for us. We then contacted Wendy to see if we could give the school nurse her name. She gave us permission and the school nurse took it from there. Fortunately, we found out later that Wendy was not pregnant.

Session 4. The school nurse and school counselor were guest speakers for this group session. The girls were given a mini "sex education" presentation. Both women stayed the entire session and answered all of the girls' questions. Five minutes before the session ended, we gave each of the girls a journal. We told them if they had something they wanted to discuss with us or comments that they did not want to talk about in the group, they could write it in their journals and we would respond to them. They seemed very excited about this.

Below is an example of the issues the girls discussed in their journals.

Journal Entry from Elizabeth, April 21

I've been wanting to write to you guys but I haven't had the time. I just wanted to share an awful experience I had to go through for a week. I met this guy through my sister, this guy is my sister's boyfriend's brother. This guy has been wanting to meet me for over a week. Well finally my sister introduced me to him and he seemed like a nice guy. He was kind to me, he respected how I was and my morals. Well the very next day we went out for a movie and had a great time. After that day he asked me to be his girlfriend and stupid me said yes. The next day he came over to my house after school and we went out, he took me to the beach and of course there weren't any people there well he tried to take advantage of me. He got on top of me and wouldn't get off of me and guys and girls had told me before when they heard that he was interested in me that I should be very careful of him, that he could hurt me. Well I did not pay attention because he was so nice to me when I met him. Anyway when he saw that I was mad he apologized to me. But the next day he took me to the park and the same thing happened but he was taking my clothes off and his and I couldn't move or hit him because he was holding my arms. I couldn't tell anyone because my mom and him got along so great. My mom treated him like a son and he told her that she was like a mom to him. I was so afraid and still am afraid of him but the only thing I could do was to pray and I got an answer so I told my sister and my best friend. They both gave me advice. But I was still afraid because he had shown me a weapon that he shouldn't have and he had been in jail because he almost used it, Oh yeah he is 17 years old.

Well the next day when he came to my house he took me out and I had to tell him I could not see him anymore but I couldn't because I was so afraid. Well he took me home because he saw that I was mad, when I got home, he and I were sitting in the living room with my mom, but my mom left because she saw that something was wrong. When I told him I did not want to see him anymore he started to cry and when he was leaving my mom stopped him and they started to talk and I went to my room. The very next day when I came home from school there were balloons and a card from him. He would call every hour to talk to me but I didn't want to talk to him.

When he saw that I wasn't going to take him back he decided to tell my mom lies that we had sex and that one day I got on top of him and I wanted to do it with him, but he was pulling me back, but my mom didn't believe him and she is not talking to him anymore.

It was very hard for me to tell my mom what he did to me because they were really good friends but I always tell my mom everything that happens in my life, but this one was really hard. Now I know why his brother and my friends didn't want me seeing him but they just wouldn't tell me why they would only tell me "you better be careful." I am so glad this is over, now I know why I've been wanting to cry and scream and hit something, and I did. I just let everything out when I told my mom.

I just wanted to say thank you to you both Terrie and Diane for letting me have the opportunity to be in your group so I could express my feelings. Thanks again. Liz Williams

Session 5. We started this session by writing thank-you notes to the school counselor and school nurse. We explained to the girls that when someone goes out of their way for you it is nice to send them a note. They liked the idea, and each wrote her own personal messages. After writing the notes, the day's activity was to decorate cookies. One of the school staff members was a cake decorator, and she came in to help the girls with their cookies. She brought decorating bags and showed the girls how to fill and use them. The idea was for each girl to decorate one cookie as a gift to herself and another as a gift for someone else. The cookies were donated by a local grocery store, and Diane and I made five different colors of frosting. The girls were so excited. They all worked well with each other and helped each other during the activity. In fact, the girl who had been suspended a few weeks earlier, for stalking and assault, created a bag from wax paper to carry her cookies in and then assisted the other girls in making their own. It was great to see them cooperating with each other and having fun in the process. At the end of each group's session, we collected the girls' journals, just as we had at the end of each previous session.

Well, Diane's and my joyous mood quickly changed when we read one student's journal over lunch. Ellen stated in her journal that her father hits her, and she described some instances when it had happened. It did not seem like an unusual occurrence. We did not know what steps to take. We had read in our textbooks that we are required to report suspected cases of child abuse, but we did not know the process.

We went straight to Linda and described the dilemma. She directed us to call the principal and the school nurse, and report it to them. We did, and the principal asked for a copy of the journal. She told us that our job was done, and she would talk to the student and make the decision whether to report the case. After discussing it with Linda, we did not feel it was ethical to give the journal to the principal. We had promised the girls confidentiality with the journals and told them they would be read by only us. We used the journals as a means of personal correspondence with the students, and they wrote to us because they trusted us. We asked her to allow us to speak with the student first and remind her of when we had to break confidentiality. We realized we had to report the abuse but did not want to break trust with the student.

Linda suggested we talk with our professor. He informed us that we are required by law to report the abuse ourselves. Fortunately for us, Linda, in compliance with the state rules, filed a report within the 36-hour timeframe and explained the situation to Child Protective Services (CPS). On Friday, Diane and I made individual reports to CPS. We were upset that we were not able to talk with Ellen before all of this took place, but we scheduled a private meeting with her for the next week. When we met with her, she was very upset because a social worker had come to her house and talked with her dad. She felt that we had done more harm than good. In spite of this, she decided to stay in the group.

Session 6. We again started the session by writing thank-you notes, this time to the people who donated the cookies and the staff member who helped us make them. We also reviewed confidentiality. The chair of the University School of Education came and spoke to the girls about high school and college. They had many questions for him. We also had a guest from Mary Kay cosmetics come talk to the girls about makeup and skin care. She brought samples so each member could choose colors and make up her face. The girls were so excited. I had not realized that some of them had never had the opportunity to try on makeup. One student, after putting it on, said, "I look much better without it." This was a fun day. It was exciting to see the girls work together to help each other apply different types of makeup. They each left with a paper picture of a face with the makeup they liked on it.

Session 7. Again we started the session writing thank-you notes to our guests. As we had started several sessions previous, we did a check-in to get a feel for how each member was doing. The discussion topic for this day was values, and we had the girls take a values inventory and discuss it. Our activity was the Web Game (Devencenzi & Pendergast, 1988). This game, along with the Knot Game

(Devencenzi & Pendergast, 1988), helped develop cooperation, team-building skills, and group cohesion.

Session 8. To incorporate the girls' art interests, Diane and I decided to do collaborative drawing. The girls were paired up and told they had to work together to create a picture. One pair split their picture in half, labeling one side "Being in the girls group" and the other "Not being in the girls group." The first half was in color, with groups of people talking, saying things like "We have fun in the girls group." "We get to talk about stuff." "We have friends." The other side was black and white, with people standing alone, saying things like "I have no friends." "I am so lonely." "I wish I had someone to talk to." Diane and I were shocked to see that this group was having such an impact on the members. We spent the rest of the time role-playing positive solutions for problems the girls may face in high school.

Session 9. Our objective for Session 9 was to start the closure process. The girls had voted in the previous session to have a formal dinner to celebrate the end of our group. We discussed attire, and they agreed it had to be formal. They decided on the menu. We played the Knot Game (Devencenzi & Pendergast, 1988) and then sat in our discussion circle. The girls shared a sense of sadness over the group's ending. We presented each member with a certificate of completion that was signed by Diane, the principal, and me. The girls were very excited and discussed where they would hang their certificates.

Session 10. Our final session was held in the evening. I know we had decided the dress was to be formal, but I had not expected really formal. Some members wore long dresses; others had had their hair done. They took this last session very seriously. Diane and I tried to make it as special as we could. We brought formal tablecloths, cloth napkins, flowers for the table, and real silverware. Diane and I had made the dinner—spaghetti, garlic bread, salad, and cupcakes. We taught the girls how to set a table, fold a napkin, and which fork to use when. We let them decorate the cupcakes for dessert. They presented Diane and me with certificates of appreciation, which they had each signed. It was a wonderful evening of laughter and sharing. We promised to see them all again at their eighth-grade graduation ceremony. We both attended and watched our group members with pride.

▪ Results

Some of the comments we received on the survey we gave each member during our last session together indicate the impact of the group experience.

What did you like and/or dislike about the group?
"I liked that we could have confidence in our group and talk about private stuff."
"I liked the makeup and cake-decorating activities."
"I disliked the first week when we didn't do anything."

"I like all things that we did. The only thing I did not like was sitting around."
"I like the way we got to talk with each other and have fun, and not worry if we did something. I felt good when we got in groups together."
"I liked the knot game and the only thing I disliked is when everyone just started talking."
"I really enjoyed everything but there were some girls that made the girls group not so fun."
"I liked everything about the group cause it made me feel good and when I was mad and I went to group it made me so happy."
"Yo pienso que el grupo esta muy interesante para me, y me siento muy bien [sic]." [Translated into English: "I think that the group is very interesting to me, and I feel very good."—Editor]

If you could change something about the group, what would it be?

"I would not change anything. I think it is perfect like that."
"I would make it one hour and a half instead of 40 minutes."
"I think I would change how much time because I feel so comfortable in the group."
"Just do more stuff."
"I would want it to be longer."
"I would like to make it for more than 10 weeks and more than 40 minutes."

What are your future goals?

"My biggest goal is to graduate from high school."
"Graduate from high school and go to a university."
"Graduate from college and become a pediatrician."
"To travel for a year after high school and then go to college."
"I would like to be a hairstylist."

All the members except one wanted to finish high school and go to college to pursue a variety of careers, including: nursing, law, medicine, journalism, modeling, fashion design, directing movies, and business.

What skills or new ideas did you learn from the group? Was the group helpful?

"I learned how to work with other people."
"I learned that working together helps everyone."
"I learned to express my feelings with other people."
"Yes, the group was helpful. I learned how to put on make-up, control my feelings, and express my feelings to others."
"I learned that it's okay to talk to adults. I think that this group was very helpful 'cause it brought people together."
"I learned how to deal with certain kinds of problems like when I go to high school."
"Sometimes the group was not helpful."

Personal Reflection

In textbooks we have read the formal procedures for starting groups for adolescents. It is suggested that, ideally, the leader or coleader meet with each member individually before the first group meeting, all members attend a planned orientation meeting, and leaders select the members they feel will have a good experience and screen out those who would not be appropriate. We did not have the opportunity to perform any of these steps. We felt that the first few sessions clearly lacked organization because of the manner in which the groups were formed, the lack of coordination by school staff, and our inexperience.

Leading a group was a new experience for Diane and me, and we felt that we were thrown into the situation. Our self-confidence was clearly tested. We had not had time to research the particular needs of adolescents. The group dynamics changed on a weekly basis as a result of absenteeism. We had to draw on our own experiences and basically "wing it." We had limited knowledge of school rules, policies, and laws. Before the group selection took place, we had not set any goals and objectives or planned the process and procedures. We had some informal ideas and a rough outline of activities. In the parent permission slip, we stated, "The purpose of this group is to improve self-esteem and communication skills through discussions and activities." This broad description left our options open. We also had not discussed a time limit for the total number of group sessions. In fact, we were two weeks into the group before we decided on the number of sessions. We chose 10 sessions, since we had read that 8 to 12 is optimum.

The lack of preparation was evident when it came time to sign up our members. This is probably what we regretted most. We had no way to limit the group, and we did not use a fair selection process. As a result, the groups were too large to reach a true working level. We would have liked a maximum of six to eight members in each group.

Also, if we had had a way to clearly define our selection process, then we might have been able to individually screen each of the members. Then maybe we could have targeted the girls most in need of the prevention activities we presented. After the groups began, we were continually apologizing to girls who claimed that they signed up on the original list but were never informed that the groups had started. Every week, girls who wanted to join a group approached us. Through the experience of leading these groups, Diane and I came to realize that the level of need for students this age is great. They all need to experience successes that will lead to a sense of self-confidence and respect.

Our self-assurance was definitely tested from the beginning. We felt we had to prove ourselves before we could be accepted. We felt resistance from agency and school staff members. At times we felt like we were in the way. We were even intimidated to a certain degree. The view we were presented with was that our personal safety could be at risk on school grounds, and it was questioned if interns could handle the students. We also heard negative comments from staff at the school about working with "those girls"; they made it sound like we would be working with some terrible adolescents. This, of course, was not the case, but at the beginning, we had developed a bit of a negative perception before meeting the girls. Those who supported our efforts the most were the school nurse, counselor, and psychologist. They seemed to believe in our efforts and saw the value in the group experience. Their support was reassuring.

All of these experiences provided a sense of personal growth for Diane and me, but it is difficult to truly measure our own development. The feedback on the survey we had at the end was helpful and encouraging.

As coleaders, we took time after each day to reflect on the sessions. We talked about the general overview of the group, mistakes, successes, problems, and solutions. It was easy to try to become "one of the gang," but we reminded each other that these girls needed role models and leaders, not two more friends. As counselors, we were willing to share ourselves with the group and to take personal risks; we were able to display genuine caring attitudes, enthusiasm, and openness. We feel that we gained their respect and know they gained ours.

The most meaningful development from the group experience for Diane and me came from learning to be professionals. We both struggled with taking many of the girls' issues home with us. The teenage pregnancy and child abuse dilemmas had a large effect on both of us. We continually worried about these young women, which added stress to our personal lives. We realized that we would have brief careers in counseling if we continued this pattern.

Our university has a "Learn by Doing" philosophical approach to producing professionals. We learned so much from this practical experience—perhaps more than any single text could have taught us. The experience of developing the group was very rewarding. All of the trials and tribulations aided our learning and growth as people and as counselors. Being able to provide information, to foster hope, to develop a sense of belonging, and to increase feelings of self-worth is difficult, but these are basic requirements for adolescents. We can only hope that we made a difference in at least one of the girls' lives.

Reference

Devencenzi, J., & Pendergast, S. (1988). *Belonging: A guide for group facilitators: Self and social discovery for children of all ages.* San Luis Obispo, CA: Belonging.

Suggested Readings

Billow, R. M. (2004). Working relationally with adolescents in group. *Group Analysis, 37*(2), 187–201.

Hall, A. S. (2002). Interventions and preventions strategies for counseling adolescents. *Journal of Mental Health Counseling, 24*(2), 95–101.

Ripley, V. V., & Goodnough, G. E. (2001). Planning and implementing group counseling in a high school. *Professional School Counseling, 5*(1), 62–67.

Biographical Statement

Terrie J. House, PhD, is now a counselor educator at Boise State University. She worked in a school for four years and is a licensed school counselor and elementary school teacher. You can reach Terrie at terriehouse@boisestate.edu.

Just Leave Me Alone

Jered B. Kolbert

John is a sixth-grade student who scores in the "very superior" range on intelligence tests and has been in the gifted and talented program since third grade. However, his teachers refer him to counseling because his grades aren't consistent with his potential and because he's isolated from peers. Jered Kolbert meets with John in 10 individual counseling sessions. He uses a variety of approaches, including client-centered, cognitive-behavioral, and solution-focused counseling. Kolbert's goal is to help John find his social niche as a means to lifting depression.

T he community was undergoing a rapid transition from rural to suburban, with many parents working in Richmond, Virginia. Some families were wealthy professionals and some even owned horse farms. The majority of the families were middle class. A sizable minority of the student body was from economically lower class families. Fifteen percent of the students received free lunch, and an additional 3% received a reduced-price lunch.

The School

The student population of our middle school was comprised of 1,350 sixth through eighth graders. Seventy-nine percent of the students were Caucasian, 20% were African American, and 1% were of another ethnic origin. There were three school counselors and each was assigned a specific grade level, comprising approximately 450 students each.

Student Need

John, an 11-year-old sixth grader, was referred to me by his teachers, who were concerned that he wasn't receiving grades consistent with his potential and was isolated from classmates. It was still the beginning of the school year and I didn't know John. His records revealed that he had been in the gifted and talented program since third grade. His last intelligence test from fifth grade indicated that John fell in to the "very superior" range for both verbal and performance abilities. He had received mostly As and Bs for both his fourth- and fifth-grade years.

Goals and Strategies

On my first interaction with John, he claimed that he wanted, as he put it, to be "left alone." We were able to more clearly define this vague desire as his wanting a cessation to the bullying he was experiencing from peers, and a desire for more freedom in his relationship with his parents. While in the process of assisting John to meet his goals, I also simultaneously worked to achieve several goals that I saw as most relevant to his developmental and unique personal needs, which included the following: (a) improving John's self-esteem and identity exploration through enhancing his awareness of his strengths and resources, and (b) increasing his connectedness to a compatible peer group through the acquisition of new social and cognitive skills. I used an eclectic approach, integrating client-centered theory, cognitive-behavioral theory, solution-focused theory, and family systems theory. I met with John in 10 individual counseling sessions, conducted an informal observation of his social interactions, and held several conferences with his parents.

Process

<u>Session 1.</u> I have several goals when I first meet with a student. Of course, I establish rapport. Client-centered principles help with this. Second, I am clear about the reason for the meeting, explaining to the student who referred him and why. Third, I assist the student in identifying goals that could be achieved through counseling. Finally, I gather data.

My first impression on meeting John was that he had some of the physical characteristics that I associate with children who are bullied. He was short and skinny, wore glasses, had disheveled hair, and his clothing was outdated.

Counselor:	My name is Dr. Kolbert. Ms. Smith and Mrs. Brown asked if I would talk with you because they were concerned that you haven't been turning in your homework and also because they said that you seemed not to be enjoying yourself at school. But John, I want you to know that my job is to help people work on whatever goals they have. I thought we could spend some time together so I could get a sense of whether or not there is anything you would like to work on. How does that sound to you?
John:	Well, I guess so.
Counselor:	John, I also need to tell you that whatever you tell me is confidential, meaning that I don't tell other people like your parents or teachers, unless I thought that you might harm yourself or somebody else.
John:	I just don't see what the big deal is. I mean everyone just seems to be on my case. I wish they would just leave me alone.
Counselor:	You see others as concerned about you?
John:	Yeah . . . like my parents . . . they always want me to do things with them and my brother. I'm just not into what they do.
Counselor:	So, if I'm hearing you, you see your parents as wanting you to do more things with them.
John:	Yeah. And my teachers. I like Ms. Smith and Mrs. Brown, but they always seem to be checking in on me when they don't need to. I just don't like school much . . . I mean, what can they really teach me anyway? They just have to figure out that I want to be left alone. The people here are just a bunch of jerks.

My perspective at this point is that although John is overtly communicating a desire for his parents and teachers to stop pursuing him, he also seems to have a fairly strong desire to express his frustrations to me. Typically, boys at this age are unlikely to communicate as openly as John. For instance, if they were experiencing strong emotions, they would avoid expressing them, either by not talking or by discussing superficial things such as sports. My sense is that underlying his feeling of frustration were hurt and confusion regarding the "jerks," which I interpreted to mean his classmates.

Counselor:	You seem pretty frustrated. Would you like to tell me how things have been going so far this year?
John:	I guess okay . . . I just don't like people here.

Counselor:	Don't like people here?
John:	I mean the other students. They are just really obnoxious. I mean they will just ignore what I have to say in class, or they will say nasty things.
Counselor:	I appreciate that you are telling me some of the things that are bothering you. I can understand how you would be annoyed with how you see others treating you.

I focused on reflecting his feelings of frustration and annoyance rather than on what I sensed to be his hurt stemming from rejection, because I have found that boys are uncomfortable identifying with vulnerable feelings until there is a high level of trust. John proceeded to detail several incidents in which other students ignored and made fun of him in class.

Counselor:	While I can understand that it is probably pretty hard to tell me about these things, I am also glad that you are, because I don't think it is something you should have to put up with. I would call what is happening bullying. How have you been handling these situations?
John:	Usually I just don't say anything. Sometimes I just say something nasty back, and then I get into trouble.
Counselor:	John, I think it pretty wrong of what some of these students have done to you. I think this problem sometimes can be pretty difficult to handle by yourself, and it has been my experience that teachers can often help.
John:	I don't know. I have thought about it, but I think they would make fun of me even more. But at least maybe they would understand what I'm trying to do.

John and I discussed the advantages and disadvantages of complaining that other students are bullying him. He decided to inform the teachers about the bullying and then we role-played how to approach them. I asked John if it would be okay if I checked in with him next week to find out how it went. I encouraged John to discuss the issue with his team teachers because I believed that these teachers were sensitive to students' personal needs and had good classroom management skills and thus would be able to assist him. However, I do not make such a suggestion when I perceive either that the teacher would not be concerned about bullying or would not have the skills to intervene.

I decided not to discuss the issue of grades with John at the first meeting, for several reasons. One is that it has been my experience that raising the issue of grades early in a counseling relationship with middle school students tends to interfere with rapport. Most middle school students receive enormous pressure from both teachers and parents to excel in school, and students seem to perceive school counselors as working in the interests of their parents when they also align with this goal. I see the school counselor's job as assisting students in enhancing their self-awareness and assisting them with identifying and pursuing their own goals while also helping them to recognize the advantages and disadvantages of fulfilling societal expectations. Another reason that I did not raise the issue of John's academic performance is that he was identifying a socioemotional stressor. According to Maslow's hierarchy of needs, people are unlikely to be motivated to learn, which is considered a higher order need, when needs at lower levels have not been met. In this case, John's lower level need for psychological safety and the respect of others was not being met, and thus he was not likely to focus on the higher order need of academic achievement.

Session 2. The following week I checked in with John to ask how it went in talking with his teachers about the bullying.

Counselor: So, John, fill me in—how did it go in speaking with your teachers?
John: Well, they seemed to understand and they said that they would keep an eye out for bullying situations. Ms. Smith even talked with the class one day, without mentioning names, about the need for people to be respectful. I guess those jerks are leaving me alone more now.
Counselor: Wow, how does it feel in having these guys off your back?
John: I guess good. Now I wish I could get my parents off my back.
Counselor: Fill me in on what you mean.
John: Well, my parents are just always telling me what to do. They keep telling me I need to stop reading all my science fiction books, and do more schoolwork, and play more sports.

John proceeded to spend the next 10 minutes telling me about his love of astronomy and his goal of being an astronomer. I demonstrated interest by encouraging him to talk more about astronomy.

Counselor: So, John, when your parents tell you they want you to stop reading and do other things, how do you handle it?
John: I usually try just to ignore them and go to my room. I mean, I don't understand, I do what they usually ask of me. Can't they just leave me alone? I don't see why I have got to play sports or why I have to get good grades since these grades don't count anyway for getting into college.
Counselor: It sounds like you see your parents as pressuring you to play sports.
John: Yeah, my dad makes me play basketball in the recreation league each year. He and my brother love basketball, but I could care less. Now he told me I have to try out for basketball after the Thanksgiving break. I know I won't make it and even if I did, I wouldn't enjoy it. Not only that, but some of the people who were bullying me in my class also will be going out for the team. I don't want to be around those people any more than I have to be.
Counselor: John, as you are getting older, you are finding out more about your goals and interests and you gradually get to have more say in what you do. If it was up to you at this point, what would you be doing when you are at home?

John:	Well, I could just read my science fiction books and play on the computer.
Counselor:	And what about schoolwork?
John:	Like I said, grades aren't important now. I'll worry about them when they count.
Counselor:	I know it can be very difficult in talking with your parents about what you are interested in. What do you think if I talked with your parents about the pressure you are feeling about playing sports?
John:	I guess so. I mean, anything you could do would help me out.
Counselor:	Well, okay. Just to make sure you know what I would talk about, I would talk with them about how much you are not interested in sports. My goal, John, is that they will be able to talk with you more about your interests. Does that sound okay?
John:	Yeah.
Counselor:	John, I encourage you to do more thinking about what you would like to be doing.
John:	Okay.

In this second session, I did not focus very much on his grades or the bullying situation because my perception was that he wanted to discuss his relationship with his parents. I suggested that I speak with John's parents for several reasons. One is that from the little John told me, I feared that he seemed to be isolating himself from others. I wanted to know the degree of his isolation and how his parents were responding to his withdrawing. Second, my perception was that John genuinely dreaded playing sports and that having this expectation of John was completely inconsistent with his interests and self-concept. Finally, although it was evident to me that John was intellectually advanced, the fact that he did not seem to recognize the potential long-term consequences of his continuing to isolate himself, along with his view that grades were completely irrelevant, suggested a moderate degree of immaturity. I wanted to work with John's parents because I believed he needed guidance and structure in learning to deal with his emotions and the importance of academics.

Phone Call. I contacted John's mother at work. I was vague about the nature of his concerns because I wanted to meet John's parents in person. John's mother seemed surprised to hear from me but readily agreed to meet with me. She explained that both she and her husband worked for the police department, she as a dispatcher, and he as a police officer. We arranged to meet at the beginning of the following week, which would give them both time to coordinate their schedules.

Parent Conference. My first impression of Mr. and Mrs. Applegate was that they were a fairly attractive couple in their late thirties, and both appeared to be physically fit and very tall, a large contrast to John.

| Counselor: | I appreciate you and Mr. Applegate coming to speak with me. I think it really shows your care for John. |
| Mr. Applegate: | Actually, we were glad that you called, because we have been having some concerns about John. We cannot get him to do anything. |

	I mean, he just wants to sit in his room and read those damn science fiction books. I try to get him to go outside all the time but not much seems to work.
Mrs. Applegate:	Yes, I don't know what to do either. John is just so different from our older son, Mark, who is at the high school. Whereas Mark looks forward to school and generally seems happy, John just doesn't want to do much and won't talk to us. I try to get him to open up but he won't say anything to me.
Counselor:	So it sounds like you guys see yourselves working pretty hard with John.
Mr. Applegate:	Yes, I just don't know what else to try. We have been really fighting over doing homework lately.
Mrs. Applegate:	He rarely brings work or school books home, and when we ask him about how things are going, he just clams up.
Counselor:	Mr. and Mrs. Applegate, I can see where you are concerned. One of the things that I think John is dealing with, as are most students in middle school, is figuring out who he is and where he fits in. It helps that he has some interests like astronomy.
Mr. Applegate:	I can see where his love for science fiction might be positive, but not when he won't interact with anybody, including us. I have been really pushing to get out more and do things.
Counselor:	Mr. Applegate, I really support you in encouraging him to connect with others. While I think it is fairly common for a lot of boys this age to distance from their family members, I agree with you that his withdrawing could lead to more loneliness. Like I said, I think your requiring him to do social activities can be really helpful to John. I also think John is getting to that age where he could use more say-so in terms of the activities that he wants to do.
Mrs. Applegate:	But knowing John, if we allow him to make that decision, he won't do anything.
Counselor:	So you want John to be involved in social activities but you might be open to allowing him to choose what the activities are?
Mr. Applegate:	I see what you're saying, but I just wonder if there is anything that John will want to do.
Counselor:	Well, that is something that I talked with John about . . . how he can do some thinking about what things here at school or in the community he would like to do. John will probably need help in better understanding his interests and how he could pursue them.
Mr. Applegate:	Well, I guess I'll talk with him more about it.
Counselor:	Great. Once again, I think it is wonderful that you are open to exploring all of this with John.

I informed the parents they could monitor John's schoolwork through the school's homework hotline or by getting John to use his agenda planner to record his assignments with teacher verification.

My perspective following the conference was that John had concerned and loving parents who were unsure of how to help a boy who had different interests from them and their eldest son. Mr. and Mrs. Applegate seemed to recognize that their son needed opportunities to develop peer relationships, but they were requiring him to connect with others in ways that were familiar to them, primarily sports. The parents were fairly flexible and seemed to comprehend my message of the importance of negotiating with John.

In this conference with John's parents, I joined with them by acknowledging their love and concern for John. This helped to minimize the defensiveness that most parents experience when interacting with a school official who is indirectly implying that a different approach would be more effective with their son. Furthermore, I acknowledged their parenting effectiveness by affirming their decision to require John be more socially active. However, although the parents seemed aware that one of the developmental challenges confronting John was learning to develop more intimate peer relationships, what the parents seemed not to recognize was the importance of providing John with more influence over decisions that directly confronted him. As long as John saw this requirement as being forced on him, I believed his energies would be wasted in resisting.

Session 3. The following week, I met with John to discuss both the bullying situation and the results of the parent conference.

John: (looking somewhat annoyed, with his head down) So my parents told me that I have to pick an organized activity after school. I thought after they talked with you that they wouldn't be on me anymore.

Counselor: Well, John, I could see where you would be annoyed. At the same time, John, I must admit that I can see where they are coming from.

My perception is that although he was annoyed, he also seemed to think that his parents' new position was fair. For the next 10 minutes, I showed interest in John's excited discussion of the most recent science fiction book he read.

Counselor: Well, John, I was wondering how things are going with the kids who were being disrespectful with you.

John: Things are going okay. They are generally leaving me alone. (John says this with somewhat of a sad, lonely tone, leading me to think that he might be ambivalent about the fact that these students now seem to be ignoring him.)

Counselor: Well, John, I am wondering if you have done some thinking about what types of things you can do or people you could see yourself hanging out with.

John: I don't know. I wish there was more to do with science fiction here. I mean that they don't have anything good at this school. We have

Counselor: the science fiction club, but it only meets, like, a couple of times a month and we don't really do anything interesting.

Counselor: As you and I know, bullying can be a real problem here. Next year it looks like the school will be having lessons on bullying and figuring out how to put a stop to it. Are you interested in helping us with a project like that?

John: Yeah, I guess. I mean, teachers don't really do much to help anyone with this problem anyway.

My goal now was to decrease his isolation by encouraging steps toward connecting with others. One of the other school counselors and I had coauthored a grant application to fund a bullying prevention program. Our application was successful, and the program would kick in when John started seventh grade. The grant required us to involve students, teachers, parents, and community members. The other school counselors and I formed a bullying student council, which met once a month to generate ideas. We wanted this council to include students who had frequently been bullied, such as John, student leaders both in terms of academics and social popularity, and students of varying ethnicity. The council performed skits at a schoolwide assembly and held an art contest for artwork that depicted antiviolence messages.

At the council meetings, I observed John interact with other students and I could see how he contributed to his social isolation. John alienated council members by denigrating the suggestions of others, using his sarcastic wit. For example, John would criticize students' ideas about how to stop bullying, saying, "Yeah, and I'm going to be president someday." Although I found his sarcastic sense of humor appealing during our individual sessions, it clearly didn't win friends among his peers. I looked forward to talking about this at an individual session. However, a crisis arose that put this issue aside.

Session 4. The following week, a student appeared at my office reporting that one of John's elective teachers, Ms. Bancroft, needed my assistance immediately. When I approached the classroom, the teacher was standing outside the door, looking down at John, who was staring at the floor dejectedly. The teacher's facial expression indicated annoyance. She proceeded to tell me in front of John that I needed to take him out of her classroom and talk with him because approximately 15 minutes prior, he suddenly shouted in front of the entire class, "Leave me the [expletive] alone or I am going to kill myself." The teacher seemed rather insensitive about the situation, as if John had created a problem for her. I asked John to go and sit outside my office, and then I proceeded to gather more information from the teacher. Her perception was that several male students, who I noted were some of the same students who John had complained were bullying him a month ago, were probably teasing him. She had not overheard or observed the interaction. It is important to note that Ms. Bancroft, as an elective teacher, was not one of John's team teachers, and thus she, unfortunately, had not been informed of the fact that these students had been bullying John. I was not surprised that Ms. Bancroft had never directly observed any negative interactions between John and these students because my impression was that she had poor classroom management skills, rarely moving from her desk at the front of the room. I returned to my office to speak with John.

Counselor: Hey, John, I get the feeling you are pretty upset. Would you like to tell me what happened?

John: I just can't take it anymore. Those jerks are always doing something.

Counselor: I can sense how angry you are. So what did they do?

John: I was talking with Jennifer while we worked on the projects, and Jason purposely bumped into me, sending my stuff flying, and then Mike called me a fag.

Counselor: So it sounds like you also felt pretty embarrassed, with their doing that in front of Jennifer.

John: Yeah. I mean, things have sort of been going better until I got to Ms. Bancroft's class today.

Counselor: So after Mike called you that, what happened next?

John: I don't know . . . I just . . . I just didn't know what to say . . . I wanted to tell them off but nothing came out . . . I just yelled.

Counselor: Ms. Bancroft said that you said something about wanting to hurt yourself.

John: (His body language indicated to me that this was difficult for him to admit but also confirmed for me that he did make such a threat.)

Counselor: John, remember when we first got together, we talked about confidentiality and how if I thought you might harm yourself or somebody else that I would need to tell other people who could help you?

John: Yeah.

Counselor: Well, this is one of those times that I need to find out about how you are feeling and if you are thinking about hurting yourself or somebody else, and I may have to tell other people who can help you. John, tell me more about what you said about hurting yourself.

John: I mean, I was just angry, I didn't mean it.

Counselor: Believe it or not, I talk with a lot of students who have mentioned that they have thought of suicide. Have you been thinking about it lately?

John: No . . . I mean . . . I think about it for a short time and then it goes away . . . I would never do it.

Counselor: Tell me what thoughts you have had about it.

John: Well . . . you know . . . just like it may be better if I didn't have to put up with this . . . but I would never do it.

Counselor: When you have thoughts about suicide, did you think about how you would do it? . . . Do you have a plan?

John: No.

Counselor: For how long would you say you have been thinking about it?

John: Not long . . . maybe since the beginning of the school year.

Counselor: Have you ever tried suicide?

John: No.

Counselor: Well, John, I just want to say again that suicidal thoughts are common, but when people think about suicide, it indicates that they are having some really strong feelings that are difficult to deal with, and what can help is figuring out how to deal with difficult feelings. You mentioned that you have had thoughts of suicide for a short time. How do you manage to make the thoughts go away?

John: I will go play on my computer . . . or I go play with my dog. Just get my mind off it.

Counselor: What else do you do?

John: Nothing really.

Counselor: John, sometimes when people are picked on they tend to start to question themselves, thinking they have done something wrong. Have you ever done this type of questioning?

John: What do you mean?

Counselor: What I'm trying to say is, sometimes people think this says something bad about them . . . they think negatively about themselves. . . . Have you been doing that?

John: I think so . . . I mean, sometimes I wonder why this is happening to me.

Counselor: What answers do you come up with?

John: Like something is wrong with me.

Counselor: The reason why I am asking about this is because the level of our feelings depends upon what we say to ourselves. Often when we think negative things about ourselves, we feel really upset or even angry to the point where it is hard to think about how to handle things. Sort of like today in the classroom. I totally understand where you would be really angry with what happened, but what you were saying to yourself also should be looked at.

John: Maybe . . . I'm not sure.

Counselor: Earlier you mentioned that you said something to yourself like, "Something is wrong with me." What are you feeling when you are thinking this?

John: Sort of down.

Counselor: What I am trying to get across is that often our emotions are based on our thoughts and that we can actually change our thoughts to be less upsetting.

John: I see what you are saying. I know one thing that helps me is when I am thinking if something is wrong with me, but then I will think it is not about me, it is about them just being jerks.

Counselor: Exactly! So you are able to say this isn't about me, this is about their problems. What do you notice about your feelings after you say that to yourself?

John: I usually feel a little better.

Counselor: Well, John, this idea of how thoughts can increase anger and other feelings is somewhat complicated, but it sounds like you sort of have the hang of it. Maybe over the next couple of weeks we can talk more about it.

I raised the issue of self-castigation as a result of bullying because students internalize negative messages sent by peers. I proceeded to obtain from John more specifics how the students were bullying him and who they were. I asked him to identify other students in the class who were not involved but who may have observed the event. After speaking with one of the students who John thought observed the incident, I made a discipline referral on the students who were bullying John to their team teachers. Because there had been several other incidents between John and these students a month ago that had been documented, the team teachers were able to take disciplinary action, having them serve lunch detention for a week.

Counselor:	John, not that we can change what happened today, but looking back on it, what do you think you might do differently if a situation like this comes up again?
John:	That is a hard one . . . I could tell the teacher, but I don't think that will help . . . I want them to know what jerks they are.
Counselor:	So you want them to leave you alone. How do you get that message across in a way that won't lead them to get really angry or get you into trouble?
John:	I guess I could tell them to leave me alone. (John actually says this in a fairly assertive tone with appropriate eye contact and body language.)
Counselor:	I really like how you said that. You told them what you wanted using a firm voice but you weren't too aggressive. I really appreciate that you were open with me about your thoughts about hurting yourself. While I heard you when you said that you do not think you are thinking seriously about hurting yourself, would you be willing to promise me that you will seek me out or find another counselor if you are having such thoughts here at school?
John:	Yeah.
Counselor:	How about when you are at home? Who would you let know about it?
John:	I guess my mom.
Counselor:	Now, John, I am required to let your parents know about that what you said in the class today, and what you told me about having some thoughts of suicide. What I will say to them is essentially what I just said, that you made that statement today and that you have thought about suicide but you will talk with your mom when you are having such thoughts. Is there anything you want me to know before I call your parents sometime this afternoon?
John:	No, I guess not.

I achieved most of my goals for Session 4. I first wanted to assist John in decreasing his emotional intensity through use of client-centered skills of empathy and reflection so that he could process the experience. I then shifted to my main priority of conducting a suicide assessment. My assessment indicated that John was not a high risk, due to a lack of a specific plan, not having tried in the past, and willingness to

contract with me and his mother. I then introduced him to cognitive theory principles regarding the relationship between the thoughts and levels of emotional intensity and the ability to dispute or challenge one's thinking.

I called Mrs. Applegate early that afternoon before John arrived home and informed her about his suicide statements and thoughts, and that he contracted to speak with her and me or any of the other school counselors. She seemed remarkably calm. She informed me that she was not aware of any suicidal ideation in John's past. I also shared my perspective that I didn't think he was at a high risk for suicide. Mrs. Applegate also informed me that she and her husband were maintaining the plan of requiring John to seek social outlets of his own choosing. She believed that some progress had been made, in that John had recently mentioned some options.

Session 5. Since John made the statement in the class about killing himself on a Friday, I met with him on the following Monday at the start of the schoolday to assess his current suicidal ideation, process the experience further, and help him prepare for any negative reaction from other students.

Counselor:	So, I am wondering how things went over the weekend. Did you have any thoughts about hurting yourself?
John:	No . . . but I talked with my mom about it.
Counselor:	How did that go?
John:	Well, she just said that she was really concerned about me and that she wanted me to tell her if I were feeling that badly.
Counselor:	What do you think about her wanting you to tell her?
John:	I guess . . . I guess . . . I would.
Counselor:	John, I imagine it can be very difficult to talk about it. I think it takes courage to be honest.
John:	(silent for about half a minute) Guess what I was reading about this weekend? I got the new book on . . .

John told me about his new science fiction book for about 10 minutes. My interpretation of his silence was that he did not want to process the situation any further.

Counselor:	How are you feeling about being back at school today?
John:	Okay, I guess . . . I hope those guys don't make fun of me.
Counselor:	Well, I wanted you to know that I referred those guys to your team teachers so I imagine that they will be getting some type of consequence. If they say anything to you, I do encourage you to let me or your team teachers know. John, you know how word gets around fast in a school. I imagine that people may be talking about what happened. How do you plan on dealing with that?
John:	I don't know . . . ignore them? I mean, I was just really angry. I guess I could tell them that.
Counselor:	So it sounds like you plan on showing them it was really no big deal?
John:	Yeah.

Session 6. The following week I met with John for what essentially had become our weekly individual session. My goal for this session was to gradually address the issue of John's social isolation by discussing how John related to others.

Counselor:	I was wondering how things have been going with your decision about what types of social activities you want to do.
John:	I don't know. If it were up to me, I wouldn't do any.
Counselor:	Well, John, I know that you are annoyed with your parents' expectation. While I understand that you might not agree with them, I was wondering if you understood why they thought it would be a good thing.
John:	They told me that I need to learn how to deal with all different types of people. I sort of see where they are coming from. It is just that they don't understand what it is like here at school.
Counselor:	So you sort of understand what you parents are saying. . . . Since your parents are requiring this. . . . What would John like to get out of this?
John:	I don't know . . . some more people to hang out with?
Counselor:	A little bit ago you mentioned that it is pretty difficult here at school trying to deal with people. . . . What has John learned about dealing with people?
John:	If you don't get along with them, just avoid them.
Counselor:	I was talking more about meeting your goal of having more people to hang out with. What has worked for you?
John:	Not much . . . I mean, people here only like you if you are good at sports or suck up.
Counselor:	I do think it can be really hard to make friends in sixth grade. A lot of students tell me how hard it is. Tell me, what are those things that you think people would like about John?
John:	I don't know. I like science fiction?
Counselor:	Yeah, I got to admit, John, that is something I think is really neat about you. You have a real passion for science fiction. It also says to me that John is a pretty bright guy. (John looks down, seemingly embarrassed but also with a slight smile.) What else?
John:	Well, I guess I'm pretty smart when it comes to math and science. I . . . I also know a lot about computers.
Counselor:	You know what another thing is that I like about John? I think you have a real good sense of humor . . . you can be pretty sarcastic . . . do you know what that means?
John:	Yeah. My dad calls it my dry sense of humor.
Counselor:	While I imagine that not everyone appreciates your sense of humor, I imagine that there are people who would, and even more as you get older and go to the high school. Who are people here at school that you think would appreciate your wit and intelligence?
John:	I do like some of the people on the bullying council. They seem a lot nicer than most of the jerks in my class.

Counselor:	I get the sense that you are thinking about developing closer relationships with some of those people on the council?
John:	Yeah . . . somewhat.
Counselor:	Tell me how you have been going about that?
John:	I guess talking with them. Some of them seem to like science fiction also.
Counselor:	Wow, I imagine you feel somewhat excited to find people with similar interests?
John:	(looks down with a slight smile)
Counselor:	I think it takes a lot of courage to take the risk of talking with new people. How do you manage to motivate yourself to do that?
John:	I don't know. I guess I just did it.
Counselor:	There is something I want to mention. John, while I love your sarcastic wit, there is a danger in that you can use that power that you have to put down others. For example, if you don't like somebody's idea, it's easy to tell them in a way that gets a laugh but may also be hurtful. Do you know what mean?
John:	You mean like when my mom says I have a real smart mouth?
Counselor:	Smart mouth?
John:	Well, if someone is saying something obnoxious, I might say something nasty back, like with those jerks who have been bullying me.
Counselor:	I could see where you would want to protect yourself. We have talked about telling them what you want in a clear, firm way. Are there any other times when you see yourself "being smart with others"?
John:	(At this point, he gives me sort of a knowing look, indicating to me that he understands that I'm talking about his tendency to criticize others.) I guess sometimes I can seem to say things in a way that people don't like.
Counselor:	Could you give me an example of one of these times?
John:	Like the other day, Mrs. Brown had us working in groups. This one guy in my group claimed he knew what Mrs. Brown wanted, but I knew she wanted something else, and I just said something about him not knowing what he was talking about.
Counselor:	What happened next?
John:	Hmm . . . he didn't say much the rest of the group.
Counselor:	Well, trying to put yourself in his shoes, what do you think he was feeling?
John:	I guess he was annoyed.
Counselor:	Tell me about what you were thinking and feeling while you were in the group.
John:	Well, I was getting annoyed because I thought his ideas were pretty stupid. I knew what the teacher wanted.
Counselor:	On a scale of one to ten, with ten being really high, the highest you have ever been, how annoyed were you?
John:	Like an eight.

Counselor:	Remember how we talked about how thoughts often influence our feelings? What were you saying to yourself?
John:	This guy is an idiot and I don't need to listen to him anymore.
Counselor:	How do you think this thought influenced your level of annoyance?
John:	I see what you are saying. My mom often tells me that I have to learn to better tolerate other people.
Counselor:	John, tell me about times when you see yourself as being tolerant?
John:	Like, when I am hanging out with my cousin. If he doesn't want to do something I want to do, I will go along with him since he is younger.
Counselor:	Ah . . . so it sounds like you say something to yourself like, "Just relax, he is younger and I need to understand that."
John:	Something like that.
Counselor:	Well, great. You are using what we call positive coping statements in that situation to relax yourself. How about in the situation with the guy in the group? What could you say to yourself that would help you to feel less annoyed?
John:	Maybe something like "I think my idea is better but I can listen to his idea."
Counselor:	Sounds great.

John and I proceeded to use cognitive rehearsal in which I role-played the guy in the group while asking John how he could employ cognitive coping statements throughout the interaction. I assigned John the task of using positive coping statements when he recognized that he was becoming annoyed with other people.

<u>Sessions 7–10.</u> Over the next month, I met with John on a weekly basis and we continued to explore his developing relationships with one male and two female students whom he met on the bullying student council. John made the additional observation that he used sarcasm not only when he was annoyed with others, but also when he was anxious. He recognized that this had become an obstacle to developing new friendships. We cognitively rehearsed positive self-statements that helped him decrease his anxiety, and we explored the relaxation technique of deep breathing.

The students with whom John was seeking a greater connection were involved in the school's theater activities. At the beginning of the next marking period, I was able to honor a schedule change request made by John to change one of his elective classes to a dramatic arts elective in which these three students were enrolled. John shared that although he was terrified of acting, he really liked doing stage production, working with the camera, lights, etc.

After the Thanksgiving holiday, my sessions with John decreased to about once every several weeks as there seemed to be less of a need for counseling. John appeared to be happier and readily talked about his activities with this group of friends and his newfound interest in stage production. His teachers reported that although his academic performance was not consistent with his potential, he completed his homework on a more regular basis and was now making mostly Bs. During the spring, John was selected to be one of the stagehands for the school play. John reported that his parents were happier with his grades and recognized his work on the school play as meeting their requirement of a social activity.

Results

I attribute what I consider to be a rather successful case to a number of factors. One, John was highly intelligent and he readily understood complex concepts such as the principles of cognitive theory and was able to apply them outside the counseling sessions. For example, although he did not at first seem aware of how his sarcastic wit had a negative impact on others, he quickly grasped what I was referring to. He also had the requisite level of perspective taking to understand that he had hurt others.

I believe that John was motivated to change, despite his initial claims that he wanted to be left alone, because of the pain he experienced from social ostracism. According to Erik Erikson's theory of psychosocial development, adolescents are confronted with the challenge of establishing an identity. One of the primary ways in which they seek a sense of who they are is through developing peer groups that provide both an opportunity for social comparison necessary for developing self-awareness, and a sense of emotional support as the adolescent gradually individuates from his or her family. It has been my experience that students lacking such a support group are frequently depressed and at much greater risk to be a victim of peer aggression. My goal with such students is to assist them in finding their "social niche."

Finally, another major resource to the successful outcome of this case was the flexibility of the parental subsystem. A central principle in family systems theory is that families frequently experience difficulty when individual members are entering a new developmental transition, by tending to react through increased rigidity of their rules and patterns. Although I am not positive, my perspective was that John's parents initially responded to his social difficulties, and subsequent emotional withdrawal, by increasing their control. For example, the couple insisted that John develop social outlets in the ways they would have—through sports. This contributed to a negative feedback loop in which John responded to their enhanced control through withdrawal, which most likely reaffirmed their sense that they needed to do what was best for John. However, John's parents seemed willing to question the appropriateness of their reaction to John, which suggests a fairly high level of differentiation. They were responsive to my interpretation that John was experiencing a developmental transition that required a new way of relating to him; namely, providing more autonomy while still maintaining some basic and crucial expectations.

Personal Reflection

I believe that my training and experience as a family counselor provided me with somewhat of a unique perspective on the issues that were confronting the family. Although my intervention with John's parents was limited to one conference and several phone calls, I believe that this was sufficient to allow for a slight reordering of the family structure. Another effective contribution that I believe I made was my understanding of issues specific to boys, and the issue of bullying. I have found that boys are particularly fearful of being shamed. Some of the implications of this shame phobia include the importance of helping boys first identify feelings of anger before moving on to the more vulnerable feelings such as hurt and sadness. Also, boys need more space and time in the processing of emotions, and the counselor must tolerate interruptions in the counseling process to discuss their specific interests, such as John's love of science fiction. As evident in my interactions with John, I tend to take more risks in counseling boys, being more willing to express the implied feelings and thoughts of boys because I find that they lack the language of emotional expression. My hope is that by providing more interpretive reflections, I help boys learn such a language. Another example of my risk taking was my willingness to pursue goals that were not necessarily expressed by John. John reported wanting to be left alone, and he did not utter desires for greater social connection until the end of counseling. However, I did not trust that this was what John truly wanted, and thus I was supportive of the parents' pushing John to develop social outlets. At the time that I was counseling John, I had been developing an interest in understanding the phenomenon of bullying, as I saw it as a major contributor to the emotional disturbance of most of the children I was counseling. My reading and experience in dealing with bullying had taught me the importance of shifting responsibility away from the victim, who typically internalizes many of the critical messages received, and to the perpetrators. Although John stated that he saw his victimizers as jerks, implying that it did not reflect on him, I sensed that this was negatively impacting his self-concept. I think he used his sarcastic wit, even when in the company of more accepting students, as a defense mechanism, which, unfortunately, was counterproductive in that it became an obstacle to greater connection with others.

Suggested Readings

Davis, K. M. (2001). Structural-strategic family counseling: A case study. *Elementary School Counseling, 4*(3), 18–186.

Metcalf, L. (1995). *Counseling toward solutions: A practical solution-focused program for working with students, teachers and parents.* West Nyack, NY: Center for Applied Research in Education.

Murphy, J. J. (1997). *Solution-focused counseling in middle and high schools.* Alexandria, VA: American Counseling Association.

Rogers, C. (1961). *On becoming a person.* Boston: Houghton Mifflin.

Wilde, J. (1992). *Rational counseling with school-aged populations: A practical guide.* Bristol, PA: Accelerated Development.

Widerman, J. L., & Widerman, E. (1995). Family systems-oriented school counseling. *School Counselor, 43,* 66–73.

Biographical Statement

Jered B. Kolbert, PhD, is currently an assistant professor at Slippery Rock University and is the coordinator of the school counseling program. He was a middle school counselor for three years. Prior to working as a school counselor, he was the codirector of an innovative counseling agency that provided family counseling within the public schools surrounding Williamsburg, Virginia. He currently works as a part-time therapist at Catholic Charities in Pittsburgh, Pennsylvania, working with adolescents, couples, and families. You can reach Jered at jered.kolbert@sru.edu.

15

Being Real: A Long-Term Counseling Group for Children of Divorce

George McMahon and Sheila Gold

George McMahon invites Sheila Gold to cofacilitate a divorce group for seventh- and eighth-grade girls that McMahon has "inherited" at a private middle school. By combining Adlerian theory with Yalom's goals for group counseling, they create a process-oriented group that includes psychoeducational strategies. Through participation in this powerful group experience, the girls learn that they don't have to use "divorce" or running away as their only problem-solving strategy.

A blue-and-white ceramic bowl sits on a small table by my front door at my house. Whenever I come home, I empty my pockets of the essentials that I carry with me—wallet, keys, and change—into the bowl for safekeeping. The bowl was a good-bye gift to me from members of a very special counseling group I co-led when I was the school counselor at St. Matthew's. Around the edge of the bowl, the members painted their names, as if I might otherwise forget them. Inside the bowl are the words "It's been real," a message from youngsters who had difficulty putting the significance of the experiences we shared into words. I guess I now face the same problem— attempting to describe a continually evolving and dynamic group experience in some sort of linear, narrative form. To present a snapshot here will not do the group experience justice. Nevertheless, Sheila and I, the co-facilitators of the group, will try.

The School

St. Matthew's is a small private school in a fairly large southern city. Associated with the Episcopal Church, St. Matthew's has approximately 400 students in Grades Pre-K through 8, or about 40 students per class. Although in the heart of a rather poor city, it is situated in an upper-class neighborhood and has the feel of an exclusive private school. While many of its students come from the immediate neighborhood, St. Matthew's excellent academic reputation draws students from throughout the city. In spite of the school's well-developed financial-aid program and a recent increase in the school's efforts to recruit a more ethnically diverse student body, the majority of the student body, like the school's faculty, were White and primarily from a higher socioeconomic status. In addition to the teachers and three administrators, the school employed two learning specialists, who gave academic and learning support to students with learning differences, and a school chaplain, who led morning chapel, taught classes on Christian and world religions, and provided pastoral counseling. During the 4 years I worked at St. Matthew's, I was the only professional school counselor and was responsible for academic, career, personal, and social development for all 400 students.

Student Need

The group actually started five years prior to my arrival as St. Matthew's first professional school counselor. Because of an unusually high number of children of divorce in one particular class, all of them boys, the administration sought the help of a local counselor in private practice. He began meeting with the boys in a group, but rather than starting a 6- to 10-week psychoeducational group that school counselors are familiar with, the counselor chose to meet with them one morning a week over doughnuts for the entire school year. Eventually, time constraints led the counselor to transfer the group leadership duties to a middle school teacher who had some counseling training and met with the group over lunch.

The success of the group convinced the school to hire a full-time school counselor, me, George McMahon, fresh out of graduate school and full of ideas of starting my own comprehensive school-counseling program. Those involved with the group made their expectations that the group be a part of my program very clear. Parents introduced themselves to me before classes started by saying, "My son is in your group." The boys themselves came by the first day of school to meet their new group leader and to ask when we would get started. As a new school counselor looking to make a good impression and as someone who was overjoyed to see students so excited about a counseling group, I agreed to start right away and continued the group's tradition of process-oriented weekly meetings over lunch.

The popularity of the group spurred interest among other students in similar situations. Diana, a charismatic eighth grader, began lobbying for me to start a girls' divorce group as well. Seeing this as an opportunity to start a new group that fit my counseling style more closely, I agreed. The first thing I wanted to do was recruit a female co-leader. I thought it would be valuable for the members to see a man and a woman modeling a healthy, professional working relationship. Sheila Gold was a recent graduate with a master's degree in clinical social work and she agreed to co-lead a group with me.

Although we refer to one girl's group in this case study, there were actually several children-of-divorce groups. Because of the number of students interested in participating, groups were broken down by various means such as gender and grade level. The groups were open-ended and membership changed as members graduated and new members joined. For the purposes of this chapter, we will combine experiences from different groups and present them as if they occurred within one group over the course of one school year. There are two reasons for our decision. First, because St. Matthew's is a small school in a very close neighborhood, combining experiences from various groups protects the anonymity of the members. Second, we think it is less confusing to the reader to read about one group rather than to have to keep several groups straight. While some of the events presented have been manipulated in regard to their details, the significance of the stories—what they say about the group's dynamics and their importance to understanding the group's impact on the members and leaders—are presented honestly.

◼ Goals and Strategies

Two years into my job, in addition to the children-of-divorce group, I had initiated several skill-building groups on various topics that had a more traditional psychoeducational, highly structured format with a limited number of sessions. I liked the proactive nature of the psychoeducational format, delivering specific information or leading skill-building exercises that would help the students manage difficult situations that would arise in their future. At the same time, they did not provide the opportunity for the members to build relationships within the group or to work with group dynamics the way the process-oriented counseling groups did. We envisioned a process-oriented group that would also include psychoeducational strategies.

At the time, I was really getting interested in Adlerian counseling. I realized that my groups had always been democratic in nature, with the group members taking a great deal of responsibility for the group process and direction, and I wanted to continue that. I also liked Adler's idea of style of life, fictive goals, and basic mistakes. I used these concepts in the groups by looking for members' thought or behavior patterns that emerged as the group discussions became more personal. I wanted to help the group members recognize these patterns, both within themselves and in each other, and begin to identify how these thoughts or behaviors might be helping them achieve some goal that they have.

As for Sheila's perspective, she's a "Yalom girl." Irving Yalom identifies 11 therapeutic factors that make group therapy effective. We'll say just a little about four of them that seem to apply to our group.

The first therapeutic factor is *Imparting Information*. This includes didactic instruction, suggestions, and direct guidance and works best in psychoeducation groups.

The second therapeutic factor is *Recapitulation of the Primary Family Group*. This means that group members interact with other group members in a way similar to how they interact at home or with their family. Essentially, each group meeting is an opportunity for the co-leaders to reparent and the group members to refamily each member. One of the strengths of our group is that the co-leaders were male and female, thus setting up a parent–children paradigm.

The third therapeutic factor is *Imitative Behavior.* Preteen girls love to imitate each other, so this goal was not all that difficult for each to achieve. The challenge was to create an atmosphere where the girls could learn positive behaviors from each other.

Yalom's fourth factor is *Group Cohesiveness.* An effective group is a place of trust and acceptance. Our group was incredibly cohesive. The girls felt a sense of camaraderie and protectiveness of each other.

We decided to open the group to any seventh- or eighth-grade girl who was experiencing some sort of family change, provided that she returned a permission slip signed by a parent and that she met with one or both of the group leaders for a pregroup interview where Sheila or I would discuss group norms and expectations and hear what the student wanted to get out of the group. We expected group members to come to every meeting. If they decided they did not want to be part of the group at some later date for any reason, we expected them to tell the group about their decision to leave and attend a good-bye session.

The group would meet off-campus during lunchtime throughout the school year. We would start each group with a quick check on new developments and updates on past situations. If any member wanted to request group time to talk more in depth about a situation, she would let us know at this time. After the check-in, we would go back to those girls who had requested extra time. If there was time left, we would present a topic for discussion. Examples of topics and exercises we brought to the group include looking at roles the members play in their families, understanding family communication styles, identifying current relationship patterns, identifying stages of grief, assessing attitudes and feelings about marriage, finding relationship role models, dealing with parents who are struggling with the divorce, and understanding and asserting the rights of children of divorce.

We decided on a few basic goals for our new group. We wanted to create a safe and supportive environment that would promote personal insight, responsible decision making, and coping skills.

Process

Because our group met weekly for an entire school year, it would be impossible for us to recount the happenings of each and every group session. We are describing some of the critical situations that highlight the group's development.

<u>September.</u> At our first meeting, the girls arrived in my office and introduced themselves. There was Diana, who originally approached me about starting the group. Her parents had been divorced since she was very young, but she had just recently started visiting her father again. Shawna came from a neighborhood several miles away from St. Matthew's, and her style, reflected by her clothes, her hair, and her personality, was different from many of the St. Matthew's students'. Her parents had been divorced for several years, and she continued to struggle with managing life in two houses. Lindsey was from the St. Matthew's neighborhood and her family was very involved in the community and with the school. Lindsey came to me the previous year to discuss her parents' divorce, and then went through a long phase where she did not want to talk about it at all. Eventually, her friends convinced her to join the group.

After the eighth graders, the four seventh graders arrived in one loud, giggling pack. Sherri told everyone hi and dramatically welcomed Sheila Gold to the group. Sherri is African American, which caused her to stand out in a primarily White school like St. Matthew's. Sherri was known for her gregarious personality and her spontaneous routines, dramatically acting out stories or imitating people. Her parents were divorced when she was in elementary school, and her father passed away as a result of a long illness three years later. She was living with her aunt and uncle. Darcy also had an exuberant personality and was a close friend of Sherri's. Her parents were recently separated, and her mother had initially refused to allow her daughter to participate in the group or discuss the divorce with anyone, saying that it invaded their family's privacy. Only after plenty of convincing from Darcy did her mother relent and sign the permission slip. Carmen was biracial, and she and Sherri were the only students of color in their grade, and they seemed to have a special bond. Carmen's parents had been divorced for several years. Holly was new to the school. Her parents had recently completed their divorce and still fought. Both maintained their own residences and were burdened with the financial cost of divorce. To help her parents, Holly was expected to take care of her younger brother, a fifth grader at another school.

When everyone was present, I introduced Sheila to the group. I reminded them that we would be leaving school and walking to a nearby lunch spot and that when we were talking in the restaurant, we all would have to be aware of who was around us and to keep our voices down. The girls made the most of the quick walk, asking Sheila all kinds of questions as they tried to get to know the new co-leader.

In subsequent sessions, as each member shared her story, we encouraged the others to ask clarifying questions while we tried to sum up the major themes in their stories. As more of girls told their stories, we began to link their stories together. A few weeks later, once everyone had finished telling her story, we asked each girl to think about a goal related to her family situation and something that the group could help her with. For example, Shawna wanted to renegotiate her visitation schedule, Carmen wanted to become more organized with her schoolwork between her two houses, and Diana wanted to build a relationship with her dad.

The girls' relationships with their fathers seemed to be a prominent theme. Some members were separating from their fathers a bit, feeling that their mothers understood them better as they grew. Others wanted to get their fathers back into their lives. The most common issue with fathers, however, seemed to be the girls' wanting to take care of their fathers. Many of the girls whose parents were divorcing or who had recently divorced reported having a tough time seeing their fathers struggle. They saw their fathers as strong men in many ways and hated to see them sad, lonely, or lost. Lindsey talked about taking over some of the roles and responsibilities that her mother used to have, including cooking for her father, shopping for groceries, and even waking him up in the mornings. We asked the girls to think about what was going on inside of them that led them to take over these responsibilities.

October. We asked about the roles the girls played in different contexts, such as in their families, in their class, with their friends. We asked them how they felt about those roles (e.g., the clown, the caretaker, the quiet one) and whether they chose those roles or if they felt "forced" into them. We looked at the positives and negatives of playing those roles, and encouraged the girls to picture themselves playing some other roles. What might that look like? Sound like? What would be different?

November. As we completed our check-in, Diana said she had heard that children of divorce were more likely to get divorced themselves. She was scared that she was going to go through what her parents went through and that she might put her kids through what she went through. We acknowledged the discouraging statistics but asked the girls to think about why that might be. They generated several ideas, from genetics (some inherited trait) to personalities (some people just like to fight) to what they learn from their parents (divorce is an acceptable way of solving problems). A few of the girls stated that they thought they would be less likely to get a divorce because they know how hard it is. Many of the girls identified what *not* to do in a relationship, such as yell at each other or insult each other. We asked them about people they knew who had good relationships, and we said we could talk about that next week.

The girls came back with several relationship role models, including aunts and uncles, grandparents, and parents of friends. Many had talked to their role models and asked them what they did to help their relationship, particularly when they fight. The girls discussed several things they thought were important to a marriage's working out, such as picking the right partner, being your partner's best friend, fighting fair, managing anger, and talking problems out rather than ignoring them or yelling. We asked the girls to think about how they tended to solve problems with people who were important to them, such as their close friends. Many of the girls acknowledged that they have had times when they got mad at their friends and their fights led to their not being friends anymore. Over the next few sessions, the girls talked about difficult situations they had with their friends and the group gave feedback about how they could better handle those conflicts and maintain their friendships.

January. As soon as the eighth-grade girls walked in, we could tell there was something wrong. They looked as serious as they had ever been, and as the seventh-grade girls began to file in, we saw very little eye contact between the two subgroups. Lindsey, an eighth grader, spoke first: "I have something very important to talk about, Mr. McMahon." I said okay and I asked if she was all right. "Not really" was the response, followed by a quick "Let's go." As we walked out of the office, Sheila and I acknowledged the event through silent eye contact and a little shrug of the shoulders.

At the restaurant, no one else said they had anything to talk about, so we gave Lindsey the floor. She reported that there was a story going around the seventh grade about her, something that she had talked about in group. She did not know who talked, but she figured the only way that it could have gotten out is if one of the seventh-grade girls had broken confidentiality.

Sheila asked the seventh-grade girls if they knew what Lindsey was saying. They denied that they had talked about Lindsey outside of the group. Lindsey said that she had talked to the other eighth-grade girls and they had a solution: "We think we should split into two separate groups, one for eighth grade and one for seventh grade. Then we won't have to worry about it."

Sheila and I looked at each other. I wanted to tell them, "That's not going to happen," but I had always encouraged them to take responsibility for their group, and I wanted to respect the decisions they made.

"Okay, I'll tell you what," I finally said. "Let's talk about this and give us some time to think and if all of you still want to break up into two groups, we'll see what we can do. But before we get into that, I want to ask you, does this situation remind anyone of anything?"

Most of the girls looked around the room, confused. Eventually, however, the lightbulbs started to go off. Diana's moment of realization was marked with a verbal "Wow. We want a divorce." Sheila observed that when the group hit a rough spot, their way of solving the problem was to split up. "And like Mr. McMahon said, if, in the end, you still want to do that, that's an option. But maybe there are other ways to handle it, too. What do you think?"

We talked for a while about they how they felt about splitting up, but as the session was closing, the girls decided unanimously to try to work things out. We agreed to talk more next week about how to rebuild trust between the group members. Sheila and I let them know we were impressed that they had the courage to try to fix a difficult situation.

March and April. Toward the end of the school year, we learned that Darcy was leaving St. Matthew's to attend another private school in the area. Sherri and Darcy were extremely close, but it was obvious that, in many ways, Sherri needed Darcy more than the other way around. While the issue of Darcy's leaving was never directly addressed in group, it festered. Little comments would be made and slowly the girls were developing coping strategies to become more independent from each other. Previously, Sherri would frequently borrow money from Darcy to get food at whatever fast food restaurant we would be having group at that week. It was so habitual, that Darcy just anticipated what Sherri would need. Darcy was certainly in a caretaker role from that perspective. It was sad and encouraging to see these girls separate and stand on their own a bit. The group was there for them. I do believe that their hard work in the group made it possible for them to part in a healthy way, as opposed to resorting to maladaptive behavior such as purposely picking fights. It was good for the group to experience a "breakup" and see that it can be done maturely and without blame.

May. Closure is an important part of any group process, but we felt that it would be particularly vital in this group. The group members had been through separations when their parents divorced, and many of those good-byes were very difficult, even traumatic. For this reason, we thought it would be especially important to help the girls learn how to say good-bye appropriately. Furthermore, because Darcy was not coming back to St. Matthew's, we wanted to give her and the group members the opportunity to say good-bye to each other.

The group decided that for the final session, we would go to a nicer restaurant to celebrate. When we got to the restaurant, we all ordered, and then Sheila and I asked each girl to talk about one moment from the group that year that seemed particularly important, something that they would take away with them. We also asked them to think of something they wanted to continue working on over the summer. Sheila and I told each of the girls about a strength we saw in her, something special that she brought to the group. The girls thanked us, as well.

■ Results

Sheila and I informally evaluated the group throughout the process by checking in with the members, making sure the group was meeting their expectations, and assessing new situations and altering the group to respond to those situations. We both think that the group was a positive experience for the girls. In hindsight, however, I wish we would have evaluated the group in a more systematic way, such as through exit interviews.

I also wish we could have had more parent involvement. One idea we had was to create a monthly newsletter that would go to the parents to let them in on the general topics that were discussed. Of course, the group members would have final say about the newsletter, but we believe such a newsletter would promote communication between the parents and their children.

Of course, I want my students to learn something valuable from their experiences in my groups, but I am always amazed at how much I learn. This group helped me appreciate the resourcefulness and resilience of young people in difficult situations, and reaffirmed my faith in group process.

Sheila and I have presented this group experience at local conferences, and we have heard school counselors say, "That group would never work in my school." That may very well be true, but we still encourage those school counselors to be creative and find their own way to lead groups that meet their particular students' needs. As school counselors, we too often feel limited by the obstacles we see, like school schedules, limited financial resources, noncounseling duties, limited physical space, or "traditional" practices of school counselors. Find what will work in your school. If scheduling is a problem, see if you can run your group as part of an after-school program. If you have time constraints, bring in school counseling interns or LPC interns who need hours to run groups under your supervision. Hold groups outside if there is not enough space. There are creative solutions to the obstacles. Find a way to meet the needs of your students.

I want to say a few things about ethics and legal issues and groups. Confidentiality, and its limitations, is always a concern. We needed to be clear that the group was not a place for students to discuss their parents' private and sensitive concerns. Groups for children of divorce bring special demands, such as knowing the custody status of each parent. Although we required only one parent to sign the permission slip, we had to anticipate that in cases of joint custody, both parents had to agree.

Walking off campus also created some practical and ethical problems. As the group leaders, we were responsible for a bunch of middle school students walking city streets. We acknowledge that not everyone will be comfortable with that risk. We also talked with the students about the possibility of seeing someone they knew at a restaurant. Overwhelmingly, the students reported that they were willing to take that risk and that they actually felt safer expressing themselves away from the school grounds.

I guess the students whose names are on the ceramic bowl were right—it *was* real. The group provided the members an opportunity to be real with themselves and with each other. That's what made the group so special. It was a place where everyone could be honest, and that is something special.

■ Personal Reflection

George. Not too long ago, I was back in my hometown and I ran into a couple of my former group members. Although they were spread out across different high schools and some had even moved out of the state, these two students were able to give me an update on how everyone was doing. They were not all friends, even when they were in the group, but the bond that they had through the group was strong enough to keep them in touch. They even suggested that the next time I came to town, they would contact everyone so that we could have a reunion at one of the restaurants we used to go to.

I am proud of the program I was able to start at St. Matthew's, and I have countless positive memories. Although the children-of-divorce groups were a small part of my overall program, they have left a lasting effect on me. The group members taught me about what it is like to live through a divorce. I learned how powerful it was to have adolescents put so much trust in me, and I learned how important it was for them to have an adult who believed in them.

__Sheila.__ Looking back on my experience coleading the girls' divorce group, I have nothing but fond memories. While I was decidedly the outsider, the girls willingly brought me up to speed. At that time, I was working at a local United Way agency counseling convicted felons recently paroled for drug offenses. The divorce group provided a drastic and positive change, clientwise and settingwise. I did feel anxious about not being an employee of the school. I was unclear as to how the girls might perceive my introduction into the group and whether they would feel my assistance was unnecessary or due to some inadequacies on their part. However, on reflection, those anxieties were unwarranted.

Suggested Readings

Berg, R. C., Landreth, G. L., & Fall, K. A. (1998). *Group counseling: Concepts and procedures.* Philadelphia: Accelerated Development.

Jacobs, E. E., Masson, R. L., & Harvill, R. L. (2002). *Group counseling: Strategies and skills.* Pacific Grove, CA: Brooks/Cole.

Smead-Morganett, R. (1990). *Skills for living: Group counseling activities for young adolescents.* Champaign, IL: Research Press.

Yalom, I. D. (1995). *The theory and practice of group psychotherapy* (4th ed.). New York: Basic Books.

Biographical Statement

H. George McMahon, PhD, was a school counselor at the elementary and middle school level for four years. Having completed his PhD in Counseling Psychology from the University of Georgia in 2004, he is now working as an assistant professor in the School Counseling Program at Georgia State University, where he teaches a variety of classes, including group counseling. You can reach George at gmcmahon@gsu.edu.

Sheila Gold is a licensed master social worker living in suburban Atlanta, Georgia. Before taking some time to raise her beautiful daughters, Sheila's area of practice was clinical group work with addicted populations. Sheila can be reached at golds@bellsouth.net.

16

Suicide in the School: A Personal Perspective

Brenda Melton

An eighth-grade girl shoots herself in the school's parking lot. Brenda Melton describes her work during the aftermath of the suicide as a member of the school district's crisis response team. She works with classrooms full of grieving students, distraught teachers, school staff members, and parents. She answers phones and speaks with the media. Melton describes the procedures and resources her school district has in place so that when these terrible incidents occur, there is direction about what to do.

work at Mission Middle School, an inner-city school in San Antonio, Texas, in a low-socioeconomic area. Mission had seen much tragedy, including drugs, violence, and gangs. Many of these problems centered around a public housing project, but its closure two years ago improved the neighborhood environment.

The School

The principal and staff had worked hard to provide a safe, welcoming, and friendly environment, where success and academics are stressed. The incident described in this case marked a return to the "old image" of Mission as a troubled, violent school.

Student Need

A quiet Friday morning in October was interrupted when I received a disturbing phone call to immediately report to Mission Middle School, where a shooting had occurred. I quickly gathered my resources on violence/suicide, grief, and trauma and drove to the school within 15 minutes. Having visited the campus before and not knowing the nature of the shooting, I approached it cautiously and noticed a number of emergency vehicles around the school campus. A cafeteria worker, trying to enter the building from the rear, told me that everyone needed to enter through the main entrance. I walked with her as she told me that something bad had happened: "I knew that we would have a shooting someday."

An eighth-grade student had fatally shot herself. The Mission Middle School students were traumatized. For the week of the incident, I was part of the Crisis Response Team attending to the immediate needs of the students. The Crisis Response Team is contacted initially through the leadership at the district level for Student Services, Health Services, Special Education, and Communications. In the event of a suicide (or other critical incident, including car accident, trauma, or murder), these key people are notified and then they send specialized staff to the school site. Crisis Response Teams include school counselors, social workers, and psychologists. I am a counselor at one of the district's alternative high schools, but as a team member, I can be sent to any campus in need.

Goals and Strategies

As stated in the "District Emergency Response Plan" (Guidance and Counseling Department, 2002), the goals of a Crisis Response Team are prevention, intervention, and postvention:

Prevention:

- To provide workshops for the staff on depression and suicide prevention/intervention
- To provide information for parents on suicide prevention and ways to help their child

Intervention:

- To provide crisis counseling for students
- To identify students who need more intense counseling and posttraumatic intervention for grief/loss
- To provide information to the media on the incident (without revealing personal information about the child) and the role of school counselors in providing support to the students, as directed by the communications officer
- To support parents, teachers, and staff in providing for the students
- To stabilize the school environment and assist students in returning to normalcy
- To provide expertise in long-range intervention and crisis response for the district
- To join in the community efforts to improve the school environment

Postvention:

- To provide follow-up support at intervals (such as 3 months, 6 months, and on anniversary dates)
- To evaluate and assess the information received about the emergency
- To call a consultant to come to the school if necessary
- To inform the communications officer to handle the media

Following the "Crisis Response Plan Checklist" (Guidance and Counseling Department, 2000), the strategies we used included:

- Assess the situation.
- Plan for the day, including a triage process to provide counseling.
- Determine the needs of the campus and resources available.
- Provide information to staff and parents on suicide and grief.
- Generate a list of "students of concern," who have been impacted by the loss.
- Check with all of the student's classes and teachers.
- Determine which students may need specialized care and intervention.
- Generate information in the form of a letter home to parents and staff and include information about suicide, grief, depression, and community resources.
- Provide support in a "safe room" with counselors for students for the next few weeks.
- Debrief staff (administration, teachers, support personnel, office, cafeteria, custodial, bus drivers, and others) and volunteers, and provide mental health support community resources. Provide breaks, drinks, and food for the staff and volunteers as needed.
- Return to a regular routine as soon as possible.
- Prepare for memorialization and funeral rites.
- Organize three types of support groups: for students, for parents/community, and for faculty/staff.

■ Process

As I entered the main entrance of Mission Middle School, I told a police officer I was a school counselor and a Crisis Response Team member. The campus was under "containment," surrounded by school district and city police. One of the first to arrive on the scene, I was then directed to the school's main office, where I offered my assistance. I showed the administrator the materials I brought and indicated what sections would be helpful to the teachers and staff. After signing in, I was directed to room 110, down the hall, and pointed in a general direction.

Finding no one in the room, I walked down the hall in the other direction. As I passed room 103, a visibly distraught teacher stood with his first-period class. The sixth graders were crying and hugging each other. I introduced myself and asked the teacher, Mr. Garcia, if he needed some assistance. He eagerly welcomed me into his classroom. He explained that these students had witnessed the incident in the parking lot that morning. Mr. Garcia, one of the first adults on the scene, brought most of the students in the area into his classroom and then realized he had no idea what to do.

I did not know the name of the girl who shot herself, who she was, or any of the details, but the drama unfolded as the students, who were now in my charge, told their stories. They all knew the girl who shot herself; many had been close to the incident. After explaining to the group that I was the counselor at the alternative high school, I observed several students walking around the room caring for others who were very upset and crying. I sat in the middle of the group of students as they gathered closer to me and told them I was proud of them for taking care of each other at a time like this. I said, "Tell me what happened."

The children took great care in talking about their friend, Sylvia, an eighth-grade girl who had brought a 9mm handgun to school in her backpack and told her friends she was going to kill herself. Sylvia gave away her things and told her friends that she loved them. She then went to the parking lot, put the gun to her head, and pulled the trigger. Several of the students were very close to the incident and had feared that she was also going to shoot them.

For the next 2 hours, I stayed with Mr. Garcia's class. All the students on campus were contained in their classrooms with their teachers. Several of the students were taken to the campus crisis center for counseling. Students focused on me as I listened and asked them about what had happened and what it meant to them. Most of the students in the room, Sylvia's friends, wanted her to know that they cared. They knew she was troubled, had made threats to kill herself, and yet they admitted they never knew she would really do it. We talked about what to do if someone threatened to hurt himself or herself. Several of the students talked about others they knew who had threatened or attempted suicide. One boy had an uncle who had killed himself. The students were shocked and expressed disbelief about what had happened with Sylvia.

According to the students, Sylvia had "lots of problems at home, especially with her father." She also had many problems at school because people would tease her, and she had had several fights. None of that seemed to matter now. We talked about anger and blaming others as they shared their thoughts and fears. The students' questions were numerous and frantic: Was she alive? What will happen next? Are we safe? Have they searched the lockers for more guns? What are the police doing? Will this be on television? How will my parents know I'm okay? May I call my parents to let them know I'm okay?

What struck me most was the concern for others expressed by the students, and their immediate need to know that the school was safe and under control. Toward the end of the first hour, they were ready to have their questions answered. I sought assistance from an administrator. After explaining that this group had witnessed the incident and needed information and reassurance, I returned to the students in room 103 with the administrator, who had answers for them.

Brief information was shared with the students as the administrator relayed that Sylvia was still alive but in critical condition and had been airlifted to the trauma center. The school was not allowing students to call home, but parents were calling the school. The administrator reassured the students that the police had secured the campus and the school would be searched thoroughly for other weapons.

During the second hour, the students wanted to take action and do something. Ricky was on the computer and composed a find-a-word puzzle entitled "Sylvia." The embedded words were Sylvia's friends' names. As he showed me the puzzle, other students wanted their names included as her friends, and they gathered around the computer as names were offered to the friendship puzzle. I suggested other ways that the students could express their concern for Sylvia. Mr. Garcia supplied the students with paper, pencils, and markers, and some began to work together on posters. Students also composed letters and poems about their troubled friend, including things they wanted her to know. Johnny passed out tissues and continued to take care of the one or two students who was sobbing and tearful. I remained in Mr. Garcia's classroom until an announcement was made for students to go to their third-period class and then to lunch. The bell rang loudly and students left still somewhat in a state of shock, thanking me for being with them.

After the students were dismissed to go to their classes, I went to the crisis center, which was very busy. At the center, school counselors, social workers, and school psychologists met with students individually and in small groups. Several school counselors and I visited classrooms. In the classrooms, we checked with the teachers and students. Many students shared how they knew Sylvia and what they knew about what had happened, and asked for information. All of the students were traumatized, and the staff looked relieved to see professional counselors who would help address the students' emotional needs.

Parents began calling the school as soon as media broke the news. Parents who came to the school were directed to the auditorium, where a district official verified their identities and their children's names. Parents were given a list of community resources and told that counselors would be available at the school as well. After the screening process was completed, students were located and escorted to the auditorium, where their parent signed them out to take them home. Many parents later called the school because their child was crying and upset and they did not know what to do. In the classrooms, students wondered if their parents were coming to get them and seemed to feel the loss as names of students were called and their class-mates were led away.

At noon, the assistant superintendent for Curriculum and Instruction/Campus Operations and I covered the main office and took the phone calls. This allowed the office staff to take a lunch break. They were emotionally drained after answering the phones since the incident early that morning.

Being busy on the campus, the principal had chosen not to be interviewed by the media, so the district public relations representatives asked if I would be the spokesperson at the site. I was interviewed several times by television stations and radio stations. Some of the questions were tough and direct, but I focused on grief/loss, counseling, and crisis response. I had been briefed not to give any specific information on Sylvia, and in any case, my information about her was very limited. As the media hovered in the street off-campus, I was concerned about hysteria being created by the television reporters interviewing parents and children as they left. The worst of this came at the end of the day, when groups of students rallied around the television cameras and told the details of Sylvia's life and troubles.

After lunch, Mr. Garcia found me in the hallway and related an incident he found disturbing: A man came to his classroom, said he was called to help at the school, and then began telling the students that they were sinners and would be punished if they did not pray and believe in the Lord. Mr. Garcia gave me a detailed description of the individual, and I reported it to the principal, who alerted the district police on campus. The person was not a district employee or an authorized visitor. As far as I know, he was not apprehended, but this illustrated the importance of screening people who came to the school. During this time of crisis, when children were the most vulnerable, the security procedures needed to be more protective. I was grateful that Mr. Garcia trusted me and expressed his concern about the incident.

At the end of a day, a letter was given to the students to take home to explain the facts of the incident and provide information about resources families might need. After school, the staff met with the principal, the district guidance and coun-seling coordinator, and me. After the principal gave a brief report of the day to the teachers and staff, we focused on the staff's emotional needs. They were encour-aged to talk with each other and with loved ones. We suggested ways to alleviate the stress and deal with the loss. In addition, we discussed what to anticipate in the next week and the next few months for themselves and for their students.

■ Results

The "District Emergency Response Plan" (Guidance and Counseling Department, 2002) has been in place for several years for various emergencies, including school violence; bomb threats; fire; natural disasters; hazardous materials; school bus and car accidents; other emergency situations; and student/staff illness, death, or suicide. Containment or lockdown, evacuation, and student release are part of the overall plan. Responsibilities of the crisis response team, administration, the mental health team, staff, and security personnel are outlined briefly. Logistics, "code" announce-ments, command centers, and alternate centers have been addressed at the district and campus levels. The plan includes ways to define the crisis and verify facts; to respond to the media; and to notify staff, parents, students, and district and community members about the incident.

The Crisis Response Team's roles and responsibilities include identification and assessment of affected students and staff, outlining procedures to be followed during the incident, the first 24 hours after the incident, the first three days, and the first week(s) and for long-term follow-up (anniversaries and counseling support). Some items were missing from the District Emergency Response Plan (Guidance and Counseling Department, 2002). Debriefing plans for staff, community responders, and the Crisis Response Team itself need to be addressed. Sample announcements, letters to parents, and press releases need to be included, along with information on community resources, suicide, depression, and other traumas.

Since the incident, I have thought about what else the Crisis Response Team needed to consider for future situations:

- The process needs to be formalized and training should be held annually. Development of the team should include selection of members, meeting schedule and training, duties of each team member, and a flow chart.
- Evaluation procedures for the Crisis Response Team need to be formalized so that the plan may be refined and improved.
- In addition to training, curriculum for suicide prevention should be provided for all school counselors, such as the SAFE: Teen Suicide Prevention curriculum (www.safe-teen.com), or the Yellow Ribbon Suicide Prevention Program (www.yellowribbon.org).
- During the crisis, the Crisis Response Team needs to meet daily and prior to meeting with the staff.
- The automated attendance system should be turned off immediately.
- A memo to the teachers containing specific information regarding the incident is needed as soon as possible to be read to the students. The day's curriculum may need to be adapted, but teachers should be encouraged to return to their classroom routine as soon as the initial emotional reactions have been attended to.
- The school's counselor(s) should follow the victim's schedule through the day, as these classes are most immediately affected.
- Teachers and staff need extra support as well (e.g., opportunities to talk or relax, substitutes for breaks)
- Counseling attendance lists of those in the Crisis Center are needed, not only for attendance purposes, but also for appropriate follow-up.
- If possible, Crisis Team Members should have a picture of the victim.
- Honoring the victim student's empty desk may be key to closure for many students. (The desk may be moved to the side of the room for that class, rather than removed or having someone else sit there.)
- The victim's belongings (locker, desk, posted work) need to be collected and given to the family.

- Parent/community meetings should be held in the evening to address concerns and prevent further tragedies.
- An intervention team, led by the principal, should meet with the family as soon as possible. The team should discuss with the family what information may be shared. The family may want to make a statement through the school. The intervention team may recommend to the family that the funeral be held at the end of a school day so students and staff may attend. Also, the team may suggest that the family choose two friends and staff to speak at the funeral, rather than have an open microphone.
- The school needs to designate a representative to attend the funeral. Cultural differences may need to be addressed with students to explain religious beliefs, cremation, open casket, closed casket, or other family choices in a nonjudgmental way.
- School staff could be alerted to be observant at the funeral to identify other high-risk students.
- Resources such as support groups for parents of children who committed suicide, and other counseling services, should be offered to the family at an appropriate time.
- A memorial service at school is not recommended. Students may need help understanding the differences between shrines and memorials. A collection box of positive thoughts, letters, and poems may be collected and given to the family.
- A district suicide prevention task force is needed.
- A transition protocol is needed for students reentering the school from the hospital or transitioning to the hospital. The hospital staff may be helpful in developing this protocol for school counselors.
- To be most effective in responding to such a tragic event, a district Crisis Response Team should:
  - Have developed connections with campus students, staff, community, and department chairs.
  - Have a list of at-risk students at the campus.
  - Provide follow-up support groups on a regular basis—beginning weekly and then moving to biweekly.
  - Identify and plan for milestones (anniversary date, birth date, other significant dates).
  - Use a confidential box for students and others to identify students at-risk for harm. The box should be kept locked and checked twice a day. Identified students are individually contacted and parents are called.
  - Make classroom presentations on suicide prevention.

As a leader in the responses to these critical incidents, my focus as a school counselor was to provide information and support students in understanding their feelings and appropriate ways to express those emotions. The counseling sessions continued during the next week, and I returned to the campus after Sylvia's funeral to find students and staff emotionally exhausted and needing more support. I suggested that a group of students draw or write their feelings, and we began a 6-foot mural to be put in the cafeteria. Being careful not to memorialize Sylvia and her tragic death, the mural's theme was "LIFE," which was emblazoned in large letters across the entire length. As the students worked, their ideas flowed. Several worked on a large tree full of fruit; another group drew a rainbow and flowers. They wrote their thoughts: "Life is like a rainbow," "Life is a box of chocolates, you never know what you're going to get," "Life is beautiful." All of the drawings and writings were a celebration and affirmation of life. One girl said, "You know, I'm having fun, but I feel guilty about having fun." Another student quickly said, "It's okay to have fun!" and then wrote that on the mural with the other thoughts.

■ Personal Reflection

In the months following, I have stayed in contact with the Mission Middle School counselor and offered encouragement and support. The district has reviewed the Crisis Response Plan and made some revisions based on the team's recommendations. Suicide prevention materials have been distributed to all district school counselors. Crisis training is being planned to help all school counselors to be prepared for critical incidents. The Mission Middle School principal wrote a letter praising the efforts of the Crisis Response Team, and I was personally thanked for my leadership and advocacy for student safety and well-being. My only wish would be to have a copy of the "LIFE" mural to put on my office wall, but the experience is in my heart.

References

Guidance and Counseling Department. (2002). *District Emergency Response Plan.* San Antonio, TX: San Antonio Independent School District.

SAFE: Teen Suicide Prevention can be found at www.safe-teen.com.

Yellow Ribbon Suicide Prevention Program. Yellow Ribbon International, P.O. Box 644, Westminster, CO 80036–0644. www.yellowribbon.org.

Suggested Readings

American Hospice Foundation. (2003). *Grief at school: Addressing the needs of grieving students.* Washington, DC: Author.

Desetta, A., & Wolin, S. (Eds.). (2000). *The struggle to be strong: True stories about teens overcoming tough times.* Minneapolis, MN: Free Spirit Publishing.

The Dougy Center for Grieving Children and Families, www.dougy.org/srchresults.asp?catky=963572&subcatky1=3770868.

Dudley, J. (2003). *When grief visits a school: Organizing a successful response.* Minneapolis, MN: Educational Media.

Juhnke, G. (2000). *Addressing school violence: Practical strategies and interventions.* Austin, TX: Jalmar Press.

Biographical Statement

Brenda Melton, MEd, LPC, a school counselor since 1982, has been a presenter at the state and national levels on school violence, working with gangs, conflict resolution, and leadership. She was the 2002–2003 American School Counselor Association president. Today, Brenda is a school counselor at Navarro Academy, an alternative high school, in San Antonio, Texas. You can reach Brenda at MeltonBrenda@msn.com.

PART III

High School Cases

17

I Believe I Can Fly: The Transformation of Michael Greene

Rhonda Bryant

Michael Greene, a 14-year-old African American high school student, lives in a town that suffers from the difficulties associated with both racial segregation and integration. The predominantly White staff of the high school addresses the racial issues by adopting a position of color-blindness and ignores race as part of personal identity. Michael feels disconnected to school. He earns mostly Cs and acts out. Rhonda Bryant, a young African American counselor, works in the Upward Bound program. Michael joins the Upward Bound program to please his parents, who have high aspirations for him. Bryant joins Michael in listening to rap music. Then she provides individual counseling, family consultation, and career guidance to help Michael envision a future that includes college.

When I met Michael Greene, I was employed as the program counselor and coordinator of an Upward Bound program. The Upward Bound program provides support to selected high school students in their preparation for college, especially first-generation college students who live at or below the poverty level. The goal of Upward Bound is to increase the rates at which participants enroll in and graduate from institutions of postsecondary education (Upward Bound, n.d.).

My job was located in Charlottesville, Virginia, a community of over 150,000 people. The University of Virginia, a prestigious university known for its academic excellence, housed the Upward Bound program. In the two years prior to my employment, the university enjoyed great prosperity, while some of the townspeople underwent a number of financial setbacks. The town had many affluent members, mostly due to faculty appointments at the university. Due to successive closures of several plants and factories, though, many townspeople lost their jobs. Families who depended on these jobs to maintain middle-class status found themselves thrust into financial chaos and unable to find employment. Thus, the need for Upward Bound's services intensified as state revenues decreased and state contributions to county school budgets dropped to record lows.

As the program coordinator, I worked with 11 high schools across eight rural counties and two cities. Every fall semester, I visited each school to explain the program and to encourage students to apply. Students whose parents had not completed college and fell within the poverty guidelines were eligible to apply for the program. Applicants were required to complete an interview, submit grades, and obtain recommendations from their counselor and one teacher. The program required that students participate in a Saturday enrichment program twice a month during the academic year and live on the university campus for five weeks in the summer, taking college preparatory courses.

The School

One of the high schools I visited was located in an urban district. The State Department of Education had placed the school on probation during the latest round of statewide testing because so many of its students had not passed basic writing and mathematical requirements. The school building was over 30 years old and had not been renovated at the time of my visit. Racial relations had been a problem in the school off and on since integration in the 1960s, and although it was not overtly addressed by the school's staff or administrators, some African American students often discussed their mistrust of teachers and staff members among themselves. One of these students, Michael Greene, came to my attention when he applied for admission to the Upward Bound program.

Student Need

Even though desegregation had integrated most of the town's schools, neighborhoods remained racially separated into the 21st century. The railroad tracks quietly distinguished between the haves and the have-nots. Michael Greene lived on the

poorer side of the railroad tracks, in a predominately African American community of working-class families who depended on factory work to maintain lower
middle-class status. Michael applied to the Upward Bound program at the urging
of his parents, who felt he could benefit from the encouragement and positive
peer interactions Upward Bound offers. Michael, aged 14, had experienced a number of critical incidents in his family that seemed to shape what his ninth-grade
counselor saw as a "lack of motivation" and "apathy" toward his education and life
aspirations.

Michael earned Cs and sometimes Ds in his high school course work. His high
school performance mirrored his accomplishments in elementary school in that he
earned Cs and an occasional B there. His elementary school teachers described
Michael as "not causing any trouble at all" and did not deem Michael problematic
or exceptionally smart. In elementary school, Michael did not seem to value developing relationships with his classmates and did not have close friends. For recreation, he
spent time with family and watched television.

When he got to eighth grade, however, Michael's parents noticed a change
in him, as did his teachers. He began to get into trouble for talking in class and acting as the class clown. He could recite the latest rap lyrics verbatim and performed
the dance moves from videos during class. Frustrated, his parents tried to intervene by grounding him; however, they could not attend school conferences due
to their work schedules at the factory. Taking off from work meant loss of pay,
and the family could not afford this. Teachers, whose telephone calls were not
returned, assumed that the parents were uninterested in Michael's development.
His parents did send the teachers notes indicating that they were interested but
were unable to attend conferences. The teachers referred Michael to the middle
school counselor, but Michael would not answer her questions beyond one- or
two-syllable answers. As Michael continued his eighth-grade year, the counselor
was unable to determine the reasons for Michael's classroom disruptions. He
continued to get into trouble for this behavior, and he received detention and
in-school suspension throughout the academic year. He progressed to high
school the next year.

I met Michael when I went to the high school to recruit students to enter the
Upward Bound program. The school counselor did not formally encourage students to attend the interest meeting I held to learn about Upward Bound but did
allow access to the students. Although he had not made concrete plans to enter
college, Michael stopped to listen as the meeting began in the student common
area. During Michael's middle school years, he had not discussed career or educational planning. While his father encouraged him to "get a good education,"
neither the family nor the school had made any effort to coordinate making college
attendance a reality. Michael's first efforts to prepare for college involved his application to Upward Bound. After I reviewed his application, I discussed his situation
with my Upward Bound colleagues and we decided to take a risk. Despite his average grades and misbehavior at school, the Upward Bound program admitted
Michael Greene.

Goals and Strategies

Based on the information provided by his ninth-grade counselor and the Upward Bound application, I decided that Michael needed personal counseling to address his academic performance and his behavior at school. Family participation was a requirement of the program, and because we had Saturday meetings, Michael's parents insisted that one of them could attend any meetings that the Upward Bound program had on the weekend.

Prior to the initial meeting with Michael, I had some questions about how he would receive me as his counselor. I am an African American woman, at the time in my midtwenties, and I was not sure how much Michael valued racial issues. I was also concerned about finding a connection with Michael because so many of his teachers were women and I did not know what type of male role models he had. More than anything, I wanted to assist Michael in clarifying his educational goals, and if he wanted to attend college, I wanted to get him on the college preparatory pathway as soon as possible.

Process

Session 1. Michael and his father came to the first session on time. Michael's father is a stern-looking man who seemed a bit surprised to find out that I was Michael's counselor. After reassurances that they were indeed in the right place, I opened the session by sharing with them my background and interest in working for Upward Bound. I told them how I grew up in the heart of Washington, DC, and had always planned to attend college so that I could escape the inner city. I shared that I was a graduate of the university that housed the Upward Bound program and was grateful for the opportunity to work as a counselor. This seemed to ease their tension a bit, and I continued by asking the father, whom I called Mr. Greene, and his son about their expectations of our time together.

Mr. Greene:	Well, I hope you're going to give some pointers to this boy about stayin' out of trouble and minding his teachers. (Michael seemed embarrassed but showed his father respect and courtesy by sitting up straight and maintaining eye contact with the floor.)
Counselor:	Mr. Greene, from my prior interview with Michael, he seems to understand why he gets detention and in-school suspension. Michael, what's it like going to your school?
Michael:	It's all right.
Counselor:	What's all right about it?
Michael:	There's some nice-looking girls there.
Counselor:	(laughs) That is very important to the young men that go to the school. You are now an Upward Bound student too. How is your school going to help you with this? (Michael grew noticeably agitated, as did his father.)
Michael:	I don't think that school will help at all.

As we continued the session, Michael talked about how the successful young people he knew were the ones who had athletic ability, musical talent, or "hustled"—sold drugs. While he knew that these were not options for him, he did not see how he could get into college, because he was only a C student. Michael's father agreed that there were a number of hustlers in the community, but there were also other successful people in the neighborhood who did not resort to crime. Both of them agreed that Michael had not gotten any assistance from his counselor about how to plan for college. His father felt that if Michael had not been acting out, his counselor would have been more willing to assist him with planning for college.

At the end of the first session, I felt that I had gained some important information about Michael. First, it seemed that Michael's father was quite invested in helping his son go to college and had entrusted his educational planning to the school counselors. Michael seemed to respect his father but recognized that his behavior was causing a rift between them—a rift that he did not seem to want. I looked forward to meeting with them again and they agreed that we would continue to meet biweekly over the semester.

Consultation. By Session 3, I felt there were some missing pieces to Michael's case. Although he attended every session of Upward Bound and his family had not missed any counseling sessions, Michael was still very guarded. I decided to consult with the school counselor to see how Michael's behavior had improved in school. Michael turned in his report card, which indicated that his grades had improved slightly from a C− average to a solid C average since he received tutoring at Upward Bound.

School Counselor:	Michael seems to be doing better in his schoolwork since he started Upward Bound. His math grades have improved the most. I really didn't think that he would stick with it.
Upward Bound Counselor:	What are your impressions of Michael?
School Counselor:	He has consistently scored in the lower percentiles on all of his state standardized tests.
Upward Bound Counselor:	Has he ever been referred for testing for a learning disability?
School Counselor:	No, he is on grade level, so he is not eligible for testing. (She spoke in a careful whisper.) We are a Title I[*] school and many of these kids struggle just to make it from day to day. Frankly, I think that you have to understand that not everyone is college material.

I left the consultation with a knot in my stomach. I asked the school counselor for her impressions of Michael and she spoke about test scores and percentile ranks. To be fair, she had a caseload of about 200 students. Nevertheless, I was still

---

[*]Title I schools are schools serving communities with high levels of poverty. The purpose of the federally funded program is to assist these schools in providing opportunities for children to meet state academic standards.

concerned that she could dismiss this young man's future based on test scores and the poverty of the neighborhood. I decided to take a different tack in the next session with Michael and his family.

Telephone Call. To prepare for Session 4, I called Mr. Greene to ask if he and his wife had a time when they both could come to counseling. He indicated that this would be possible on the next Saturday. During previous sessions, the parents had mentioned an aunt who was very interested in Michael and I asked if they minded if she participated. Surprised, the family agreed to ask. Before the end of the day, the family had called back to say that she had agreed. In case he was worried, I assured Michael that all was well and that he was not in trouble. He seemed relieved.

Session 4. My plan for Session 4 involved three goals. First, I wanted to get the family's impression of the school's helpfulness in Michael's education. Second, I wanted to determine what informational resources the family had to prepare for Michael's college preparatory studies (e.g., Did they have a computer at home? How often did Michael go to the library? How much television did he watch every day?) Third, I wanted Michael to tell me what he thought about his teachers, counselor, and school in general.

Counselor:	As I told you, I met with Michael's school counselor to talk with her about Michael's progress in his classes.
Michael:	(visibly agitated) I don't think she is going to help me.
Mr. Greene:	I've told you before, son, your teachers are there to help you. They've got theirs; you've got yours to get!
Counselor:	Mr. Greene, Michael has sounded very frustrated about his school experiences on a number of occasions. I am really interested in hearing him out on this one.
Mr. Greene:	Well, if you think it will help. Go ahead, man.
Michael:	Well, I think those teachers are prejudiced. Have you ever noticed how many Black dudes get suspended or put out? I mean, even when we do what the White kids do, they get in less trouble than we do.
Counselor:	That is a big problem for you.
Michael:	Yeah, it is. I mean, I know that I cut up with that dancing and stuff, but the only ones who get attention are the real smart ones. I am a C student. How am I going to go to a real college with that?
Counselor:	(to the family) What are your perceptions of the race relations at the school? (The family looks hesitant and Mrs. Greene begins.)
Mrs. Greene:	You didn't grow up around here, did you?
Counselor:	No, ma'am, I did not.
Mrs. Greene:	You look a little young.
Counselor:	(feeling a bit flustered) Well, I've been accused of that too. (Everyone laughs.)

Mrs. Greene began to paint a picture of the history of the town and her family that spoke volumes about the problems that Michael was having at the school. The state's budget cuts obscured the personal experiences that characterized the Greene family's survival and existence in their community. Their town reeled from the impact of Jim Crow and desegregation not only in its K–12 educational system but also in housing, salaries, and quality of life for African American citizens. Although Michael did not articulate fully his family's history, his observations of problems in race relations, poverty, and cultural mistrust in his high school seemed rooted in the town's legacy as a profitable enslavement enterprise.

Mrs. Greene, her husband, and Michael's elderly aunt gave me a history lesson that I will never forget. They shared that when enslavement ended in that region, emancipation was not without risk for newly freed African Americans. The profit that White citizens and the state made through enslaved persons' labor had subsidized the region for well over 200 years. I knew from my studies of American history that generations of forced illiteracy and miseducation inhibited African American persons' involvement in a society that valued literacy and mathematical skills. Mr. Greene added that malnutrition, high infant mortality rates, and poverty confronted the freepersons in the region. But I still was not clear what this had to do with Michael, his relationship with the school counselor, or planning for his future.

Mrs. Foster, the elderly aunt, had been quiet until this point. Speaking softly but firmly, she told me that the town's African American populace gradually moved toward relative financial prosperity from the 1890s to the 1960s. Self-directed farming initiatives and skills training led to the establishment of a vibrant African American–owned business center, which I will call Gum Hill. The business center touted grocery stores, a hospital, a dentist, and restaurants established and maintained by African Americans. Mrs. Foster noted with pride that the establishment of African American colleges and universities in the region provided African American teachers and ministers who supported the educational aspirations of community members by teaching African American history, poetry, and literature. One teacher even kept an African drum in the schoolhouse to teach the children about communicating without words.

Silent, I was intrigued by the wealth of knowledge that the family had about the town's history. Michael sat quietly but listened intently as his father became more animated.

Mr. Greene:	About 1965, some of the White town leaders came up with a plan to do us in. They knew that Jim Crow was coming to an end, so they passed some regulations that made it illegal to operate a business in that area without a special permit. None of the businesses could afford the fees, so after a while, the businesses couldn't stay open.
Mrs. Foster:	Without businesses, people couldn't keep up their homes, and finally, some town leaders offered to buy the houses in exchange for some new houses across the street.
Mrs. Greene:	What they didn't say was that those houses were federal projects and people were giving up home ownership to move to government-owned houses.

Mr. Greene: (with sadness and anger in his voice) When I got the word that our restaurant had closed, I left Norfolk State and came home to help out by getting a job. I was a junior.

Mrs. Greene: (to Mr. Greene) When you were on your way home from school, your daddy went out to the back of that restaurant and just sat on an old tree stump. He sat and sat. I know he was crying but he wouldn't let nobody see.

Mrs. Foster: (to me) We lost our best teachers 'cause the White schools wouldn't hire colored ones then. People felt like they had to go to the factories if they wanted to live. Oh, it's honest work all right, but it is hard, backbreaking work that saps your spirit and kills your dreams.

Mr. Greene: Daddy was too old to work in the factory. I don't think Daddy ever got over losing what everyone had worked so hard to keep.

Mrs. Foster: (looking at Mr. Greene) Baby, *you* ain't been right since you left school.

I thanked the family for their input and closed the session by requesting to meet with them again in two weeks. I was exhausted.

I had come to understand the pressures that Michael faced in his education. His father was determined to send his son to college but was still grieving the loss of his opportunities to finish college and, presumably, to take over the family business that had sustained the family's finances for at least two generations. As a man, he wanted to protect his family from instability and injustice, but his father had been unable to protect him and it seemed that he was unsure if he could do so for Michael. Hence, he pushed Michael to perform in school, got frustrated by Michael's lackluster grades, and could not understand why Michael did not see the opportunities that college could give him.

Mrs. Greene, eager to provide emotional support to her husband and son, seemed unsure of how to help her husband grieve the loss of his dreams and watching his father suffer the psychological pain of discrimination. Mrs. Foster, who reminded me of a female African griot,[*] helped me understand that the family had goals and dreams but just needed a road map to get there. The question was whether Michael wanted to participate.

Session 5. I decided that I would meet with Michael the week before I met with the extended family again. I asked Michael how he thought things went in that session. He told me that his family talked a lot and laughed. I told him that family is good for that and thanked him for agreeing to participate. I spent part of the session asking Michael about what he wanted to do about school, because it seemed that his family had many hopes for him. He indicated that he did want to go to college, but he felt attracted to the material things that some of his peers had, like expensive shoes, cars, and jewelry.

---

[*]In West African societies, the griot is a revered elder who serves the community by preserving genealogies and history through oral tradition.

Michael was smart enough to observe that many of those "guys" had been locked up or gotten hurt or killed. We talked about how rap videos had pretty women who seemed to like the "flashy dudes." Admittedly, I do not like rap, but in my spare time, I forced myself to watch Black Entertainment Television (BET) to see what images "entertained" my students. I asked Michael if I could listen to his CD player with him. We listened to the latest rap songs, and even though he commented frequently about how uncool I was, he explained the lyrics to me. He seemed surprised that I did not put him down even though I did not care for the angry words. Listening to the words did help me grasp why many of my African American male students seemed so angry and frustrated: The lyrics expressed emotions that Michael could not share.

After the next few sessions, Michael seemed to warm to the idea of choosing his own career path. As a part of counseling, he completed an instrument (Terrell & Terrell, 1981) measuring how important matters of race were to him. The scale indicated that Michael valued racial identity very much and was strongly oriented toward learning about African American history and culture. Now, it was understandable why Michael felt that his counselor did not care about him. He told me that when the Awareness of Black Culture club at his school tried to arrange a meeting about getting an African American–history course at the school, some faculty members, including his counselor, told the student group, "We are color-blind and we don't care about color." Disappointed, Michael said that he wished his teachers would pay attention to him and that his color is who he is. "If they don't see color, they can't see me, can they?"

I also administered a career interest inventory to Michael, which indicated that he had a strong interest in music production and recording. I sent Michael to O*NET (U.S. Department of Labor, n.d.) to discover how to accomplish this, and he was surprised to discover that many of the rap producers had been to college and had degrees in business, economics, or production. Michael found out that there was a highly regarded music production program at one of the state universities. Armed with new information about himself and the career world, Michael got in less trouble at school and utilized his time in Upward Bound to read books about African American history.

We stopped meeting for formal counseling after six sessions, but I assigned readings to Michael dealing with the rites of passage for African American males. I started with Malcolm X's (1965) speech entitled "To Mississippi Youth" and sections of Richard Wright's (1940) *Native Son*. Michael completed the Upward Bound program on schedule and attended the state university the fall after he graduated from high school.

■ Results

When he entered Upward Bound, Michael was not convinced that he wanted to attend college. He did want to please his parents, especially his father, whom he respected and admired for his hard work and care for the family. Accepting Michael into Upward Bound was a risk because he did not fit the traditional criteria of a college-bound student. He was enrolled in a general studies high school curriculum and his academic accomplishments were average. Michael's school counselor did not see beyond his test scores or his behavior in class or into and beyond his color and culture. Admittedly, it is easy to understand how the lack of human and financial resources frustrated her. Michael's high school operated in one of the poorest school districts in the region; it had the dubious distinction of having the highest dropout rate in the state.

▮ Personal Reflection

Meeting with Michael's family was helpful in letting him know that I valued his resources, and it demonstrated to the family that I considered their input vital to assisting Michael. Assigning the readings to Michael also positively shaped his self-image. I enjoyed learning about the music that was so important to him.

In hindsight, it would have been beneficial to go back to the counseling staff of the school and offer some type of in-service training on working with African American children and their families. I felt embarrassed that I had not stood up for Michael with the counselor. Mrs. Foster reminded me of my elderly aunt who always encouraged me to "Never forget who you belongs to, even if ev'rybody 'round you don't know." My aunt meant that I came from hardworking, honest stock and that even if others did not appreciate the family's accomplishments, they remained accomplishments anyway.

I had underestimated the isolation I felt as the only African American educational professional in the schools I visited. One time, a staff member who either did not see or ignored my identification badge asked me if I was ready to escort my son off school property after his outburst. I told her that the young man was not my son, and she apologized. Then she proceeded to ask me to step in the other room while she retrieved another African American young man who had also gotten into trouble. I showed her my badge and she said, "Oh, I see." She laughed and walked away. I had no idea what those young men had done, but I was sure that I felt sad for them and for me. I was not quite sure why.

Michael will be successful as long as he continues to use his family as a support network. We planned how he could build a college support system prior to his attendance. The university had an African American cultural center and Michael obtained a male upperclassman as a mentor. They exchanged letters during the summer, and Michael reported on his breaks from school that making the contact helped him deal with homesickness better than if he had been alone.

One song that Michael and I listened to was entitled "I Believe I Can Fly" (Kelly, 1996). This beautiful song tells of dreams and courage and achievement. It had profound meaning for Michael and me.

Michael came to see himself as a young man with a future and a purpose. Counseling started Michael's transformation from a young man unsure of his talents and abilities to a young man who claimed the dreams of his ancestors and father as his own.

References

Kelly, R. (1996). I believe I can fly. On *SpaceJam soundtrack* [CD]. New York: Zomba Recording Corporation.

Malcolm X. (1989). To Mississippi Youth. In B. Perry, *Malcolm X: The last speeches*. New York: Pathfinder. (Speech delivered December 31, 1964)

Terrell, F., & Terrell, S. (1981). An inventory to measure cultural mistrust among Blacks. *Western Journal of Black Studies, 5,* 180–185.

Upward Bound. (n.d.). *Purpose.* Retrieved August 16, 2004, from http://www.ed.gov/
    programs/trioupbound/index.html

U.S. Department of Labor. (n.d.). O*NET can be found at http://www.doleta.gov/
    programs/onet/.

Wright, R. (1940). *Native son.* New York: Harper & Brothers.

Suggested Readings

Coker, A., & Bryant, R. (2003). Counseling African Americans: Understanding racial
    tasks and cultural values. *American Association of Behavioral and Social
    Sciences-AABSS Journal, 7*(18).

Delpit, L. (1996). *Other people's children: Cultural conflict in the classroom.*
    New York: New Press.

Ladson-Billings, G. (1997). *The dreamkeepers: Successful teachers of African American
    children.* San Francisco, CA: Jossey-Bass.

Tatum, B. D. (1997). *Why are all the Black kids sitting together in the cafeteria? And
    other conversations about race: A psychologist explains the development of
    racial identity.* New York: Basic Books.

Biographical Statement

Rhonda M. Bryant, PhD, NCC, NCSC, is a counselor educator at Albany State
University. She has worked as a school counselor and counseled young adults in a variety
of other settings, including Upward Bound, Job Corps, and community centers. She has
been a counselor since 1988. You can reach her at rhonda.bryant@asurams.edu.

18

The Hidden Issue

Neal Gray

Neal Gray's client, 16-year-old Joe, discloses that his father is an alcoholic and that his parents are getting a divorce. These serious family problems contribute to Joe's declining grades in school. When Gray discovers that Joe, himself, is on the road to alcoholism, he makes a referral for substance abuse counseling. For a successful referral to occur, the school counselor must first build rapport with the child and engage the child's parent. Gray, who has had previous experience in counseling substance abusers, says, "I would hear persons in recovery talk about points in childhood or adolescence where they reached out for help but no one was there for them. I remembered those stories when I was working with Joe."

My caseload consisted of approximately 200 students in the eighth and tenth grades. My duties included individual and group counseling, academic advising, and group guidance. Administrative duties accounted for 10% to 15% of my time at the school.

The School

The school I worked in was a private middle and high school in a large city in the southern United States. There were 800 students, predominately middle class, 60% male and 40% female. Caucasians accounted for 65% of the student population, and 35% was African American. There were four counselors, each having a caseload of 200 to 300 students.

Student Need

The student's name is Joe, a 16-year-old Caucasian male in the tenth grade. I was walking down the hall between classes and Joe stopped me and asked to talk. I asked him if he wanted me to get him out of his next class, and he said, "No, it isn't that important. I'll come up at lunch tomorrow."

Prior to the above interchange, I had been Joe's counselor for two years and had established fairly good rapport. Five times during his freshman year, Joe had come to see me about an issue he was having with his parents, who were going through a divorce. Joe reported that his father went on drinking binges for three to four days and the family would not hear from him until he ran out of money or phoned from jail. Joe's grades had dropped. He told me he couldn't concentrate in class because he was worrying about his family, particularly his mother and his younger sister.

During our third meeting, Joe asked about counseling not just for him but for the whole family. I asked him to have his mother call, and she did, the very next day. Joe's mother, Stephanie Smith, disclosed that she and her husband were finalizing the divorce. She informed me that her husband hid his alcohol use from her until the third year of their marriage, when he was picked up for drinking and driving. She said that since that incident, over the course of the past 10 years, his drinking had gotten out of control. Mrs. Smith told me that she had tried a family intervention three years ago, but her husband was resistant and got drunk later that same night. She said that he was currently living in a car. I told her that Joe had spoken to me about counseling for the family, and she was also very open to family counseling. After counseling began, I checked in with Joe two more times that year and contacted the counselor twice (after receiving a release of information from the mom), and things seemed to be better. Though I didn't know it at the time, Joe, himself, was also dealing with the beginnings of a potentially serious substance abuse problem.

■ Goals and Strategies

I believed that a referral for Joe to receive substance abuse counseling was necessary. While I have significant substance abuse counseling training and experience, I didn't have the time to provide treatment in my role as a school counselor. My goal was to find a counselor with experience in treating substance abuse in teenagers and family counseling.

■ Process

<u>Session 1.</u> The day after I saw him in the hall, Joe came to my office during his lunch period. He seemed anxious and immediately sat down on my couch and said, "I don't know what to do."

In most of my previous meetings with Joe, he joked around initially and it took a while for him to open up and discuss what was troubling him, but this time, he got right to it. I asked him what was going on, and he told me that he was feeling guilty about "letting his mother down over the weekend." I asked him to clarify what he meant by "letting her down."

Joe replied that on Friday night, he had come home extremely drunk, 2 hours past his curfew. He said, "Since my dad left, I have needed to take care of my mom and my little sister. I feel like I really let her down. Saturday morning she was crying and she told me that she and my little sister were very worried and that she didn't sleep. She has never been this hurt and upset with me. Mr. Gray, I want you to tell me how to get her trust back. What can I do? I promised her I will never drink again."

I remembered our discussion from the previous year about his father's drinking. I asked Joe to tell me more about what happened on Friday night. He had gone to a party at a senior's house with two students from another school. He said he was excited about the party and just wanted to unwind because it had been exam week at school. He drank one beer casually during the first half hour. Then, someone gave him a shot of whiskey. "Mr. Gray, this really loosened me up. After this, I wanted to party."

From 8 P.M. until midnight, he drank 10 more beers. Binge drinking is defined as consuming five or more drinks in one sitting! Now I was very concerned, particularly about Joe's tolerance level, as he was approximately 5 ft 7 in and could not have weighed over 125 pounds. Joe could have died from alcohol poisoning from drinking this much alcohol.

I asked Joe if he passed out or got sick from the alcohol. He said, "I remember leaving the party and feeling very sick. I drink every weekend, but it's usually only a few beers a night." He did not remember how he got home. It appeared to me that he had experienced a blackout.

He said, "When I got home, I went into the bathroom and that's all I can remember, and then the next day I woke up in my bed feeling worse than when I broke my leg skateboarding."

I asked if he had ever come home drunk before. He replied, "Yeah, but not wasted. You know, just a head buzz."

I asked, "What is a head buzz to you?"

"Two to three beers," Joe replied.

I asked if he was talking about 12-oz beers, to which he replied, "No, twenty-ounce beers." I was becoming alarmed about these red flags.

I asked Joe at what age he took his first drink, and he answered that it was when he was 11. This was another serious indicator. He followed this up by telling me that at the ages of 11 and 12, he mostly snuck beers and whiskey that his father had left in his car, where his father hid them. He would fill up the whiskey bottles with water to make it look like he had not taken any. Recently, he had made some new friends, and they would sneak into one of their parents' liquor cabinets or have an older brother buy alcohol for them. He said that before this current incident, he was drinking seven to eight beers each weekend.

I asked Joe if he did anything else besides drinking. He replied that he had smoked marijuana twice but that he didn't like the way it made him feel. I then asked him about ecstasy, heroin, cocaine, and speed, to all of which he said, "No way." I asked Joe if he drank in the morning, to which he responded with an emphatic "No." Next, I asked him about his peers' usage. He responded that his friends at school didn't use, but that most of his friends in his neighborhood, whom he hung out with on weekends, did.

Then I asked, "Who do you think is someone who has a drinking problem? What would he or she look like?"

Joe commented, "My dad," and then elaborated by saying, "A drunk is someone you see passed out, living on the streets, with a bottle of whiskey in their hand and asking for money."

I asked him if he thought his dad had a problem, to which he replied, "Yes."

I then asked Joe, "Do you think you have a problem?"

He said, "No. I am just doing what my friends do." He then contradicted himself by saying that the way his mom responded to him the last weekend bothered him.

I asked him if he had ever tried to quit, to which he responded, "Yes. I got really drunk after the first football game and was sick for three days and I decided to quit for three weeks."

I asked, "How did that go?" and he said, "No problem."

Then I asked, "Why did you start drinking again?"

"At a party one night, a couple of my friends were making fun of me because I was the only person at the party without a drink. I felt foolish because I was talking to a girl I liked, so I told him to get me a beer. But after that game, until this weekend, I really tried to slow down and not get drunk, and that's been over two months. I don't know what happened over the weekend."

After a few moments, he stated, "Mr. Gray, I will never drink again. My mom said she found me passed out in my underwear next to the toilet and put me into bed. She said that she thought about taking me to the emergency room but that after I was in bed a while I seemed better. She was so scared, she watched me all night. And then, the next day, the way she cried. I can't believe I did that to her. What can I say or do? I wish it never would've happened. I never meant to drink like that, but sometimes, once I start partying and having a good time, especially if whiskey is involved, I can't stop."

Then, Joe said, "I'll do anything, Mr. Gray. What can I do?"

I sat in silence for about 30 seconds, thinking about how I was going to tell him that I wanted to meet with his mother. I could not come up with any magical words, so I simply said, "Joe, I'd like for your mom to come in and the three of us talk about the situation." I assumed that he would become defensive, but he nodded his head in agreement and said, "I will do whatever it takes."

I thought about having him call his mother from my office or calling her with him present, but I knew he had a test review in his biology class, in which he was doing poorly. I sent him back to class, and as I had talked with Mrs. Smith last year, I felt fairly comfortable in calling her even under the circumstances.

Case Consultation. I saw this as an emergency and I cleared my calendar for the rest of the day, including my group guidance activity with two classes. The first thing I did was to call Ann, the head of guidance at our school. She had over 20 years of experience in schools. Ann had also been Joe's counselor in the eighth grade. At our school, at the end of every academic year, the four counselors meet and transfer case notes to their students' new counselors for the next year. Ann was just finishing a session with a senior and she told me to come to her office. I told her about Joe's weekend binge and his alcohol use. Because Ann had not been Joe's counselor in three years, she wanted to see a picture of him to jog her memory. We found his photo in the yearbook and she remembered him immediately. Ann reviewed her case notes. Joe had seen her about scheduling and a problem he was having with a female class-mate. He did not talk to her about any problems with his parents or substance use.

Ann asked me what I thought needed to be done. I replied that I would like Joe to see a counselor with a background in substance abuse counseling and family counseling. Ann had a list of mental health professionals who worked well with adolescents and had a reputation of involving the school counselor in the process. We narrowed the list to three counselors, taking into consideration that Joe's mother might want to use someone from her insurance company's provider list instead of any of the three we had chosen. My next step was to call Mrs. Smith.

Phone Call. I phoned Mrs. Smith at work. Even while we exchanged greetings, I could sense the worry in her voice. "Mrs. Smith, I spoke with Joe today, and he told me about this weekend and I am very concerned."

She replied, "Thank you, Mr. Gray. I am too. I spoke with two friends of mine with children now in college and they told me it wasn't any big deal, just kids' stuff. But I thought he might die. You know, his dad has struggled with alcoholism ever since I knew him and my brother and father are alcoholics."

I asked her, "How was it before this incident?"

She said, "Ever since his dad left the home, or I made him leave, as he says, last year, Joe has been keeping a lot of things inside. At times, I feel he is too protective of me and his sister. He is so kind and considerate. I don't want him to throw his life away."

I asked, "How did things go with that counselor you went to last year after your husband left?" She replied, "Well, he was good. We went to see him a couple of times, but I thought the kids were doing well and with my husband's financial problems, it was hard just on my salary, but I am willing to go back. What do you think?"

Very bluntly, I told Mrs. Smith that I would like Joe to see someone with training in chemical dependency counseling. "I have some names of persons who have worked well with our students, or I could look over your provider list and see if there is anyone on that list that we have used at the school who is good with adolescents. How is your money situation?"

She replied, "Mr. Gray, my financial situation has improved. Let me know who you would recommend."

"If possible, Mrs. Smith, I would like for you to come to my office. We'll meet with Joe and discuss the steps we have just talked about. Then, we can talk in detail about your options in obtaining a counselor. Can you come in today?"

She replied, "Today is good. I am picking up Joe from school anyway."

Session 2. I went to Joe's classroom and asked his teacher if he could step out into the hall to speak with me. In the hall, I told Joe that I had spoken to his mother and that he needed to come to my office when the bell rang. He agreed and asked, "How is she?" to which I replied, "She is very concerned."

Joe sat on the couch across from his mother, who sat in a folding chair next to me. I began by summarizing the day's events and asked the two of them what they would like to say.

Mrs. Smith's eyes were watering and her face was red. She began, "Joe, I am very concerned. You know how much I love you, but you are a different person when you drink. I talked to Mr. Gray earlier and I would like for all of us to go back to counseling, but I would like for you to see someone who has some experience working with drugs and alcohol."

Joe responded, "I won't do it again. I have learned my lesson."

His mother said, "Joe, I know how sorry you are, but I don't want you to have the same problems my dad and your dad have. Joe, for the past four weekends, I haven't been able to sleep on Friday nights when you have been out. I know I grounded you, but it's more than that. You need help."

After a long silence, I asked Joe, "Are you willing to give this a try?" He did not make eye contact with his mother or me but nodded slightly and said, "Yeah." I sensed that for now, his guilt and concern over hurting his mother were the reasons for his acceptance of help. His understanding of the real issue would come later.

Mrs. Smith went over to Joe and hugged him. Joe said, "I've let you down. I need to be the man around the house." His eyes were watering and he was shaking his head.

After embracing him for several minutes, Mrs. Smith talked about the past year, "We are still healing and this is one more step. It's not just you. The three of us need someone to talk to. Joe, you and your sister are the most important things in my life. We are going to make it."

Mrs. Smith asked Joe to go down to his biology teacher's office to talk about tomorrow's test, and then she and I discussed finding a counselor. I provided Mrs. Smith with the three names. She chose an LPC who was conveniently located.

I called and made an appointment for that Friday after school. She signed a release of information for me to talk with the counselor. I believe communication between a school counselor and a private counselor can benefit treatment.

I was very tired. It was already 3 o'clock. I had spent the majority of the day focused on this case. Looking back, I felt the meetings had been very fruitful. I hadn't wanted this issue to rest for even a day. I had wanted to use Joe's guilt as a motivator for treatment, and it had worked.

Session 3. Monday, I sent a guidance pass to Joe's gym teacher so that I could talk to him about his first session with the private counselor. He jokingly fussed with me, asking why I did not get him out of geometry or biology.

First, I asked Joe how his weekend had been, and he responded that it had been good and that he stayed in with his mother and little sister all weekend. Next, I asked him how his session with the counselor had gone. He said that he liked him and that it had gone well. He said both he and his mother met initially with the counselor for about 15 minutes, and then Joe met privately with him for about 45 minutes. I asked him if he thought that he would go back to the counselor, and he said that he had an appointment for this coming Friday.

Jokingly, he complained that the counselor gave him homework. Joe was supposed to write down reasons to continue drinking and reasons to think about quitting. He said the man was very nice and didn't judge him. Joe noted that he talked to him for about 10 minutes about skateboarding and music, and he seemed to really think some of the tricks Joe could do on his skateboard were really cool.

Joe ended the session by saying, "My mom told me to tell you that she was going to call you either later today or tomorrow."

Session 4. Early the next morning, Mrs. Smith came to see me. She said that she liked the counselor even though she had met with him for only about 15 to 20 minutes. "It was good to get things out in the open."

She said, "This Friday, I am going to meet with the counselor alone after Joe's appointment. I have a lot I need to talk about. I feel like the last 14 years, I have been trying to keep peace with my husband and take care of my kids. I don't know who I am anymore. The counselor said we would discuss the possibility of seeing me individually or referring me to another counselor. Once this gets going, the next step may be my daughter. He gave me some numbers for support groups for families of alcoholics. I attended a meeting with a friend at work five years ago, but I had so much going on at home, taking care of myself was the last thing I had time for. The counselor also talked to Joe about some teen Alcoholics Anonymous meetings. Joe seemed pretty resistant. I don't think he believes he has a problem at all."

I said, "It may not be a short road but I always feel much more encouraged when I am dealing with a supportive family situation, as we have here. When parents who suspect or even know for sure their child has a problem do nothing about it, it only makes things worse in the long run."

Mrs. Smith thanked me and asked a few questions about graduation requirements and Joe's electives for his junior year. We said our good-byes and I reiterated
that if she needed anything, she could call me, and that I would call the counselor
that day.

Phone Call to the Private Counselor. The counselor assured me that Mrs. Smith and
Joe had signed release of information documents. Of course, I had also obtained these
releases. "Mr. Gray, most of the time was spent developing rapport. That is usually the
biggest part of my first session with adolescents. I work from a reality therapy–oriented
approach. My goal is to see what Joe wants, and then ask him if his actions are helping
him get what he wants. After having him evaluate how his actions and what he wants
are not matching, we will make a plan. At the end of our last session, I asked him to
make a list of negative consequences associated with alcohol and I also asked him
to write about the positives of usage. After finishing up a chemical dependency
assessment, I am going to provide him with education about alcoholism and chemical
dependency. If Joe commits to treatment and an alcohol-free lifestyle, we will work on
developing coping skills that will achieve this."

I shared my information about red flags and academic problems. "At our school,
the students take four classes a semester, and currently Joe has three Ds and a C in
physical education. In both the eighth and ninth grades, Joe was a B student. I can
send progress reports to his teachers and give them to you if you would like. He has
never been a discipline problem."

He asked me about Joe's attendance.

"He's missed six days this year. The limit is ten. Last year he had eight absences."

He then asked about his peer group, and I said, "Joe told me that most of his
friends who use alcohol are from his neighborhood, but here at school, I haven't noticed
him hanging out with the drug-and-alcohol crowd. Of course, I don't know everything
that's going on."

He asked about learning disabilities, and I let him know that Joe didn't have a
learning disability and that he had average scores in math and reading.

We agreed to be in touch with each other about the case every other week. I was
glad about this because sometimes I never hear from the outside practitioner. I told
him that for the next few weeks, I would try and see Joe weekly, though it would be
hard with the large numbers of students in my case load.

■ Results

I consider this case a success in that the student felt comfortable coming to talk to me,
facilitating identification of the core issue. Although it appeared that his goal was to
relieve some feelings of guilt, his openness and our relationship made me aware of
the deeper substance abuse problem. Although I believe he did not fully realize that
he had a substance abuse problem, I was able to support his mother's concerns and
provide a channel for help. I really don't know how this case will turn out. Of course,
I hope that Joe will eventually see how dangerous alcoholism can be. I saw my intervention as a seed-sowing process.

■ Personal Reflection

I believe my training and experience as a substance abuse counselor were beneficial. While counseling adults, I would hear persons in recovery talk about points in childhood or adolescence where they reached out for help but no one was there for them. I remembered those stories when I was working with Joe. I wanted to be there for him. I hope that Joe won't have to hit rock bottom. In hindsight, I wish I would have discussed broader topics in my three meetings with Joe earlier, during his freshman year. He was always very open and I believe I could have reached him that much sooner.

Suggested Readings

Hogan, J. A., Gabrielsen, K. R., Luna, N., & Grothaus, D. (2003). *Substance abuse prevention: The intersection of science and practice.* Boston: Allyn and Bacon.
Lewis, J. A. (1994). *Addictions: Concepts and strategies for treatment.* Gaithersburg, MD: Aspen Press.
Stevens, P., & Smith, R. L. (2004). *Substance abuse counseling: Theory and practice* (3rd ed). Upper Saddle River, NJ: Merrill/Prentice Hall.

Biographical Statement

Neal D. Gray, PhD, LPCC, is an assistant professor in the Department of Education, Division of Counseling and Educational Leadership, at Eastern Kentucky University (EKU) in Richmond, Kentucky. He came to EKU in 2002, after spending two years as a middle school and high school counselor in New Orleans, Louisiana. Prior to this, Neal was a mental health and substance abuse counselor in Cincinnati, Ohio. You can reach Neal at neal.gray@eku.edu.

19

Implementing a Career Guidance and Educational Planning Program at the High School Level

Brenda Jones

High school counselors are charged with helping students set educational and career goals and guiding them through the implementation of goal-related plans. Brenda Jones describes the way that a high school counseling staff provides developmental guidance to all 3,000 students in her school. Jones provides sufficient detail for counselors to replicate the actual guidance units for each grade level.

*O*ne aim of the staff of Sandra Day O'Connor High School is to create an environment that promotes achievement and provides a sense of belonging for each student. I regard our school's counselors as true professionals who go beyond the call of duty. The following is a detailed description of our guidance program as it relates to career and educational planning.

The School

Sandra Day O'Connor High School is located in Helotes, just outside of San Antonio, in the heart of the Texas Hill Country. It was opened and dedicated in the fall of 1998 and is one of seven large, comprehensive high schools operated under the auspices of the Northside Independent School District in San Antonio. The district has a population of over 70,000 students.

O'Connor is a four-year public high school and is a member of the College Board. It is accredited by the Texas Education Agency and has been designated by the agency as a Recognized School in Texas. O'Connor is an academically oriented school in which the curriculum is innovative and progressive. It is a school where a full range of rigorous academic and career and technology exposure is strongly encouraged. A goal of the school is to produce effective leaders of the 21st century by allowing students to sample various forms of technology. Equipped with over 700 fully networked multimedia computers, O'Connor is one of the most technologically advanced high schools in the San Antonio area. Special programs, support services, and classes are also available for students with special needs and varying learning abilities. The school features a fully computerized, technologically advanced media center that is the hub of the school and an agriculture center consisting of technology labs, shops, classrooms, and a greenhouse.

The school year is divided into two semesters. Each day is composed of seven 50-minute periods, allowing students to earn up to seven credits each school year. Entering freshmen, starting with the class of 2005, are required to complete the 24-credit state "Recommended Graduation Program" and pass all sections of the Texas Assessment of Knowledge and Skills (TAKS)—the state's student proficiency test. The total student enrollment is approximately 3,100, with a total faculty and staff of approximately 240. The socioeconomic status of the school is such that less than 10% are economically disadvantaged. The racial and ethnic makeup of the school is as follows: 58.5% White, 33.3% Hispanic, 5.7% Black, 2.1% Asian or Pacific Islanders, and .3% Native American.

The Guidance Staff

The Career Center, which is manned by a full-time technician, is an on-campus facility in the guidance department that serves students, parents, staff, and the community with many valuable services. One primary goal we have is to empower our students to successfully transition from the high school to postsecondary settings. Through the Career Center, students are able to explore postsecondary education and training options and possible career choices.

Our counseling staff includes 10 well-qualified counselors. They are active in professional organizations and attend and/or present professional growth workshop sessions at the local, state, and national levels. Students are assigned alphabetically to seven comprehensive counselors who work with a caseload of 400 students each. Three specialty counselors—a counselor for students in special education, a part-time SDFSCC, and a head counselor—are also on board.

The counselor assigned to students with special needs has a caseload of approximately 150 students. These students are considered the most needy special education students. These are students whose primary handicapping condition is emotional disturbance and those who will graduate by decision of the "Admission Review and Dismissal Committee"—Texas's name for the group responsible for special education students' development and implementation of their individualized education plans. The goal of the decreased caseload is to allow the special needs counselor more time to do consultation and small group counseling with students in his assigned caseload. All other special education students not in the two categories mentioned are assigned to the comprehensive counselors.

Students refer themselves or are referred to the SDFSCC by their parents, teachers, administrators, counselors, or other students. She provides individual and small group counseling services to students exploring or recovering from use of illegal substances or who are living in substance abusing environments. She also provides in-service training to counselors about such work.

I, as the head counselor, am the program manager and am not assigned a student caseload, although I do provide direct guidance and counseling to students as well. The primary role of the head counselor is to ensure that guidance activities are in alignment with district guidelines and to ensure that program activities are implemented properly and in a timely manner. Other responsibilities include providing professionally relevant supervision and leadership to the counselors and assisting the principal to meet campus objectives. Parental involvement is seen as crucial and is encouraged and welcomed. My goals as program manager are: (a) to enable counselors to be visible and proactive in the delivery of services to students, parents, teachers, administrators and the community; (b) to provide a means for parental involvement in guidance activities; and (c) to minimize nonguidance activities so that counselors may be readily accessible to students.

For a campus program to be successful, several factors must be in place. There must be strong support from the administrative staff, teachers, and parents. The unique talent and ability that each counselor brings to the staff must be utilized in such a manner that services are extended to a greater segment of the student population. In other words, even though each counselor is assigned an alphabetical caseload based on students' last names, I believe counselors with strong expertise in certain areas should be allowed to work with students in small group sessions or other special settings to extend their services to all students, including those outside their assigned caseload. This greatly eliminates duplication of efforts.

Four paraprofessionals are assigned to the department. A full-time secretary serves as the office manager. She also copies group and classroom guidance handouts for counselors to use with students. Our registrar assists the counselors in evaluating transcripts. He updates student files, obtains official records from students' previous schools and sends records to other high schools, colleges, and special programs. A grade-reporting secretary assists with data entry. A Career Center technician disseminates numerous materials and forms to students, which are explained by counselors in group/classroom guidance sessions—these are detailed later. From time to time, all of these individuals assist in the standardized testing program (e.g., counting test booklets, sorting of test materials for dissemination and interpretation).

As head counselor, I perform many duties that also allow students more access to counselors. I train and mentor all counselors new to our school. I sometimes see students and parents in the absence of a counselor. I frequently organize parent volunteers to copy, collate, staple, file, and alphabetize guidance material. Parent volunteers and/or the guidance paraprofessionals prepare all of our mail-outs. I edit, with all counselors' input, and prepare for printing all guidance material (senior, junior, and sophomore guidebooks; preregistration and parent-night program handouts, etc.) so that counselors assigned to students are not strapped with this time-consuming responsibility. I also serve as the building test coordinator and work with teachers on organizing, preparing, and communicating test logistics for all standardized tests given.

■ The Guidance Program

To ensure that the guidance program is responsive to the individual students' and the community's needs, careful program development, monitoring, evaluation, and redirection occur on an ongoing basis. Evaluation instruments are developed and used at the end of each guidance activity. The results of the evaluations dictate changes in the delivery of the guidance services. At the end of each school year, all counselors participate in a planning session for the upcoming year. The calendar for the year is evaluated for effectiveness in implementation and appropriateness of content. Departmental and professional development goals are also evaluated for levels of accomplishment and anticipated student outcomes. The students evaluate counseling groups at the end of the sessions for effectiveness and participation. An annual calendar is then compiled for the upcoming year listing those activities that were effective and needed. Other items are deleted or added depending on student needs. Goals and strategies are developed from all of the above sources.

In addition to the activities described below, counselors participate in the delivery of other guidance services. In the guidance curriculum component of the comprehensive guidance program (Gysbers & Henderson, 2000), activities such as orientations to cooperative work-study programs and safe and drug-free lessons are presented. O'Connor High School's counselors' time is consumed mostly in the individual planning and responsive services components, doing both individual and small group counseling. The series of guidance activities described below fit into the individual planning component. Other individual planning activities include the following: career day/volunteer fair, prep days, open house, service academy/ROTC scholarship brown-bag sessions, test interpretation, local community college orientations and registration, summer school, night school, correspondence and credit by exam programs, dual credit informational sessions, new student groups, and career exploration sessions. Every other year, Breaking Away, an evening program designed to assist parents and students in making successful transitions from high school to college, is also presented.

Efforts are made to ensure that all students are exposed to the same types of general guidance information. Information is presented to students in age- and grade-appropriate formats. Special education students have the same access to guidance services and activities as regular education students do. In all grade-level unit topics, counselors are available to see students and parents in individualized sessions to address additional concerns that might come up after the sessions.

In the responsive services component, counselors provide the following counseling groups: families in transition/changing families, alternative education placement/transitioning back to campus, girls/boys in crisis, Unity Club, anger management, conflict resolution, new student, grief and loss support, and career exploration. Consultation services to outside agencies and to other on-campus programs, such as "504" and special education, are also provided.

Efforts are made to communicate guidance activities to parents, students, faculty and staff through the newsletter of the Parent, Teacher, Student Association (PTSA), "The Panther Track," mail-outs, the O'Connor High School Web page (www.nisd.net/oconnor), classroom guidance materials, individual conferences, Parent Preview Night (which gives parents a chance to preview guidance materials), parent-night programs, the Career Center, and large group guidance sessions (i.e., grade level conferences). Evening workshops are provided to parents based on annual needs assessments done by our Parent Teacher Association. The calendar of guidance activities is also disseminated to teachers at the first faculty meeting on the teachers' return from summer break. I also strive to maintain constant, updated communication with my staff. I attend monthly head counselors', campus department coordinators', and the school advisory committee meetings as well as weekly campus administrators' meetings, and communicate campus, departmental, and district guidelines and policies to counselors in our weekly staff meetings. I also conduct periodic staff meetings with the guidance paraprofessionals regarding monthly guidance activities and the roles that they play in the carrying out of these activities.

Student Need

The vision of our department is that counselors are a part of an energized force to provide appropriate behavioral and educational support for students in need. We are led by goals (departmental and individual) and professional development plans. Both the goals and the growth plans are affected by community influences and societal changes. Both generate identifiable student needs.

When O'Connor first opened a few years ago, counselors met with all students through their English classes. The role of the counselor, counseling services, and how to access those services were explained to students. Each year thereafter, counselors have greeted incoming freshmen through World Geography classes—required of all ninth graders—and have given that same information. In addition to this information, the Counseling Support Group Referral Form is explained and left in the classroom for interested students to pick up, complete, and return to the appropriate counselor. (The referral form is printed on page x.) Copies of this same form can be picked up in the counseling office by parents so that they, too, can make referrals. This referral process is shared with members of the faculty and staff, who also make referrals. The needs of our students are partially determined by feedback from these referrals. Another way student needs are determined is from the Request to See Counselor Form. (This form is printed on page x.) The needs most often expressed by students and their parents are: getting help to succeed academically; exploring career options; exploring college entrance information (2- and 4-year colleges, trade/technical schools); dealing with stress; dropping out of school; obtaining information on NCAA rules for high school athletes transitioning to college; military enlistment, academies, and ROTC scholarships; goal setting/making plans; understanding graduation requirements; getting involved in clubs and organizations; volunteerism and community service (to build good resumes); making good decisions; improving study/organizational/time-management skills.

■ Goals and Strategies

As mentioned earlier, a primary goal of the guidance program is to empower our students to successfully transition from middle school into high school and from the high school to postsecondary settings. A standard, sequential program for educational and career planning is offered. The counselors and the Career Center technician provide sessions in which the language and topics are adjusted to meet the needs of different groups. Groups differ by age and grade and by levels of academic achievement. Counselors provide a series of activities appropriate for each grade level that focus on self-assessment, evaluation, decision making, career awareness, and exploration of post–high school educational and training opportunities. The head counselor is an active participant in the teaching of guidance lessons. Special materials and testing information are provided to students with special needs and their parents by the guidance and special education departments. Related individual counseling is made available, and parental involvement is invited.

Students are encouraged to start early with personal career exploration. Even students who are still very undecided about their career choices benefit from this exploration. By starting early, students are better able to enroll in high school courses that are consistent with their career choices. Students learn flexibility by having several options to consider as they prepare for the ever-changing adult world.

The ACT DISCOVER program is the career guidance tool that we use. It has four "Halls" for students to explore. Hall 1 enables students to learn about themselves and careers. They can explore their interests and find out about their abilities and values as they relate to career choices. Hall 2 allows students to choose occupations by exploring various inventories, the World of Work map (ACT, Inc.), and job characteristics. Hall 3 allows students to plan for their post–high school education. Students can find majors aligned with occupations to consider. Students may also find schools aligned by certain characteristics to explore. Hall 4 enables students to plan for work. Students have the option to explore topics such as earning and learning through apprenticeships, internships, and military opportunities or to define ideal jobs by values. Students can prepare for job searches and job interviews.

There are four folders (sections) in the district-provided portfolios that students develop. The first folder is on education and career planning. Students update their Graduation Status Report, which tracks their progress toward graduation. Spaces for preemployment experiences, honors, awards, work experiences, volunteering, planning future goals, and a career skills checklist are provided for student updates. The second folder has spaces for students to list and update skills employers want, detailing which skills they have already acquired and which skills they need. The third folder is for personal information. Students may keep copies of their birth certificates, social security cards, certificates and awards, test scores, school activities, calendar information, class schedules, report cards, and so forth in this folder. The fourth folder has employability information such as resumes, samples of job applications, a listing of work and volunteer history, a list of school and community activities, letters of recommendations, transcripts, et cetera.

Teachers encourage students to utilize the Career Center to conduct research on possible careers to integrate the high school disciplines with career and college exploration. This is done by giving an assignment and having students come to the Career Center on an individual basis. Teachers may also bring students to the Career Center to do research during class time. Students are provided with a list of the fastest growing occupations and the top 25 projected annual average job openings in Texas and the nation. This information is projected for up to 10 years.

In addition to the career information, catalogs from numerous colleges and universities are available in the Career Center. Information is also available on technical schools, military enlistment, community service agencies, the admission process, and financial aid and scholarship. College and military representatives frequently visit the Career Center to discuss postsecondary options with students.

Volunteering is an excellent way for students to invest in themselves. Volunteering provides students with many benefits: Students (a) prove their dependability and competency; (b) develop out-of-school job skills; (c) use their time wisely; (d) get to know people in positions of authority who can later provide them with job contacts and references; and (e) build a range of experiences that will prepare them to take advantage of opportunities later on. In the Career Center, interested students are given a list of volunteer programs and agencies in our community and are encouraged to participate in these activities. Students are also given a Student Volunteer Evaluation Form that is to be completed by their volunteer supervisor and mailed back to their counselor. This completed form, then, becomes a part of the student's credential file and will be used by counselors in writing letters of recommendation for students.

■ Process

Unit Topic #1: Assisting ninth graders in transitioning from middle school to high school and in being knowledgeable about themselves.

Meeting with Ninth Graders. This occurs in the spring when counselors meet with the incoming ninth graders at the middle school campuses that feed into our school. Counselors start off with an energized "Welcome to O'Connor" session. O'Connor student leaders who have attended these middle school campuses assist us in this effort. Counselors conduct an icebreaker session next in an attempt to help students connect with O'Connor. Our student leaders also encourage participation in campus activities. A video prepared by students in our Independent Study in Technology class is shown to give incoming freshmen a view of the O'Connor family and the campus features and atmosphere. A guidance brochure answering questions commonly asked by incoming freshmen is distributed and discussed. Students are assisted in the completion of the ninth-grade course-selection card and are given information regarding the eighth-grade orientation night for students and parents.

Meeting with Eighth Graders. The eighth-grade orientation night occurs in August, prior to the start of school. The principal primarily organizes it, and counselors are very much involved in this schoolwide activity. It is a night session in which parents and students have the opportunity to rotate to four informational sessions, one of which is the administrative/counseling session. The other sessions are core academics—English, math, science, social studies, and international languages; band, pep squad, cheerleading, dance team, and athletics; electives; and clubs and organizations. A counselor presents along with an assistant principal at this session. In addition to this, counselors are stationed at a table outside the door of this session for parents needing more individualized information. In early August, teachers, administrators, and counselors work together in conducting the Panther Preview Night. This night is planned to assist freshmen in getting the school year off to a great start.

Welcome to High School. This classroom guidance session is done in mid-September. It consists of a PowerPoint presentation and is scheduled through World Geography classes. The role of the high school counselor and ways to access the counseling services of the counselor are described. The district-provided portfolio, *My Career and Life Planning Portfolio,* is introduced. In the past years, students were given a portfolio folder with blank hard copies to complete. Each year, students, with the aid of the teachers and Career Center technician, were given an opportunity to update this portfolio. We are currently in the process of changing over to new software that will allow students to prepare portfolios electronically.

Important Forms. This classroom guidance session is conducted during World Geography classes in early November. Students receive copies of a blank academic achievement record (AAR) and permanent record card (PRC)—our transcript forms. The following items are discussed:

1. Building a high school record—students are made aware that their permanent record is a clean slate and that they are now in control of their academic and career destinies;

2. Understanding graduation requirements, grade-point average computation, and the effect that the grade-point average has on future options and school honors, such as the National Honor Society. Preparation for their first high school semester exams is emphasized, and the Graduation Status Report Form is introduced to students;

3. Becoming involved in school and community activities and how factors such as attendance, conduct, and attitude affect future teacher recommendations, scholarship, and employment opportunities. Students are given a list of clubs and organizations with names of sponsors and are shown criteria for a scholarship application;

4. Understanding the roles and expectations of high school teachers and how these as well as study habits, time management, and organizational skills differ from those required at the middle school level.

Visiting the Career Center. Following the November classroom guidance session, all freshmen visit the Career Center with their World Geography teachers. The Career Center technician conducts an orientation to the center. Students are introduced to the resources available and to the DISCOVER program. Hall 1 of the DISCOVER program is incorporated in this session in conjunction with folders 1 and 3 of the portfolio. After students have had hands-on experience with the DISCOVER program, the Career Center technician asks the students to complete a scavenger hunt worksheet using the DISCOVER program and other resources in the center. The teachers incorporate these activities in their lesson plans and assist the counselor and the Career Center technician in implementing these activities with the students.

Preregistration Information. This is a classroom guidance session conducted in early February in which the counselors work with freshmen during English 1 classes. Information and materials are disseminated on preregistration for next year's courses. An elective fair is held after the classroom session. At the elective fair, students are allowed to visit teachers of certain electives for more information before enrolling.

Unit Topic #2: "Making Tentative Choices About Your Career Pathway," for tenth graders.

College and Career Interest. Students are introduced to college entrance testing and career interest assessment. Counselors work with sophomores through the English 2 classes and discuss the upcoming PSAT (the College Board) and PLAN (ACT) tests. Registration information and deadlines for the PSAT are given. The district pays for each sophomore to take the PLAN.

Planning for High School. This focuses on assisting sophomores in planning, decision making, and organizing their remaining years of high school. Sophomores and their parents attend one 2-hour session held in the auditorium. During the first hour, counselors assist students in understanding how a realistic self-assessment—understanding their abilities and interests—is a valuable component of educational planning, career search, and goal setting. They are also encouraged to define personal goals, goal paths, and alternate plans. The importance of personal initiative and self-motivation is stressed. Various options to consider beyond high school, such as apprenticeship, on-the-job training, military training, business/trade schools, community/junior colleges, 4-year colleges/universities, and professional schools, are discussed.

Students are given a handbook entitled *It's Your Journey, Prepare Well,* developed by the O'Connor High School guidance department. Students are asked to write their personal career choices/goals on page 1 of this booklet. Various ways to get information on career choices, course selection, and new college/career terminology are introduced. Students' PLAN results are disseminated and interpreted. Students are asked to compare their results with the career choices they have written on page 1 of the *It's Your Journey, Prepare Well* booklet and check for consistency. Students are challenged to start making future educational and career plans. Career pathway booklets are discussed.

During the second hour, students attend a small group session with their assigned counselors. In this session, students are assisted in understanding graduation program requirements for the next 2 years of high school. Information such as grade-point average computation, grade averaging facts, class rank, school and community involvements, tutoring information, and academic recognitions is reiterated. Students are given a copy of their official academic records (state and local) and are assisted in the charting of their progress toward graduation on the Graduation Status Report.

Visiting the Career Center. Immediately following the February classroom career guidance unit, all sophomores visit the Career Center with their English 2 teachers. The Career Center technician and the teachers reacquaint the students with the resources in the center and assign them a career exploration report to write. The DISCOVER program and other Career Center resources are used to complete this report. The "My Career and Life Planning Portfolios" are updated to further personalize student planning. Students work in folders 1, 2, and 3 of the portfolio.

Preregistration Information. Counselors also work with sophomores through their English 2 classes in February to disseminate preregistration information and related handouts. Sophomores also participate in the elective fair after the classroom guidance sessions.

Unit Topic #3: "Becoming Aware of the Many Facets Involved as You Prepare to Graduate," for eleventh graders.

Junior Testing Programs. Counselors work with juniors through English 3 classes. Students are given a partial year junior calendar and information on the upcoming PSAT test. Registration information and deadlines for this test are also given.

Exploring Postsecondary Options. Juniors are helped to understand the importance of the choices they make and that the choices made at this time will greatly influence the rest of their lives. Juniors and their parents are invited to attend this 2-hour conference—the "Junior Conference." During the first hour, students receive our locally developed guidebook that guides them through a step-by-step process to prepare them for the senior year. In addition to being introduced to new information, students are also reminded of the following: understanding final-year graduation requirements, getting organized, fine-tuning career plans, understanding new terminology, seeking college/career information, understanding what colleges/employers look for in an applicant, choosing the right college, understanding NCAA information (for student athletes), understanding the process of entering the military (including service academies and ROTC scholarship programs), understanding and preparing for the many different types of college admission testing programs, and becoming familiar with the financial aid search process.

Students are taught by the counselors about the value of building a credential file, and provided information to start the completion of theirs. The credential files contain important feedback from various sources, such as an updated resume that includes student's school and community activities, teacher evaluation forms, volunteer evaluation forms, and parent brag sheets. These files also assist the counselors in writing letters of recommendation. Counselors encourage juniors to use their summer well and prepare for the beginning of the senior year. This extra time gives them a chance to do further research, take all of the necessary admissions tests, complete campus visits, and accomplish other steps needed to fulfill their plans.

During the second hour, students meet with their assigned counselor in a small group format. Students are, again, given an updated copy of their academic records (AAR and PRC). Counselors guide the juniors in updating their Graduation Status Reports, ensuring that students and parents have a clear understanding of their courses passed and credits earned, courses currently enrolled in, and the courses required for graduation next year. Individual questions regarding the information presented will be answered.

Visiting the Career Center. Immediately following these conferences, juniors visit the Career Center again with their assigned English 3 teachers. The Career Center technician and the teachers guide students in further use of the center. A research paper is developed by each student, which includes the information gathered through career exploration, resume writing, college applications, and financial aid/scholarship searches using Halls 2 and 3 of the DISCOVER program. Students work on updating folders 1, 2, 3, and 4 of the portfolio.

Preregistration Information. Again, counselors work with juniors through their English 3 classes in February and disseminate information and handouts. Juniors also participate in the elective fair following the classroom sessions.

Unit Topic #4: "Implementing the Steps Needed to Meet Postsecondary Planning," for twelfth graders.

The Senior Year. Seniors and their parents are invited to a 2-hour conference around mid-September. During the first hour, seniors are given another user-friendly guidebook that takes them month by month, one step at a time, through their senior year. Some of the topics highlighted include getting organized and prepared for the year, reviewing their options after high school, understanding the application process for college admission and employment, requesting transcripts, planning for a productive campus visit, understanding required testing, NCAA and financial aid application requirements, obtaining teacher recommendations, and being aware of support services for students with disabilities.

Students with disabilities are encouraged to take the same steps to postsecondary options. They are helped to evaluate each option based on their individualized needs and to ensure that the requirements of the Americans with Disabilities Act (ADA) are met. We strive to ensure that students are aware of what their handicapping conditions are and what to look for in the next environment, so that they are prepared to advocate for themselves.

During the second hour, seniors again meet with their assigned counselor in a small-group format. Students are, again, given copies of their academic records (AAR and PRC). The students and counselors cooperatively complete each student's Graduation Status Report, arriving at mutual understanding of credits earned and courses passed, courses currently enrolled in, and courses needed for graduation. Additional questions are answered during this portion of the "Senior Conferences."

Visiting the Career Center. Immediately following the conferences, seniors visit the Career Center with their English 4 teachers. Halls 3 and 4 of the DISCOVER program are used heavily by the students as they are guided by the Career Center technician and their English teachers. Students continue to work on completing all four folders of their portfolios, primarily adding to folder 2—updating their employability skills and knowledge. The completed portfolios are given to the seniors to assist them in completing the necessary paperwork for implementing their postsecondary plans. Seniors independently come to the center on a continuous basis to research scholarships; colleges and universities; trade/technical schools; apprenticeship programs; and state, local, and national job market reviews. Students may also type various applications and apply online in the center.

Financial Aid. The goal of this session is to allow students and parents hands-on opportunities with the many facets of the financial aid process. A Financial Aid Night program is scheduled for seniors and parents around mid-November and is planned by one of the counselors on our staff. Financial aid experts are invited to acquaint parents and seniors with options as plans are being finalized as to how to pay for college or other postsecondary training costs. An additional opportunity to continue this process is offered by the district in January. Co-Step, a nonprofit organization, drives a mobile unit equipped with computers onto campus to allow parents and students the opportunity to process financial aid applications online and have additional concerns addressed and questions answered.

■ Results

As you can see from the many guidance activities and services presented, there are never dull moments on our campus. Time is a major factor. There never seems to be enough. In spite of this, we attempt to remain proactive in empowering students and parents to engage in the counseling/guidance process on our campus. Each semester over 4,500 students sign in to see their assigned counselors. The annual evaluation of our activities demonstrates that the majority of our students achieved reasonable resolutions to their concerns that initiated their requests for our services. I am still surprised, however, by the low to average parent turnout at our evening programs that focus on helping parents communicate with their teenagers; however, high turnout *is* experienced for those programs that relate to the students' educational and career planning.

There are three documents that I think would really help other counselors who want to replicate our programming. Please e-mail me and I will be happy to send the following documents: *Calendar of Guidance Activities*, *Request to See Counselor Form*, and *Counseling Support Group Referral*.

I've found some resources that I can recommend. *Developing and Managing Your School Guidance Program* by Gysbers and Henderson (ACA) provides a great overview. I also like these Web sites:

ACT, Inc. at http://www.act.org;
DISCOVER at http://www.act.org/discover/index.html
PLAN at http://www.act.org/plan/index.html
The College Board at http://www.collegeboard.com/splash
PSAT at http://www.collegeboard.com/counselors/psat

■ Personal Reflection

Counseling at the high school level is a job that presents daily excitement, challenges, and rewards. Teenagers present constantly changing concerns and needs. I get to see tangible results; for example, at-risk students rising to cope with concerns that were inhibiting their academic achievement, students moving on to the next phase of life and continuing their education/training at various postsecondary institutions, graduating seniors receiving over $3.9 million in scholarship awards. Knowing that I have been an instrumental part of this whole process is priceless to me.

We counselors help each other face the high stress, the "no closures," and the constant prioritizing of tasks by taking care of each other. We have summer counseling retreats. We keep humor in many of our conversations. We make attempts to spend time together to consult and to laugh.

References

ACT, Inc. (n.d.). www.act.org.
ACT, Inc. (n.d.). *DISCOVER*. www.act.org/discover/index.html.
ACT, Inc. (n.d.). *PLAN*. www.act.org/plan/index.html.

Gysbers, N. C., & Henderson, P. (2000). *Developing and managing your school guidance program* (3rd ed.). Alexandria, VA: American Counseling Association.
The College Board. (n.d.). www.collegeboard.com/splash.
The College Board. (n.d.). *PSAT.* www.collegeboard.com/counselors/psat.

Suggested Readings

Gysbers, N. C., & Henderson, P. (2006). *Developing and managing your school guidance and counseling program* (4th ed.). Alexandria, VA: American Counseling Association.
Henderson, P. (1994). *Northside Independent School District comprehensive guidance program framework.* San Antonio, TX: Northside Independent School District.
Krueger, D. (1995). *Student goal setting program.* San Antonio, TX: Northside Independent School District.
Texas Education Agency (2004). *A model: Comprehensive developmental guidance and counseling program for Texas public schools.* Austin, TX: Author.

Biographical Statement

Brenda Jones has completed 30 years in the field of education, including 9 years as a business education teacher and more than 20 years as a school counselor. Currently, Brenda is head counselor at O'Connor High School in San Antonio. Brenda has been active at the leadership level in counseling organizations at the local, state, and national level. You can reach Brenda at Brenda_Jones@nisd.net.

Clear and Imminent Danger

Mary G. Libby

Working with high school students when they are contemplating suicide is one of a school counselor's most horrendous challenges. Mary Libby shares insights into her own reactions and feelings in these situations as well as her experience in working with one such student, 17-year-old Lenny. Before the suicide event began, Lenny had been assigned to a counseling intern as part of her caseload. Libby, the school's head counselor, gets involved as soon as his suicidal ideation surfaces. The value of consultation among counselors is underscored.

Libby's title for this case refers to the ethical standard that the school counselor "keeps information confidential unless disclosure is required to prevent clear and imminent danger to the student or others" (American School Counselor Association, 2004).

Responding to students in need is one of the primary roles of a school counselor. These student needs are generally related to academic concerns, career exploration, or personal/social issues that are interfering with their academic success. Often enough, however, issues arise that cause a counselor to be concerned about a student's safety.

When students come to the school counselors' office and share information that indicates an adult is harming them physically, sexually, or emotionally, the counselors' responsibility is to report our suspicions of abuse to the appropriate authorities—in Texas, it is Child Protective Services (CPS). Our role does not involve finding out enough information to support or negate the "outcry." Rather, our role is to support the student and help the student get through the trauma of the outcry. Sometimes a referral to a community counseling agency may be necessary and appropriate, but typically this is CPS's role.

When students come to our offices and share that another student has made a threat to hurt them physically or sexually or that they intend to hurt another physically or sexually, our responsibility is to refer these cases to administrators, and they, then, investigate the validity of the outcry and follow through as appropriate. Our role is to support these students and help them to work through issues related to such events. Again, referrals to outside counseling agencies may be necessary.

However, when a student comes into our offices and shares suicidal intentions or someone tells us about a student who has made a suicidal outcry, we as school counselors are the first-line investigator and responder. Our professional responsibility, whether it is the student's first outcry or an ongoing pattern of outcries, is to respond immediately to that student. We do not have the luxury of allowing CPS or an administrator to investigate the outcry. We are it.

For many counselors, the very word *suicide* conjures up fear and apprehension that may inhibit their ability to respond appropriately and effectively to a student in crisis. Even now, with 11 years of experience, when I work with a suicidal student, or even consult with another counselor about such a case, I feel uncomfortable. My uncomfortableness is not about my abilities as a counselor but about my concern for the student's behavior and safety. (If the uncomfortableness *is* about my abilities, then it is imperative that I consult with another professional.)

When first confronted with a student who seems to be considering suicide, my overall awareness heightens and triggers a fight-or-flight response similar to the response I have when *I* am in danger. I feel a change in my physiology. My heart beats faster, my palms get a bit sweaty, and my adrenaline flows.

To me, the choices of fighting or taking flight are at opposite ends of the same continuum. Operating in the flight response keeps me away from the topic, away from being fully attentive to the student by avoiding the obvious or delaying the encounter. I am reluctant to touch the uncomfortableness of the situation. At the same time, it allows for more objectivity, a fuller observation of the "big picture," than the fight response does. Operating in the fight response fills me with a sense of urgency. It allows me to approach the uncomfortableness and challenge the instability and stickiness of the situation. It gives me energy to get through the situation to "safety."

The immediacy of the fight response, however, narrows my focus and prevents fuller observation of the whole situation.

As a professional counselor, I must control whether to let these reactions inhibit or enhance my interaction with the suicidal student. It is necessary to be aware of my reactions but not directed by them. I strive to balance my reactions. Not finding a balance impedes my ability to manage the intervention process. Finding the balance allows me to be fully attentive to the student. When I arrive at the balance point on the fight–flight continuum, I am ready to work with the student productively.

As the intervention process begins, it is important that I monitor my responses to maintain the balance. My heart has slowed, my voice is even, my hands are no longer sweaty—for me, these are good indications that I have reached a balance. "Okay, this is what the student has shared. This is what I know from past experiences"—with the student or in similar situations. "This is where I'm at." Now I can ask myself, What are the steps I need to take as the professional counselor to provide a safe physical and emotional environment for the student? I can take charge of the situation on the student's behalf: "You are safe in here, but I am concerned about this situation and we need to explore this." The process of assessing the clarity and imminence of the danger begins.

For me, assessing for suicide is not a clear-cut formula-driven process. The goal of the assessment is to determine if it is clear that a student is in imminent danger of harming him or herself and needs to be referred to an agency counselor, psychologist, or psychiatrist. In the schools, we are not in the position or trained to use formal diagnostic psychological assessments, but we are qualified, by training and experience, and have the responsibility to assess how clear and imminent the danger is.

As a school-counselor-in-training and then as a new counselor, I was taught to use a checklist format when assessing a student's suicidality. Ask the questions and the student replies "yes" or "no." If I was lucky, the responses fit the template and the assessment moved along:

Counselor:	Do you want to kill yourself?
Student:	Yes.
Counselor:	Do you have a plan?
Student:	Yes.
Counselor:	Do you know when? Where? How?
Student:	Yes, I have some pills in my dresser and I'm going to take them sometime when my parents and little brother are not home.
Counselor:	Have you tried before?
Student:	Yes, but I threw up before the pills worked.

In this dialog the responses are cut and dried. The student is clear that he or she wants to kill him- or herself, and it is necessary at this point to contact a parent and refer him or her appropriately.

Looking back on my first assessments of students who presented suicidal ideation to me, I am aware of how the list of standard questions I then used limited the students' responses. Adhering to the questions enabled me to hide behind a structure: Although they were the "correct" questions to ask, they did not allow for true exploration of the situation. The balance was tipped toward a flight response.

However, through experience, I discovered that responses rarely fit perfectly into the checklist. If the responses did not fit the format or the student was talking freely, I found myself more focused on, "Hey, that does not fit the format I'm following," and trying to make it fit rather than on being present with what the student was sharing verbally and nonverbally.

Although those questions are appropriate, I have since learned that starting with the direct-hit questions many times is not the best way to begin. I now understand that the process is far more significant than the end result. It is necessary and warranted to allow the process to evolve and not become fixated on the conclusion—answering the question, "Is the student in imminent danger?" If I allow for the process to evolve by asking myself such questions as, Where is the student right now? What is he saying? What is he not saying? I am still able to determine whether there is imminent danger. I often allow the student to lead the conversation. I am responding to the *person* in the crisis, not the crisis. Sometimes the student is in my office on his own, but more often, someone who cares about him has referred him. I prefer to begin in generalities and get more specific as the conversation evolves.

Counselor: I hear you are having a bad day (night, lunch, etc). What can you tell me about this? What's going on?
Student: (attempts to describe feelings)
Counselor: It sounds like you are feeling _____. (Frequently, people in crisis do not have words for how they feel, all they know is they feel "yuk!")
Counselor: What do you want to do about it? (Depending on how the conversation is going, this may be the place to ask the direct-hit questions. Sometimes it is necessary to start with closed or yes–no questions to get any response.)
Counselor: Have you thought about hurting yourself?
Student: Yes.
Counselor: What have you thought about?
Student: I have a knife in my room. (red flag—plan)
Counselor: What would you do with it?
Student: I've cut myself before. It doesn't hurt. (red flag—tried to hurt himself before)
Counselor: So, you want to kill yourself?
Student: No. (positive sign)
Counselor: What do you want to do with the knife?
Student: I just don't want to feel this way.

At this point I explore with the student those feelings that may be contributing to the above statements.

■ The School

I am the head counselor in a comprehensive high school with a student population of approximately 2,700, in one of the largest school districts in south Texas. We have a diverse student body with a 64% minority and 35% Anglo population. Most students are from middle-class to lower middle-class families. There are eight counselors (six comprehensive, one special education, 1 SDFSCC) to address the needs of these students. As head counselor, I do not have an assigned caseload, but I do provide counseling services. This past school year, we had a counselor intern working with us as well. The following case began with the student's regular counselor, was transitioned to the counselor intern as one of her individual cases, and ended up with me. For consultation purposes, I brought another counselor into the process.

Student Need

Lenny was 17. He seemed to show up in the counseling office during first period regularly. We fondly refer to such students as "Frequent Flyers." He and his first period teacher had a less-than-compatible relationship, and Lenny's response was to be out of class as much as possible by creating reasons to visit the counselor, nurse, vice-principal, or whoever was available.

Lenny had had difficulty being successful in school. His regularly assigned counselor worked with him as a result of his failing grades. During one of these sessions, Lenny shared that he had cut himself. The counselor determined that this was something that he had done more than once. The most recent time was on his stomach, and his stepdad took him to the doctor for treatment. Lenny also shared that he did not want to cut himself again and that he had promised his girlfriend he would not cut himself anymore.

Lenny's counselor consulted with me and we determined that Lenny was not currently a danger to himself. Also, his stepfather was already aware of the previous cutting incident. Lenny's counselor and I decided to refer the student to the counselor intern so she could continue to work with him on less threatening issues related to his academic success.

Together, the counselor intern and I set clear boundaries for Lenny on the appropriate process he would follow to access counseling services. This would hopefully meet his needs while preventing unnecessary hall wandering and manipulation of the system. The counselor intern built a counseling relationship with Lenny by establishing rapport and credibility. I observed and consulted with the counselor intern as her supervisor. This allowed me the opportunity to build a relationship with Lenny as well.

It was pretty easy to do a quick, informal assessment of Lenny's state of mind by observing his hair. If he was feeling good about himself, his hair was up out of his face in large thick spikes. Another clue was his smile, and he had a warm one. If the hair was up and spiked, so was his smile, and he was quite engaging. Lenny's sessions with the counselor intern on these days were short and more or less for check-in purposes.

If, on the other hand, he was not having a good day, then his hair was down in his face and not spiked or fixed at all. It would be difficult to see his eyes or mouth, not only because of his hair, but also because he would keep his face down. It was very difficult to engage him at all when he presented himself like this. His hair effectively kept others out. Any questions from the counselor intern were usually met with shrugs of the shoulder or mumbled and inaudible responses. Lenny's sessions on these days were generally longer. Lenny could be antagonistic and challenging when he came in like this, and the sessions would be filled with a lot of "therapeutic silence." These are the sessions that try most counselors' patience. It is as if the student is saying, "I need to see you because I'm in a bad place but I dare you to care or help!"

However, other times, his hair would be in between—spiked, but the spikes would droop over his face. He would offer a glimpse of his eyes and mouth, but never the whole picture. He was not forthright when he came in like this, but it was possible to engage him and discuss the issues that were on his mind and interfering with his classroom performance.

The repeating themes in Lenny's life that seemed to cause him the most concern were difficulty trusting his current stepdad, due to extreme mistrust of his previous stepdad and the resulting anger at his mom. He was unsure about where he fit into his "new" family because of a younger sister. These issues overwhelmed Lenny to a degree that they were interfering with his success in school.

The counselor intern met with Lenny and his mother to share with them her concerns and to suggest they seek counseling outside the school. Lenny's mother was receptive to the information and shared that Lenny was already attending court-mandated counseling for anger management. After Lenny went back to class, his mother shared with the counselor intern that she, too, was concerned about Lenny. She stated that on the previous Saturday evening, they had an argument. Although it was late, Lenny left the house on foot. Once she was able to go after him, some time had passed, and she found Lenny walking on a dark, heavily trafficked road. When she found him, she said, "What are you doing on this road? It's dangerous. You could get hurt." He replied, "I know. That's why I'm here." Lenny got into her car and they went back home. Things seemed to go back to "normal." His mother told the counselor intern that this was the first time he had said anything like that. Mom took a referral list and stated she would look into further counseling once his current counseling concluded.

■ Goals and Strategies

Although there were times Lenny presented as sad, depressed, withdrawn, or antagonistic, and he had a stated history of self-mutilation, the issue of Lenny's being suicidal had not arisen—until now.

Several weeks later, Lenny was in his regularly scheduled meeting with the counselor intern. His hair was not spiked and it hung over his face. He stated that he and his girlfriend had been arguing and if they broke up, he was "not sure if he could make it." The counselor intern tried to clarify this statement by asking him if he were going to kill himself. Lenny replied, "I could go to the top of the school and jump." With this information, the counselor intern sought consultation with me.

I believe that consultation is a necessary tool to the professional school counselor. Although we are aptly equipped to handle students and their issues as they are presented, sometimes it is necessary to bounce a case off a colleague who does not have an investment in the case—a colleague offers objectivity. Colleagues can help ensure that important aspects of the case are not being overlooked. They can also validate a counselor's initial instincts, or not, and help develop a particular course of action. Consultation is especially crucial when we respond to a suicidal outcry. With the fight-or-flight response feelings, sometimes it is just too scary to go through the process without the support and objectivity consultation brings.

    After hearing the information from the counselor intern, I was not so sure that Lenny was in imminent danger of harming himself. Yes, there were many red flags: His girlfriend was a stabilizing force in his life and a breakup could be extremely painful for him, he had a history of self-mutilation, he had made a statement that he would jump from the building, and he had sometimes exhibited reckless and impulsive behavior. Even with these red flags, I thought more exploration was necessary before a determination of his current condition could be made. Because of my own investment with Lenny, I did not trust my own level of objectivity in this case, and I consulted with another counselor who had no previous interactions with Lenny. This counselor validated the concerns regarding the red flags, and also agreed that more information needed to be gathered.

■ Process

I continued dialogue with Lenny to assess the intensity of his suicidal intentions.

Counselor:	Do you want to kill yourself?
Lenny:	No [shrug of the shoulders]. (This is a red flag—the shrug negates the "no" response. If a student cannot give an answer that verifies his safety, I assume there may be intent.)
Counselor:	Do you just want to not be here?
Lenny:	Kind of.
Counselor:	Do you want to hurt yourself? (It was necessary to ask this question because of the previous history of self-mutilation.)
Lenny:	[Shrug of shoulders] (Up to this point, I chose to use closed questions because Lenny was not in a place to elaborate.)
Counselor:	On a scale from one to ten, one being for sure, where are you on wanting to hurt yourself?
Lenny:	[After a minute or two] Eight. (Red flag—an 8 out of 10 suggests high intent.)
Counselor:	How do you want to do that?
Lenny:	I know how to get to the top of the roof. (Red flag—there is a plan.)
Counselor:	Then what would you do?
Lenny:	I could jump, but I probably would just hurt my legs and that would be a bummer. (Red flag—more about the plan. However, he also shared that being hurt was a "bummer." Keeping in mind all the red flags, I continued to ask questions.)
Counselor:	So, what else might you do?
Lenny:	I could leave school and keep walking. (Red flag—the school is on the same heavily trafficked road that he was walking on when his mom had found him.)

Counselor:	Tell me about walking away from school.
	(Until now, Lenny's head was down in his hands with his hair hanging in his face. However, at this point, he raised his head just enough to look at me and he responded with some exasperation and a slight grin on his face.)
Lenny:	Miss, don't you ever feel like just walking so you can get away and think?
Counselor:	So you didn't want to get hit by a car?
Lenny:	[looking at me] No. (The red flags go to half-mast because of the "no" response and because he is making eye contact.)
Counselor:	Lenny, do you want to hurt yourself at all? (I am re-asking the same questions because the intensity of the session has shifted. My fight-or-flight response has eased a bit, but I need to make sure.)
Lenny:	[looking at me] No. [still making eye-contact]
Counselor:	Are you wanting to kill yourself? (again, re-asking)
Lenny:	[Looking at me] No. If you would just get Tina in here we can talk and things will be better. (Tina is his girlfriend. This is an indication of hopefulness.)
Counselor:	I can't do that right now, Lenny, but let's talk about that later. I'm going to step out for a second to chat with another counselor. I will be right across the hall. If you need anything come get me.

The consultant counselor was available. We consulted again and agreed that the student was sad, overwhelmed, and worried about issues with his girlfriend but did not appear to be suicidal. The plan of action was to continue meeting with Lenny, and to help him learn to identify his feelings and to give him better language to use when these feelings overwhelmed him.

It is not unusual for an adolescent or teenager to make statements like, "I want to kill myself," "I want to die," or "I don't think I can go on if we break up." The words themselves suggest dangerous intent. What these words do *not* say, though, is what is really going on, and that is more like, "I have all these feelings. I don't know what to do with them. I don't like them and they make me feel bad! Help me feel differently!"

Because teens do not always have the appropriate words, I have a feelings poster in my office. The feeling face in the center hub of the wheel is Anger. There are 11 other feelings faces that spoke out from this hub. These 11 feelings are what I call the uncomfortable or vulnerable feelings: jealousy, embarrassment, hurt, loneliness, et cetera, that we all have but do not feel safe about sharing with others. Anger is an important feeling, but it is also used as a wall to prevent other people from getting too close. I use this poster as a tool to help students put names to these uncomfortable feelings. This also helps students understand that there is a direct connection between denying these uncomfortable feelings and pretending they do not exist and their maladaptive behaviors such as drug and alcohol use, self-mutilation, or suicidal ideation. In case you are interested, the poster is available from Creative Therapy Associates of Cincinnati, Ohio.

To help Lenny put some names to his overwhelming feelings, I went to the chart. He and the counselor intern had used the feelings poster, so this activity was not new to him.

Counselor:	(I was standing at the feelings poster.) Lenny, it seems like you have a lot of feelings about this situation with Tina. Let's identify some of them.
Lenny:	[Before I could go to one feeling, he got out of his chair and pointed to jealousy, hurt, sadness, fear, and frustration and then returned to his seat.]
	(I found this to be an important action. When I first met with Lenny, it appeared he wanted to wallow in these feelings. Now he was showing some insight and energy to want to sort and work through them.)
Counselor:	Tell me what is going on that is making you feel jealous.
Lenny:	Tina has a friend who is a guy and she talks to him a lot. And I don't like it.
Counselor:	What worries you about this?
Lenny:	[shrug of shoulders]
Counselor:	Are you worried she might break up with you for him?
Lenny:	[shrug of shoulders and nod of head]
Counselor:	That would really hurt, wouldn't it? (Sometimes it is necessary to help students identify the feelings they are expressing but unable to name.)
Lenny:	[nod of head]

We continued to address all the feelings. I reminded him to use "I" statements when identifying his feelings and behaviors because he has control over only himself. After indicating which feelings he had, Lenny held his head down with his hair partially covering his eyes. Every so often he would sniff and wipe his eyes. As he continued to identify these feelings and the accompanying behaviors, his overall body language became more relaxed. Gradually, he sat up in his chair, moved his hair out of his eyes, and made more eye contact. At this point he looked at the clock; the bell for lunch was about to ring.

Lenny:	Miss, I have to leave and meet Tina.
	(I did not respond immediately. Just an hour earlier Lenny had presented with suicidal ideation and now he wanted to leave the office and meet his girlfriend. The red flags were not waving, but . . .)
Counselor:	Lenny, I'm concerned that you want to leave the office. How do I know you aren't going to run?
Lenny:	Miss, I need to see Tina and I promise I'll be right back. (indication of wanting trust)
Counselor:	OK, I'm going to trust that you will come back at the end of the passing period. If you are not back, I will let the campus police know and they will find you.

This was a difficult and significant moment. I had just done a suicide assessment and Lenny had shared some vulnerable parts of himself. As the counselor, I had asked him to trust me with this information; as the student, he was asking for the same trust. Again, balance is important.

Many counselors choose to use written contracts for suicidal ideation. These contracts usually include statements that individuals agree not to harm themselves. If they do feel like harming themselves, they agree to see the counselor immediately. My contract with a student is not written but rather occurs through discussion. That contract includes every piece of emotional pain and struggle that a student, in this case Lenny, has entrusted to me. That contract includes the change in his body language and the eye contact he made with me. When a student agrees to check in with me the next morning, that is a contract. When we end a session with discussion about future plans—such as, "What do you want to do after high school? Next summer? This weekend?" — that is a contract. For me, using a written contract would be allowing myself to escape into the flight response. I could overly rely on the written form as evidence that everything is okay and that I have fulfilled my responsibility. I would not have to experience my own fear and alarm. In turn, this avoidance of feelings could prevent me from being fully engaged with the student. The written contract would be used more to meet my needs than to meet the needs of the student.

Results

Lenny honored our contract and returned as promised. He shared that he and Tina had talked, and he was hopeful that they would be able to continue talking after school. I reminded him that when he and Tina continued their discussion, he should use "I" statements and that he could be responsible for only his part of the discussion.

One other piece of the contract that emerged was Lenny's thoughts about his future. He had goals that were very important to him, and he acknowledged that what he was doing now was not going to help him reach those goals. I saw this as an issue that he and the counselor intern could continue exploring. In addition, before Lenny went back to class, I wanted to contact his mother to let her know that he had been in my office for serious work. Lenny was not comfortable with this. Because he had trusted me to this point, I asked him to trust me once more as I took this step to elicit his mom's support. He acquiesced. This session ended with Lenny feeling safe—both by his account and mine.

Personal Reflection

As I reflect on the processes involved in this case, there are a couple of things that stand out. The first awareness, and perhaps most important, is that Lenny trusted our relationship, was willing to go through the counseling process and do the work. Had he been resistant, not trusting of the process, or not willing to share, it would have been necessary to spend some time building a counseling relationship before proceeding to the assessment.

Another awareness is the value of consultation: Lenny's regular counselor consulting with me weeks before the event, the counselor intern consulting with me once Lenny's intent was made clear, and my consultation with another counselor when I needed reflection and objectivity. All of us working together made for a positive outcome. Suicide threats do not always end this way. There are times when the red flags do not go away, when it is necessary to contact the parent and recommend, strongly, an assessment by an outside counseling professional and, perhaps, complete supervision.

Intervening when there is potential for "clear and imminent danger to the student or others" (ASCA, 2004) is a mantra that is drilled into every counselor-in-training's head regardless of his or her anticipated counseling specialty. It is one of the few situations in which breaking confidentiality with clients is not just acceptable but legally mandated. It seems so cut and dried: They are intending to hurt (injure or kill) themselves, or not; they are going to hurt (injure or kill) another, or not; or they are being hurt (physically, sexually, or emotionally), or they are not. However, when you actually have an individual in your office presenting you with one of these issues, you realize how muddy it can be. With an individual's ability to think, reason, and answer questions or not, determining clearness or imminence becomes even more complex, but it is not unmanageable. The challenge is to find your place on the fight-or-flight continuum, the place that allows you to best meet the needs of the student in crisis.

Reference

American School Counselor Association. (ASCA). (2004). *Ethical standards for school counselors.* Retrieved from www.schoolcounselor.org/content.asp?contentid=173

Suggested Readings

King, K., Price, J. H., & Telljohann, S. K. (2000). Preventing adolescent suicide: Do high school counselors know the risk factors? *Professional School Counseling, 3*(4), 255–263.

Capuzzi, D. (2002). Legal and ethical challenges in counseling suicidal students. *Professional School Counseling, 6*(1), 36–45.

Biographical Statement

Mary G. Libby, MS, LPC, is head counselor at William H. Taft High School in San Antonio, Texas. She has been a high school counselor for eight years and prior to that was a student assistance program counselor for three years. You can reach Mary at taft26@nisd.net.

21

Those Kids

Marcia Loew

Gay students at an inner-city high school threaten to protest against harassment from other students. Fearing a violent altercation, the principal asks the counselor, Marcia Loew, to intervene. What begins as an attempt to prevent a disruption evolves into an ongoing support group for gay and lesbian students.

A

s the Safe and Drug-Free Schools and Communities Counselor (SDFSCC), a grant allows me to work with students who are using drugs, students who are concerned about family members' use of drugs, and students who are at high risk for using drugs. Since I am not assigned a specific caseload, I am available to all students in need.

The School

The school is an inner-city high school with 3,200 students. The student body is 78% Hispanic, 9% African American, 11% White (non-Hispanic), and 1.5% Asian. Sixty-two percent are economically disadvantaged. The mobility of the student population is 29%.

Student Need

Gay students have a higher rate of drug and alcohol abuse than heterosexual students do. In fact, 30% of the gay population is addicted to drugs. They are three times more likely to attempt suicide than heterosexual youth; 30% of completed youth suicides are committed by gay youth annually and suicide is their leading cause of death. Gay youths make up 20% to 40% of homeless youth in urban areas. Twenty-two percent of gay students skipped school in the past month because they felt unsafe at school, and 28% of gay high school students drop out of school because of harassment resulting from their sexual orientation.

Goals and Strategies

Before seeing students in groups, I need to have a district-approved permission form signed by a parent or guardian. The permission form is generic and does not specify the type of group the student will be attending. For those few parents who call wanting more information, I explain that many teenagers need a place where they can talk about anything on their minds, and the group offers them a confidential setting where a counselor helps them deal with social issues, school issues, or family concerns. Rarely does a parent refuse permission.

Once the permission forms are received, the student is ready to start in the group. I keep my groups to 12 or fewer students so that there is an opportunity for individual interaction. I receive referrals from teachers, counselors, administrators, parents, students, and self-referrals. All students are seen individually before I admit them to a group. This interview process allows me to determine if the student is appropriate for a group, if the student needs a referral to a community resource, or if the student is in immediate need of assistance. With the group discussed below, I used solution-focused therapy as my main strategy.

─────────────── ■ **Process**

It was early fall when the principal spoke with me about a possible violent situation on our campus. A group of gay students was mobilizing to picket for gay rights during lunchtime the following week. I was the newest counselor in our department of 10 and it quickly appeared to me that I was being assigned the title of the "at risk" counselor although, in reality, I was the SDFSCC. I had no experience working with high school students, much less gay students, but I did possess a strong, fervent devotion to fairness and equality for all humans. So there I was, facing the principal for my first directive! I was told that there had been antigay slurs written in a restroom. He was fearful of violence erupting, and he hoped I would meet with the students and stop anything from happening. The hair on the back of my neck stood up as I listened, and I cautioned myself to tread lightly—after all, I needed to make a good first impression. I replied that of course I would be willing to meet with the gay students but (I just couldn't help myself) I felt they did have a right to be heard, albeit in a safe environment. Eyebrows raised, the principal nodded and replied, "Just make sure no one gets hurt!"

I received a list of the ringleaders and called them into my office. Their response was negative from the moment they walked in. "Why are we here?" "We don't need counseling!" "Don't try and stop us!" This wasn't going to be easy. I asked the six students to sit down and to talk to me about the way gay students were treated in our school. After about an hour, I was hooked, and so were they. Things had to change, and they wanted this to be accomplished today! I bargained for more time so we could rally all their friends together and have one more after-school meeting.

The following day, I met with 22 students in my office, which could squeeze in 10 somewhat uncomfortably. They sat on the floor, on the arms of chairs, and squeezed in two to a chair! I needed to learn about them as well as gain their trust quickly because their demonstration was only three days away. There were a lot of issues that the students were sharing during the meeting, and I felt they were out of control like a runaway train. I decided to meet with them again the following day. During the meeting, they agreed not to demonstrate if we could meet on an ongoing basis to work through some school issues regarding gay students. I quickly agreed, and we set up a weekly meeting during the schoolday. I told the students that meeting under the guise of a counseling group would afford them the confidentiality that many needed. They were sure they didn't need counseling, but I knew differently.

Administrative Consult. I met with the principal and told him that I would be meeting with the students weekly and that everything discussed in group as well as the members who attended would be confidential. I assured him that if I felt anyone was in danger, I would take the proper action. He seemed relieved that an incident had been averted and was only too happy for me to work with the students.

Session 1. I read fast and furiously anything I could find about gay and lesbian teens before each meeting, although my best teachers were the students. I knew we needed to get to know each other and also for them to come up with group rules during this first session. Lisa was really angry and stated that we didn't need all this crap and all we did need was to "kick some ass." The other students confirmed her as the group leader with their nods of agreement. But a lone voice from the middle of this huge group of 24 was Eric's. He stated that he believed that for things to change, just maybe their attitude had to change, too. The group quieted down and, voilà, another leader had emerged!

Session 2. Lisa didn't show up to group and four other students were also missing. Marco stated that Lisa was dropping out of school, and her parents were getting her an apartment because they, her parents, were moving out of town. Lisa was only 16, so I knew I had to contact her. During this session, I used a get-acquainted interview activity. I could see that there were definite subgroups in this larger arena. We also came up with group rules emphasizing confidentiality as well as the limits of confidentiality. They also decided on *no put-downs* and the *right to pass.* I told them that rules could be changed or added.

Teacher Consult. Joey's math teacher caught me during lunch and wanted to know why he was in a group, what she could do to help, and would he be missing her class often. Phew! I explained about confidentiality and thanked her for her concern. I then explained that since my groups met on a rotating schedule, he would miss her class only once every six weeks, and he would be contacting her to make up the work. She seemed satisfied and left with "Anything I can do to help, you just let me know!"

Session 3. Okay! This was not a group . . . this was a mob. More students came during this session, and we were up to 36. I saw during the last session that there was a definite split between senior students and lower grade students. That's were I would start dividing them into manageable groups.

I used an opener. Going around the circle, students stated their name, how they were feeling at that moment (they could consult the emotions chart on the wall), and if they would like time to share something. All went well except the time. With such a huge group, we didn't have the time to let everyone speak who wanted to, so . . . it was a perfect chance for me to broach the subject of smaller groups. I told them to think of ways to split the group into smaller groups, and we could discuss it the next week. During the sharing time there were many voices speaking about suicidal ideation and failed attempts. I told the group I would like to explore this further and asked those students who had spoken to stay after the group. I set up individual appointments during the next two days for those who were not currently feeling suicidal. Melissa had stated she felt suicidal at that moment, so I asked her to stay.

Session with Melissa. Melissa, 15 years old, was the oldest child in her family. Because of fear, she had not come out to her family as a lesbian. She had heard many negative comments about gays from her family members. Her mother kept pressuring her to take her hair out of a ponytail and to wear a dress to school. She referred to Melissa's friends as "disgusting gays." Melissa did not want me to contact her parents, and I reminded her that her expression of feeling suicidal was something I couldn't keep to myself. I assured her that I would not be discussing her sexual orientation, but I would encourage her mother to seek outside help. I allowed Melissa to be in the room when I called her mother so that she would not lose trust in me. I also told her mother that Melissa was in the room and could hear our conversation. Her mother said she was fine with the arrangement. She sounded very anxious and wanted to know what kind of trouble her daughter was in. She stated that she was having problems with Melissa at home because she was disobedient. I told her mother about Melissa's talk of suicide and that I believed it would not be safe to leave her unattended until she received some outside assistance. I volunteered a list of community agencies, but she said she would take her to talk to their clergyman.

Two days later, Melissa stormed into my office, "Thanks a lot! Now my mother's convinced I'm going to hell because I'm gay! She wants to pull me out of this school. She thinks my friends have made me gay!" I assured Melissa that, if she wished, I would speak with her mother and clergyman and explain that being gay was not a choice. She said nothing else and stormed out of my office. The following day, Melissa's parents withdrew her from school and she was sent to California to live with relatives.

Session 4. Although I had thought to divide the group by grade level, the students wanted to be with their friends. I tried to work with that concept but found that one group had 5 and the others had 21 and 10! I suggested that we draw names from a basket to divide the groups evenly and randomly. And so four groups were formed amidst some low rumbles.

Based on what I had heard from the students themselves and also my reading, I knew that I wanted to discuss how gay teens were at high risk for suicide. We went around the circle. When we got to Raymond, he cried as he related how his family was very close but no one was aware that he was gay and he was terrified that if they found out, they would not love him anymore. Dena told the group that her mother had read a letter she had written to her girlfriend on the softball team and now she was forbidden to participate in any sports. She told the group that her mother wouldn't allow her to visit relatives because she might "try things" with her cousins.

I thought that it was now time to broach the topic of suicide. There was a lot of conversation with many students responding in healthy ways to their stress, anger, fear, and sadness. Watching the expressions on their faces and the nodding of heads, it was evident that they were teaching each other. Ah, the power of the group! We then traded phone numbers so that if anyone felt they needed to talk, someone would always be there. I also gave them the number to our local teen hotline.

Session 5. From this point, I will write about only one of the small groups. Did these students know why they were gay? Did they know the difference between sexual orientation and sexual behavior? We would explore this first. I gave them each a print out of an American Psychological Association document explaining sexual orientation and sexual behavior. We also viewed the video *Growing Up Gay and Lesbian*. I could see that these students were starving for accurate knowledge about homosexuality and for positive gay role models. I decided to bring in books and guest speakers.

Administrative Consult. Two of my girls, April and Desi, came bursting into my office midweek with the following tale. They had walked to class together and then kissed on the check as they separated to go to their classes. An English teacher grabbed them and told them they were disgusting and took them to the vice-principal's office. The vice-principal told the girls that she would suspend them from school and call their parents if this ever happened again. Despite the fact that they were terrified that their parents might be called, the girls had done exactly what I told them to do if they encountered situations at school that they believed were unfair: *Be polite. Don't talk back. Come tell me about it!* I told them that I would speak with the vice-principal and then call them into my office to inform them of the outcome. The vice-principal explained that there was a policy on public display of affection (PDA), and rules were rules. I asked her if she had ever called parents of heterosexual couples who had broken the rule, and she replied that she had not. I asked her if she had suspended students for PDA and again a negative response. I told her that there were legal entanglements that might occur if certain groups of students were being treated differently than others, and she quickly responded that she had said those things to scare the girls but really wasn't planning on doing anything more.

It was time for me to educate the faculty and administration, and what better place to begin than at the top. I went to see the principal about allowing me to speak with the administrators during one of their weekly meetings. The principal allotted me 10 minutes at their next meeting, and I was delighted. I needed to be clear, concise, and convincing. I put together a one-page handout on the statistics of gay teens. It gave facts and figures regarding suicide rates, drug and alcohol use, dropout rates, and violence. This was my chance to be an advocate for these kids. The day after my presentation, the principal asked me to repeat it at the next faculty meeting. I was elated.

Session 6. I asked a speaker to share with the students what he had experienced as a gay teen and what his life was like as a gay adult. The students posed some very difficult questions for our speaker. I told the group to remember that our group rules applied to our guest, entitling him to the right to pass if there was anything he did not want to respond to. The following are some of the questions.

When did you tell your family that you were gay?

How did your family respond?

Did you experience problems in school?

What does your church say about being gay, and do you believe it?

Do you know "married" gay people? Do they have children?

Do you know anyone with AIDS?

Do you have a boyfriend?

Our guest was honest and informative. I decided to schedule speakers from the community every month.

Session 7. During our share time, several of the students talked about partying and getting wasted on Saturday night. Thus began our discussions on drugs and alcohol. This was a difficult subject for the teens because it appeared that only two of them did not do drugs or alcohol. I thought a good place to start would be to do a modified family tree. I did a simple one on the board, including only blood relatives and going back to great-grandparents. Using circles for female and squares for males, we simply noted our family members. We then went back and shaded in those relatives who were known to have a drinking or drug problem. I was careful not to use the word *addiction,* for obvious reasons. Of the 10 students who said they used drugs or alcohol, 8 had a parent with substance abuse issues. This led to an outburst of questions and shock on their part regarding the hereditary information before them. I could see lightbulbs going on!

Teacher Consult. I had consulted my librarian about books in the school library dealing with homosexuality. She was eager to show me what was available and offered to purchase more books if I would provide her with a list. I found our library had only a few fiction books that dealt with homosexuality and one nonfiction book, but the librarian gave me a list of books for teens that dealt with homosexuality and that were approved by the state library association. I started ordering books for my groups and begged books from friends who were into gay and lesbian detective stories and mysteries. I became a lending library for my students, teachers, and even the school newspaper staff who were writing articles in the school newspaper. Our librarian also began ordering books and would share them with me as they arrived.

Session 8. Billy came into the session crying and needed to talk. We dispensed with our usual opening, with the group's approval. Billy had come out to his mother during the summer, and she warned him not to say anything to his stepfather. With increasing tension in his life, Billy decided he would go public with his cross-dressing. His stepfather saw him leaving for school in a skirt and makeup. He began screaming at Billy and punched him in the face. He called him lots of obscenities and threw him out of the house. Billy walked to his friend's house and then came to school. In the group, he talked about being afraid to go home. The other students came to his defense but offered conflicting advice. I asked him if there was a relative he could stay with until things were resolved. He said his aunt knew he was gay, was okay with it, and he would like to stay with her. I told Billy that the physical abuse he received, as well as the threat not to come home, was going to be reported to CPS. The group turned on me. They bonded against me as the enemy! I pleaded my case and a few students started to agree with me. The majority, including Billy, were furious. After an extended session only a few students remained hostile, but Billy was one of them. I released the group, asking Billy to stay. I told him I was going to call CPS and then I was going to call his mother and his aunt. He began to see that I was really trying to prevent anything more from happening to him, and he reluctantly provided phone numbers for the latter two. The report to CPS was completed, and they told me it was all right for him to stay with his aunt until they made a home visit. I then called his aunt and she agreed to pick Billy up after school and keep him as long as necessary. Next came the call to his mother. I told her that I was concerned for Billy's safety and that her sister had agreed to let him stay with her. She agreed with the plan and asked to speak with Billy. Billy cried on the phone to his mother, but he appeared more relaxed with the plan after hanging up.

Parent Consult. Billy's mother came to school to see me the day after I filed the CPS report. She was trying to understand Billy and told me that she loved him dearly but did not want him to continue unacceptable behaviors. We talked for an hour and I lent her the video *Growing Up Gay and Lesbian* and provided her with the phone number of the local Parents and Friends of Lesbians and Gays (PFLAG) chapter. She assured me that she would call me after attending one of the support group meetings. She also stated that it would be safer for Billy to remain with his aunt until she decided what she was going to do about her marriage.

Session 9. When we went around the group to check in and share, Maxi talked about her 28-year-old girlfriend who had been emotionally abusing her. The group discussion led us to issues of self-esteem and the fear of being alone. Maxi said she would talk to her girlfriend about the need for respect in their relationship. Maxi also agreed to see me individually during the week. During our last session, I had asked the group to bring in names and information about famous people who were gay. Half the group did so, and I set the others to work with my own resource books. The students were amazed at some of the names that were revealed.

Session 10. It was time for another guest speaker, and I found a minister of a local Presbyterian church who was open to having gay people participate in the church service as well as uniting gay couples in religious ceremonies. I chose a Christian cleric since all of my students were Christian and most were very concerned about biblical injunctions against homosexuality. The students approached the minister cautiously since many had encountered negative experiences in their churches. Luckily, she was terrific with the students. The students were truly uplifted after her talk and some spoke about attending her church or other churches that were gay-friendly.

Session 11. At this point, I had a total of 47 gay students who wanted to be part of a group. Most of these students were self-referred after hearing about the groups from friends. I had decided that I would have 12 sessions per group and rotate in the new students. I planned on keeping the most troubled students in the existing groups for additional sessions.

This session was again devoted to alcohol and drug use. I provided literature from our local Council on Alcohol and Drug Abuse. Some students spoke about their abuse of alcohol and drugs and I referred them to the Palmer Drug Abuse Program (PDAP), which offers a free program for teens and their families. I had witnessed the program's successes and often consulted with them.

Session 12. This was our last session, always a difficult time because the students have really bonded. I tried to keep this closing as a positive, hopeful session. I gave each student a large index card on which they wrote their name at the top. They passed their cards around the circle until everyone had written something positive about them. Comments had to be short, positive, and not about physical attributes (i.e., "You have a great figure"). I asked the students to read their cards silently and share how the group had impacted them. I suggested that they keep the card in their wallet and whenever they heard negative comments about themselves or had negative thoughts, they should just take out their cards and read. After lots of hugs, tears and picture taking, we said our good-byes and they each knew that they had made a difference in someone's life by being part of the group.

Results

My biggest surprise was the positive attitude most teachers took and the schoolwide reduction of gay harassment. I believe that running small groups for gays is essential on every high school campus if we are going to save the lives of 10% of our student population.

Personal Reflection

I learned so much from this experience. As a straight person, I had to do some reflecting as to why I had never socialized with gay people. Why were we only acquaintances and never more? It is possible that I never displayed behaviors that allowed me to be a "safe" person. Perhaps when my progay status was made public I became trustworthy. I do know that I learned more about myself and the gay population from this opportunity, and I am determined to speak out for gay rights and to educate others. I learned so many things from this experience, but most importantly I realized that as a counselor, I could be effective in dealing with issues that were new to me. I could tap into my knowledge of child development and group process and trust the group and myself enough to tackle any group. I learned that students flourish in small groups. I also learned that most people are able to deal fairly with "those" kids if they are educated about homosexuality. In hindsight, I believe I should have divided this large group sooner than I did so that more could have been accomplished. I also wish that I had gotten started sooner in meetings with the administrators and the faculty. Better late than never.

Suggested Readings

Bailey, N. J. (2003). Safety for gay and lesbian students in our schools. *Education Digest,* (February), 46–48.

Cass, V. C. (1984). Homosexual identity formation: Testing a theoretical model. *The Journal of Sex Research, 20*(2), 143–167.

D'Augelli, A. R. (2003). Lesbian and bisexual female youth aged 14 to 21: Developmental challenges and victimization experiences. *Journal of Lesbian Studies, 7*(4), 9–22.

Henning-Stout, M., James, S., & Macintosh, S. (2000). Reducing harassment of lesbian, gay, bisexual, transgender, and questioning youth in schools. *School Psychology Review, 29*(2), 180–191.

Monier, S. S., & Lewis, A. C. (2000). School counselors and sexual minority students. *Q Online Journal, 1*(1).

Rosario, M., Schrimshaw, E. W., & Hunter, J. (2004). Ethnic/racial differences in the coming-out process of lesbian, gay, and bisexual youths: A comparison of sexual identity development over time. *Cultural Diversity and Ethnic Minority Psychology, 10*(3), 215–228.

Ryan, C. (2001). Counseling lesbian, gay, and bisexual youths. In D'Augelli, A. R., & Patterson, C. J. (Eds.), *Lesbian, gay, and bisexual identities and youth* (pp. 225–250). New York: Oxford University Press.

Biographical Statement

At the time of this case study, Marcia Loew, MA, LPC, LCDC, was a counselor at John Jay High School in San Antonio, Texas, where she was an SDFSCC for 13 years. You can reach Marcia at mloew1945@yahoo.com.

Practical Gifted Kidkeeping

LeAnne North

LeAnne North is a counselor at an unusual residential high school for students who are high achievers in math and science. The students live and learn together. North describes three specific examples of how she reaches out to her gifted clients:

Case 1: Classroom Guidance and Anxiety About Violence

Case 2: Peer Counseling and Academic Pressure

Case 3: Rock and Roll and Social Skills

work at a school for eleventh and twelfth graders who are gifted in math and science. These days, people do not like to use the word *gifted*. They say *high achievers* or *academically talented*. I think *gifted* is a lot quicker to type. Also, *high achiever* implies that a certain level of achievement is expected, and what if a student does not feel like achieving some days? Or at all? Many such school programs are no longer called "gifted and talented"; programs abound with names like Soar, Leap, Eagles, Alert, Flyers, and so on. Many of these names began as cute acronyms, but what they stand for is usually long forgotten.

The School

Full-day, whole-curriculum programs for gifted students are called stand-alone programs, and I work at a school that definitely stands alone. The National Consortium for Specialized Secondary Schools in Math, Science, and Technology has 14 member schools, mostly in southern states. My school is one of these. It is residential, public, and free, but you have to apply to get in. Students are admitted based on grades, test scores, an essay, and teacher recommendations. The admissions committee also considers whether a student is being well served at his or her present school. For example, a public high school with an international baccalaureate program is probably challenging a student as well as our school can. Another consideration is representation of the state geographically; we like to have students from all areas of the state. We are a relatively poor, rural state, so there is much variance in the quality of education between well-funded, suburban high schools and underfunded small rural high schools. However, our curriculum focuses heavily on advanced math and science, so students need to be prepared for the rigors of our academic program with a sound background in these disciplines. We get about 200 applications a year for about 60 slots.

Most of our faculty has doctoral degrees. We have only a couple of traditional high school teachers. Although my business card says I am a guidance counselor, I am not a certified school counselor. I trained as a psychotherapist. Classes run on a college schedule (MWF, T–Th) plus labs for sciences and languages. The material is Advanced Placement level or above. Students generally take seven courses, a very heavy load for college-level material. They average 30 hours a week attending class and labs. They also have to complete 3 hours a week of community service and 2 hours of physical activity. We recommend 2 hours of studying for each hour in class. Sound demanding? It is. It means no hobbies, no social life, no television, no marching band, no video games, no clubs, no part-time jobs, no art, no hanging out, just school-school-school. Alumni say that college is easy compared to their experience here. The workload results in high levels of anxiety and depression among the students. For me, it is like being a medic with a box of Band-Aids in a war zone.

The students live in a traditional dorm setting. They eat in a cafeteria and have roommates; two rooms share a bathroom. There are about 20 kids on each hall. All

128 students are supervised by 12 part-time college students and 4 full-time student services professionals. Unlike many private boarding schools, the faculty does not have any responsibility for dorm life. The students have a lot of rules. Sign out, sign in, quiet study from 8:00 P.M. to 10:00 P.M., lights out at midnight, and no leaving campus after dark except in groups of three or more. No candles, no coffeepots, no incense, no hotplates or microwaves. No more than 10% of your walls covered with posters. No spaghetti straps, no cleavage, no body piercing, no cars. Check your e-mail at least once a day. Discipline includes work detail, early curfew, being confined to your room for a weekend, suspension, and expulsion (although no one has ever been expelled). Some students feel unsupervised compared with their parents' house rules; others feel unnecessarily hampered by pointless regulations.

One hundred twenty-eight teenagers live together in one building, go to classes together, study together, and date each other. Some of them are wealthy, and some cannot afford essentials like clothing and books. Mostly they are White, although the population in our southern state tells us there should be more African American students. Next year's junior class will include only one African American. We have more than our statistical share of Asian and Indian students.

Some students love our school and some hate it. Some came here because their home life was bad or school life was bad, or both, or they thought the school would get them into a better college. If they wanted a challenge, they certainly get that. And lifelong friends—the kind you make when you are trapped on a deserted island with a group of people for two years and must rely on them for survival. As for me, I stay on the island and wait for the next boatload of refugees to wash up, find their way into my office, and tell me that they have just discovered that they are not the smartest person in the world, after all. "That's okay," I tell them. "Wouldn't that be lonely? You'll see." And eventually, they do.

Student Need (Overall)

Our students have needs like any other teenagers have. They also have special needs that relate to their being gifted, and that relate to their being in this academically rigorous and highly controlled environment. I get to know them individually as well as members of their peer group. In this small environment, I get to work with them in a range of ways. In this chapter, I describe three cases that show what the guidance program looks like. The first description is of classroom guidance; the second, helping a student cope with what she perceived as a low test score; and the third, helping a boy learn new social skills.

Case 1: Classroom Guidance and Anxiety About Violence

One of my more pleasant duties is going into the classroom. Our juniors take a life-skills class, and I visit to cover stress management, depression and suicide, what it means to be gifted, the Myers-Briggs Type Indicator, substance abuse, and anything else we adults think they might need at the time. I enjoy it so much that I am an enthusiastic substitute. If a teacher is absent and the weather is nice, we often end up outside running around and laughing. (Of course, I can totally justify this with sound psychological rationale.) My students are thoughtful, well read, articulate, and opinionated, so I find spirited discussion of the topic at hand very productive and more useful than my lecturing while they take notes.

Goals and Strategies I can tolerate a fairly loose classroom, as long as everyone is pretty much engaged in the main business of what the class is doing. When I first meet the new juniors in the classroom, in groups of about 16, I let them know a few things about how I like class to go when I visit. It is a big group to manage when what I want is more of a group counseling format, so I have arrived at some techniques, which I call "Power to the People." The first thing I have to break them of is talking only to the teacher. They are very good students and are accustomed to answering the teacher, asking the teacher questions, eyes front, hand raised. I tell them we discuss things as a group, so they are encouraged to respond to what someone else has said, and to look at them when they speak. I tell them that if they look at me, I will point at my eyes and then at the other person at whom they should be looking. Rather than raising hands and having me call on people ("Power to the People!"), we use two soft foam balls, called the Orbs of Verbosity, which give students the ability to speak. If they do not have an Orb, they cannot speak. The person who has just finished speaking passes his or her Orb on to someone who obviously has something to say. Since there are two, the discussion flows smoothly, with no fighting over a single Orb. If someone who is less assertive has trouble attracting an Orb, I intercede. This method tends to alleviate the problem of one loud and obnoxious person dominating conversations, and it works gracefully and without embarrassing anyone.

Since discussions can get very spirited and loud (we were once interrupted by the neighboring teacher, who asked us to please keep it down and asked if we were having a party in there), I devised a way to instantaneously bring the class to absolute silence. I ask them to come up with a hand signal and a word. So far, all groups but one have picked a peace sign and "Peace." One group did pick rock horns (index finger and pinky extended) and "Rock on." When needed, I make the gesture and say "Peace," and one by one the students do likewise, and silence falls. We practice this until they are proud of their ability to become instantly silent. It is very impressive when, say, the president of the school appears at the door unexpectedly.

We all have bunny-rabbit brains, which hop from topic to topic in a very interesting manner, but sometimes we need to stay on task. I am just as distractible as my students, so we often wander off a bit before I even notice. I love the mental agility and intellectual playfulness of my students. So I have a back-on-task gesture, which involves both arms: left hand at right elbow, right hand pointed up, I let my right hand fall slowly to my left elbow like I am "I Dream of Jeannie" about to cast a spell, and say, "Let's bring it on back" in a weird accent. I really have no idea where this came from, but it works.

Process I followed the DC snipers' case (September–October 2002) with interest because of the younger sniper, who was only 17 years old. On the day of the hearing (January 2003) to determine if the young sniper would be tried as an adult, the students wanted to talk about it. At first, they identified solely with the victims. "They were just going about their daily lives!" "Going grocery shopping!" "Getting gas!" "Waiting for a bus!" "And then, got shot out of nowhere!" I obtained an Orb. "But," I say, "he's only seventeen. Like you guys. And that's a kid to me. Plus, he was with his stepfather." "Oh, that doesn't matter," agreed the students. "We're old enough to know right from wrong." It was like Nuremberg.

Abigail:	If my dad handed me a gun and told me to shoot somebody, I'd tell him to bleep off.
Somebody in the back:	Yeah, your dad bakes you cookies. (Meaning, we know Abigail's father, and he is obviously a really nice guy who would never snipe anybody.)

I can see that a quiet Russian girl would like an Orb, but the discussion is too spirited for her to get one, so I redirect one her way.

Daria: (slowly and thoughtfully)	We do not know what the relationship was like between the boy and been abusing the boy and brainwashing him, so that he must do whatever his stepfather says. I think that this should be considered before they decide to try him as an adult, because trying him as an adult means that he was fully responsible for his actions, and it may be that he was not, since there was an older adult involved. I think this should be considered.

There were several seconds of silence as the group absorbed Daria's words. Finally, Jake asked, "What does it mean, anyway, to be tried as an adult?" They turned to me, their walking encyclopedia.

Counselor:	The authorities want to try him as an adult so that the death penalty will be a possible sentence. Also, juveniles who are tried as adults go to adult prisons, which is why it's controversial. But if someone is tried as a juvenile in family court, he could be released at 21 or 25, depending on the state.

The discussion resumed. They certainly did not want the sniper walking the streets in a few years; he should definitely be locked up forever. But the death penalty? Everyone disagreed, and for different reasons. "An eye for an eye." "But we shouldn't kill people who kill people to show that killing people is wrong." I did the bring-it-on-back thing. "The death penalty is one of those Conversations We Don't Have Time to Have (CWDHTTH)," I said. (Other CWDHTTH include abortion, evolution, and homosexuality—topics that become circular and heated in discussion, deserving of full discussion and not as tangents.) Everyone nodded.

Scott: But aren't there people who are just born not caring if they break laws? And then they grow up to be serial killers? Like Ted Bundy. Sociopaths.

I provided a brief definition of sociopathology and its ugly cousin psychopathology.

Kathy: What if we could identify sociopaths genetically when they were little kids? Then we could separate them from society and they couldn't hurt anybody.

Kurt: Except each other. But would that be fair? I mean, is it guaranteed they'll grow up to be murderers?

Counselor: (Everyone turned to me.) Sometimes sociopaths just grow up to be huge jerks.

Jake: Well, we could still confine them to an island.

Abigail: Yeah! And CBS could install cameras and it would be a great reality show!

Everyone laughed, and I knew it was time to get back to the actual topic of today's class.

■ Case 2: Peer Counseling and Academic Pressure

Quite often, PSAT or SAT scores that seemed very good back home at one's former high school look inadequate when viewed amongst those of one's gifted peers. I often talk with students who feel that they have been suddenly rendered stupid on their enrollment here. SAT scores cause a great deal of stress among high-performing, ambitious students, especially if their parents are pressuring them to tread a certain path. Ivy League schools do not even read your application if your SAT score is below 1400. Many scholarships have a 1200 cut-off. I spend more time counseling students about their SAT scores than any other college-application criteria. To them, the score seems as arbitrary and difficult to control as their height, and it is often the one thing standing between them and their dreams. "I just can't get that last 10 points!" they wail.

__Goals and Strategies__ My goal in this session was to alleviate a student's dismay, about her PSAT score. My strategy was simply to stay out of the peer counselors' way.

__Process__ This was the day the PSAT scores arrived, and I went over to the dorm at lunchtime and passed them out to the juniors, who mobbed me like I had Beatles tickets or something. What I had was the first clue as to what they would score on their SATs.

After lunch, I was in my office with a few of the peer college counselors, my student assistants. The assistants are seniors that have received special training preparing them to assist their peers with college planning. A sweet-faced junior girl appeared shyly in the door.

Junior Girl:	Are y'all busy? I had a question about college, but I can come back later . . .
Trey:	Heck, no. Come on in. We're peer college counselors, we can help you.
Mike: (jumping up)	Here, take the comfy chair. (He ushers her into everyone's favorite tapestry armchair.) What's the problem?
Junior Girl:	Well, I got my PSAT scores today, and they seemed kind of . . .
Betsy: (from her prone position on the couch)	Looooooow. (She kicks her feet around, and the boys sigh and look up at the ceiling.)
Trey: (shaking his head)	You can't compare yourself to these people, around here. Back at your old school, would that have been a good score?
Junior Girl:	Well, yeah. It would have been, like, a record.
Betsy:	Sure, at my old school, if you broke a thousand, they put your name on the wall.
Everyone else, including me:	Me too!
Junior Girl:	But, now I'm afraid I won't get into college.
The other kids: (laughing)	Everybody goes to college here. It's just a question of which college makes you the best offer.
Counselor:	Aiming for Princeton, are we?
Junior Girl:	Actually, I want to go to State Tech. My mom went there, and that's where my brother goes, and they have a great nursing program, which is what I want to be, so that's really where I want to go.

I reached into my desk and discreetly looked at her score. It was a perfectly robust test score of which any mother could proudly boast at the book club.

Counselor:	You do not have a problem. State Tech has never turned down a single one of my kids, and they usually offer them full scholarships. (I grab my magic wand out of my pen cup and bonk her on the head.) You are admitted to State Tech. Besides, that score will probably go up fifty or a hundred points by next year.
Junior Girl:	Really? Why?
Trey:	Mine did. I just got an SAT prep book and went through it a few times. But I've got, like, the lowest score here, and I got into Tulane.
Junior Girl: (Surprised)	Really?

Mike: It doesn't matter nearly as much as you think it does. It's just,
                           some people are loud.

The junior girl was confused, but I knew what he meant. Two people get perfect scores on the SAT; it is in newspapers nationwide, leaving 126 very talented students thinking, What is wrong with me? I didn't get a 1600. I must be stupid!

Betsy: A few people got high scores. They're going around bragging
                           about it, but most people didn't, and they're not saying a thing.
                           Think about it; how many people are really telling everybody
                           what they got? Like, five. And other people lie about what they
                           got, is my opinion.

I thought she was exactly right, but because they were doing such a great job counseling each other, it was best to just stay out of the way.

<u>Results</u> Trey: (addressing   You can't go around comparing yourself to
               our patient   people here and feel bad about yourself. It's just
               warmly)   one stupid test on one stupid day and it doesn't
                                      mean anything about who you are or what kind
                                      of person you're going to be. Just forget about it
                                      and go on with your beautiful self.

He had just given a very good paraphrase of what I told him the year before when he came to me with the same concern, apparently without realizing it, which was kind of cool because it meant he internalized it. The junior girl, completely reassured and happy, thanked everyone repeatedly and made her exit. I told her I would see her in the spring for college counseling. The peer college counselors grinned at each other. Mike breathed on his fingernails and buffed them on his shirt. "Well," he said, "I think our work here is done." They bounced out; I held my giggles until I heard them clomping down the stairs.

<u>Personal Reflection</u> Having gone through the public education system identified as a gifted student myself, I can identify with the issue of coming into contact with others who seem to be smarter than you, perhaps for the first time. I faced it when I started college. "Oh, you were the valedictorian? So was everyone else." "Best writer at your high school?" Ditto. Often adults misidentify this as arrogance, but gifted students are genuinely confused. Often they really have not had to work very hard at their studies. Things have come easily for them, and they are not used to being challenged. They have become accustomed to being, if not the smartest person in the world, at least the smartest person in the room. That is easy to take as arrogance and meet with anger or dismissal: "They need to be taken down a peg or two!" However, the student will learn on his or her own about the variance of intelligences and capabilities in the big wide world. Be gentle. They don't need to be smacked down; life will do that. I got over it fairly quickly and was soon genuinely happy to have

friends who were intellectual equals. It does not take long for my students to figure this out either. A big realization is that you cannot just make up stuff and have everyone believe you. You have to either actually know what you are talking about or not say anything at all.

◼ Case 3: Rock and Roll and Social Skills

<u>Goals and Strategies</u> I first encountered Brian because one of his teachers was concerned that he might be depressed. I looked up his schedule and loitered outside one of his classes when it was letting out, and when I knew he had some free time. He was willing to talk with me, and we met several times over that first semester of his junior year. Brian was having trouble making friends—a sad situation in this intimate and closed environment. Many of my students had had social problems at their former schools but blossomed here where they were finally able to find their tribe—other kids who value chess or skills for the math team or computer programming or spirited discussions of books and ideas. Still, every year there are a few students who cannot seem to find their niche. In Brian's case, extreme school trauma had damaged his self-esteem and destroyed his confidence, rendering him shy and preventing him from reaching out to others. When we first met, he even displayed very little facial expression—part of the defenses he had developed to deal with years of daily harassment and bullying at school. He was convinced that he was ugly, worthless, boring, and deserved no human contact. All he had was his music and his studies.

Brian is an incredibly talented musician, a true prodigy. He could master difficult new techniques on his guitar in a matter of days, even though he had little time to practice at school. His dexterity and speed were amazing in one so young, and he had never had a single formal lesson. If he played the violin, his path would be clear—the finest music schools, then a position with one of the country's symphony orchestras, and finally a career as a composer and professor of music. However, there is no Juilliard School of Rock Guitar.

<u>Process</u> I was able to help Brian when he signed up for my course in rock and roll. It became apparent that he knew more about rock than I did when the class started directing their questions to him instead of me. And then one day, he brought to class a beautiful electric guitar. As we were admiring it, I could not identify its make, and when I asked him, he said that he had made it. I was amazed. He had not put it together from a kit; he selected the parts, routed the body from a block of beautiful solid maple, and carefully assembled it into a top-quality musical instrument built to his own specifications of hand size and arm length. Of course the class wanted to hear it, so he brought down his amp, plugged it in, and noodled around a little. Our jaws dropped. It was like having Jimi Hendrix stop by.

A working rock band visited the class, and Brian hung around as they were setting up. I made him go get his guitar to show them, and the guys were genuinely impressed. The guitarist even asked permission to play it, an act of high praise, and then complimented its sound in detail. Brian smiled.

Results After that, everything changed for Brian. The students respected him as a talented musician and as someone knowledgeable about rock. They sought his opinions about bands and borrowed his CDs. They begged him to play at the next Coffeehouse (open-mike night) and cheered enthusiastically at his performance. He formed a band, made friends, got a girlfriend.

As a senior, Brian was a cheerful, outgoing guy. His band performed regularly and had groupies—girls who made themselves official "backstage passes" and bought lacy panties (never worn, and with the price tags still on to prove they were nice girls) to throw at the boys when they played. That had to make them feel good. Brian developed a best friend, planned for college, and found confidence in himself. He was comfortable. He stopped by to see me regularly and we talked about music and planned his rock star career. He told me about a shy junior boy that had been hanging around band practice. "I think I know how he feels," Brian said. "I think he feels like I felt last year. I've been talking to him some."

Brian laughed a lot. He in no way resembled the withdrawn junior who so concerned his teachers when he first got there. They complimented me, saying I worked a miracle, but I marveled at the fact that I did so very little. What Brian responded to was one adult who looked him in the eye and said, "I believe in you. You can do it."

Personal Reflection There are some things about gifted kids that the gifted community does not like to talk about but that are true. We do have some social skills difficulties. Our personality traits differ significantly from the general American population. Gender roles are differently divided. We are different in many ways, regardless of intelligence. How can we help our young people work on these things if we cannot admit that we do have problems such as these more frequently than nongifted students do?

Personal Reflection (Overall) I believe that gifted education is getting better. When I was growing up, it seemed like educators did not really know what they were doing. No program or theory lasted more than one school year. Nearly 20 years later, things seem to have settled down considerably. Now, there are many grown-up gifted kids working in gifted education, bringing a greater understanding to the students they serve. I feel very well prepared to be a school counselor for gifted adolescents; not just my college education and graduate training, but my entire life from age 3 on has prepared me to work with these young people. My students can be very strange, and I am very strange in similar ways, so it all evens out. I know them before they even move in to their dorm. It is hard to imagine working anywhere else. They are funny, and wise, and naïve. They are playful and silly. Some of them are terribly damaged and complex.

Suggested Readings

Carty, L., Rosenbaum, J. N., Lafreniere, K., & Sutton, J. (2000). Peer group counseling: An intervention that works. *Guidance & Counseling, 15*(2), 2–8.

Slater, P., & McKeown, M. (2004). The role of peer counseling and support in helping to reduce anxieties around transitions from primary to secondary schools. *Counselling & Psychotherapy Research Journal, 4*(1), 72–80.

Torsheim, T., & Wold, B. (2001). School-related stress, support, and subjective health complaints among early adolescents: A multilevel approach. *Journal of Adolescence 24*(6), 701–713.

Biographical Statement

LeAnne North is a school counselor in South Carolina. She earned an Educational Specialist degree in community counseling from James Madison University. You can contact her at LeAnne_North@gssm.k12.sc.us.

Index